The Teachings of Emanuel Swedenborg: Vol III
Last Judgment

The Teachings of Emanuel Swedenborg: Vol III
Last Judgment

By Emanuel Swedenborg
Translated by John Whitehead

Last Judgment
Last Judgment Continued
Last Judgment Posthumous

Last Judgment

I. THE DESTRUCTION OF THE WORLD IS NOT MEANT BY THE DAY OF THE LAST JUDGMENT. Those who have not known the spiritual sense of the Word, have understood that everything in the visible world will be destroyed in the day of the Last Judgment; for it is said, that heaven and earth are then to perish, and that God will create a New Heaven and a New Earth. In this opinion they have also confirmed themselves because it is said, that all are then to rise from their graves, and that the good are then to be separated from the evil, with more to the same purport. But it is thus said in the sense of the letter of the Word, because the sense of the letter of the Word is natural, and in the ultimate of Divine order, where each and every part contains a spiritual sense within it. For which reason, he who comprehends the Word only according to the sense of the letter, may be led into various opinions, as indeed has been the case in the Christian world, where so many heresies have thus arisen, and every one of them is confirmed from the Word. But since no one has hitherto known, that in the whole and in every part of the Word there is a spiritual sense, nor even what the spiritual sense is, therefore they who have embraced this opinion concerning the Last Judgment are excusable. But still they may now know, that neither the visible heaven nor the habitable earth will perish, but that both will endure; and that by "the New Heaven and the New Earth" is meant a New Church, both in the heavens and on the earth. It is said a New Church in the heavens, for there is a church in the heavens, as well as on the earth; for there also is the Word, and likewise preachings, and Divine worship as on the earth; but with a difference, that there all things are in a more perfect state, because there they are not in the natural world, but in the spiritual; hence all there are spiritual men, and not natural as they were in the world. That it is so, may be seen in the work on Heaven, in a special article there, on the Conjunction of Heaven with man by the Word ; and on Divine Worship in Heaven.

The passages in the Word, in which mention is made of the destruction of heaven and earth, are the following: Lift up your eyes to heaven, and look upon the earth beneath; the heavens are about to perish like smoke, and the earth shall wax old like a garment (Isa. 51:6). Behold, I am about to create new heavens, and a new earth; neither shall the former things be remembered (Isa. 65:17). I will make new heavens and a new earth (Isa. 66:22). The stars of heaven have fallen to the earth, and heaven has departed like a book rolled together (Apoc. 6:13, 14). I saw a great throne, and One sitting thereon, from whose face the earth and the heaven fled away, and their place was not found (Apoc. 20:11). I saw a New Heaven and a New Earth, for the first heaven and the first earth had passed away (Apoc. 21:1). In these passages, by "a New Heaven" is not meant the visible heaven, but heaven itself where the human race is collected; for a heaven was formed from all the human race, who had lived since the commencement of the Christian church; but they who were there were not angels, but spirits of various religions; this heaven is meant by "the first heaven" which was to perish: but how this was, shall be specially declared in what follows; here is related only so much as serves to show what is meant by "the first heaven" which was to perish. Every one even who thinks from a somewhat enlightened reason, may perceive, that it is not the starry heaven, the so immense firmament of creation, which is here meant, but that it is heaven in the spiritual sense, where angels and spirits are.

That by "the new earth" is meant a New Church on earth, has hitherto been unknown, for every one by "earth" in the Word has understood the earth, when yet by it is meant the church; in the natural sense, earth is the earth, but in the spiritual sense it is the church, because they who are in the spiritual sense, that is, who are spiritual, as the angels are, when "the earth" is named in the Word, do not understand the earth itself, but the nation which is there, and its Divine worship; hence it is that by "earth" is signified the church; that it is so, may be seen in the Arcana Coelestia, as quoted below. I will here adduce one or two passages from the Word, by which in some measure it may be comprehended, that "earth" [land] signifies the church: The cataracts from on high were opened, and the foundations of the earth were shaken; in breaking, the earth is broken; in agitating, the earth is agitated; in reeling, the earth reels like a drunkard; it moves to and fro like a cottage; and heavy upon it is the transgression thereof (Isa. 24:18-20). I will cause a man to be more rare than pure gold; therefore I will remove the heaven, and the earth shall be removed out of her place, in the day of the fierce anger of Jehovah (Isa. 13:12, 13). The earth was agitated before Him, the heavens have trembled, the sun and the moon are become black, and the stars have withdrawn their splendor (Joel 2:10). The land was shaken and agitated, and the foundations of the mountains trembled and were shaken (Ps. 18:7, 8, and in many other places). FROM THE ARCANA COELESTIA. By "earth" (land) in the Word is signified the kingdom of the Lord and the church). Chiefly for this reason, because by "earth" is meant the land of Canaan, and the church was there from the most ancient times hence also it is, that heaven is called the heavenly Canaan. And because in the spiritual sense by "earth" is understood the nation which is there, and its worship. Hence the "earth" signifies various things pertaining to the church. The people of the "earth" are they who are of the spiritual church. "An earthquake" is a change of the state of the church. "A New Heaven and a New Earth" signify the church. The Most Ancient Church, which was before the flood, and the Ancient Church, which was after the flood, were in the land of Canaan). Thence all the places there became representative of such things as are in the Lord's kingdom and in the church. Therefore Abraham was commanded to go thither, since with his posterity from Jacob, a representative church was to he instituted, and the word written, the ultimate sense of which should consist of the representatives and significatives which were there. Hence it is that by "earth" and by "the land of Canaan" is signified the church.

"To create" in the spiritual sense of the Word also signifies to form, to establish, and to regenerate; so by "creating a new heaven and a new earth" signifies to establish a New Church in heaven and on earth, as may appear from the following passages: The people who shall be created shall praise Jah (Ps. 102:18). Thou sendest forth the spirit, they are created; and Thou renewest the faces of the earth (Ps. 104:30). Thus said Jehovah, thy Creator, O Jacob, thy Former, O Israel, for I have redeemed thee, and I have called thee by thy name, thou art Mine; every one called by My name, and for My glory I have created,

I have formed him, yea, I have made him (Isa. 43:1, 7, and in other places). Hence it is, that "the new creation" of man is his reformation, since he is made anew, that is, from natural he is made spiritual; and hence it is that "a new creature" is a reformed man. "To create" is to create anew, or to reform and regenerate. "To create a New Heaven and a New Earth," is to institute a new church. By "the creation of heaven and earth" in the first chapter of Genesis, in the internal sense, is described the institution of the celestial church, which was the Most Ancient Church.

Concerning the spiritual sense of the Word, see in the small work on the White Horse, mentioned in the Apocalypse.

II. THE PROCREATIONS OF THE HUMAN ON THE EARTHS WILL NEVER CEASE. They who have adopted as their belief concerning the Last Judgment, that all things in the heavens and on the earth are then to perish, and that a new heaven and a new earth will exist in their place, believe, because it follows of consequence, that the generations and procreations of the human race are therefore to cease. For they think that all things will be then accomplished, and that men will be in a different state from before. But since the day of the Last Judgment does not mean the destruction of the world, as was shown in the preceding article, it also follows that the human race will endure, and that procreations will not cease.

That the procreations of the human race will endure to eternity, is plain from many considerations, of which some are shown in the work on Heaven, especially from the following: I. The human race is the basis on which heaven is founded. II. The human race is the seminary of heaven. III. The extension of heaven, which is for angels, is so immense that it cannot be filled to eternity. IV. They are but few respectively, of whom heaven at present is formed. V. The perfection of heaven increases according to its numbers. VI. And every Divine work has respect to infinity and eternity.

I. The human race is the basis on which heaven is founded, is because man was last created, and that which is last created is the basis of all that precedes. Creation commenced from the supreme or inmost, because from the Divine; and proceeded to ultimates or extremes, and then first subsisted. The ultimate of creation is the natural world, including the terraqueous globe, with all things on it. When these were finished, then man was created, and into him were collated all things of Divine order from firsts to lasts; into his inmost were collated those things of that order which are primary; and into his ultimates those which are ultimate; so that man was made Divine order in form. Hence it is that all things in man and with man, are both from heaven and from the World, those of his mind from heaven, and those of his body from the world; for the things of heaven flow into his thoughts and affections, and dispose them according to reception by his spirit, and the things of the world flow into his sensations and pleasures, and dispose them according to reception in his body, but still in accommodation to their agreement with the thoughts and affections of his spirit. That it is so, may be seen in several articles in the work on Heaven and Hell, especially in the following: That the Whole Heaven, in one complex, has reference to one man ; each society in the Heavens likewise); that hence every Angel is in a perfect human form ; and that this is from the Divine Human of the Lord. And moreover under the article on the Correspondence of all things of Heaven with all things of Man. On the Correspondence of Heaven with all things on earth. And on the Form of Heaven. From this order of creation it may appear, that such is the binding chain of connection from firsts to lasts that all things together make one, in which the prior cannot be separated from the posterior (just as a cause cannot be separated from its effect); and that thus the spiritual world cannot be separated from the natural, nor the natural world from the spiritual; thence neither the angelic heaven from the human race, nor the human race from the angelic heaven. Wherefore it is so provided by the Lord, that each shall afford a mutual assistance to the other, that is, the angelic heaven to the human race, and the human race to the angelic heaven. Hence it is, that the angelic mansions are indeed in heaven, and to appearance separate from the mansions where men are; and yet they are with man in his affections of good and truth. Their presentation to sight, as separate, is from appearances; as may be seen in an article in the work on Heaven and Hell, where Space in Heaven is treated of. That the mansions of angels are with men in their affections of good and truth, is meant by these words of the Lord: He who loveth Me, keepeth my words, and my Father will love him, and we will come unto him, and make our mansion with him (John 14:23). By "the Father" and "the Lord" in the above passage is also meant heaven, for where the Lord is, there is heaven, since the Divine proceeding from the Lord makes heaven, as may be seen in the work on Heaven and Hell. And likewise by these words of the Lord: The Comforter the Spirit of Truth abideth with you, and is in you (John 14:17) "The Comforter" is the Divine truth proceeding from the Lord, for which reason He is also called "the Spirit of truth," and the Divine truth makes heaven, and also the angels, because they are recipients; that the Divine proceeding from the Lord is the Divine truth, and that the angelic heaven is from it, may be seen in the work on Heaven and Hell. The like is also understood by these words of the Lord: The kingdom of God is within you (Luke 17:21). "The kingdom of God" is the Divine good and truth, in which the angels are. That angels and spirits are with man, and in his affections, has been granted me to see a thousand times, from their presence and abode with me; but angels and spirits do not know with what men they are, neither do men know the angels and spirits they cohabit with, for the Lord alone knows and disposes this. In a word, there is an extension into heaven of all the affections of good and truth, and a communication and conjunction with those who are in the like affections there; and there is an extension into hell of all the affections of evil and falsity, and a communication and conjunction with these who are in the like affections there. The extension of the affections into the spiritual world, is almost like that of sight into the natural world; communications in both are nearly similar; yet with this difference, that in the natural world there are objects, but in the spiritual world angelic societies. Hence it appears, that the connection of the angelic heaven with the human race is such that the one subsists from the other, and that the angelic heaven without the human race would be like a house without a foundation, for heaven closes into it and rests upon it. The case herein is the same as with each particular man; his spiritual things, which pertain to his thought and will, inflow into his natural things, which pertain to his sensations and actions, and in these they terminate and subsist. If man were not in possession of them, that is, if he were without these boundings and ultimates, his spiritual things, which pertain to the thoughts and affections of his spirit, would flow away, like things unbounded, or like those which have no foundation. In like manner, when a man passes from the natural into the spiritual world, which takes place when he dies, then because he is a spirit, he no longer subsists on his own basis, but upon the common basis, which is the human race. He who knows not the arcana of heaven, may believe that angels subsist without men, and men without angels; but I can affirm from all my experience of heaven, and from all my discourse with the angels, that no angel or spirit subsists without man, and no man without spirits and angels, but that there is a mutual and reciprocal conjunction. From this, it may now be seen that the human race and the angelic heaven make one, and mutually and reciprocally subsist from each other, and thus that the one cannot be taken away from the other.

II. The human race is the seminary of heaven, will appear from a subsequent article, in which it will be shown, that heaven and hell are from the human race, and that therefore the human race is the seminary of heaven. It must, however, first be mentioned, that as heaven has been formed of the human race, from the first creation until now, so it will be formed and filled up from the same source hereafter. It is indeed possible that the human race on one earth may perish, which comes to pass when they separate themselves entirely from the Divine, for then man no longer has spiritual life, but only natural, like that of beasts; and when man is such no society can be formed, and held bound by laws, since without the influx of heaven, and thus without the Divine government, man would become insane, and rush unchecked into every wickedness, one against another. But although the human race, by separation from the Divine, might perish on one earth, which, however, is provided against by the Lord, yet still they would continue on other earths; for that there are earths in the universe to some hundreds of thousands, may be seen in the little work, The Earths in our Solar System called Planets, and the Earths in the Starry Heaven. It was said to me from heaven, that the human race on this earth would have perished, so that not one man would have existed on it at this day, if the Lord had not come into the world, and on this earth assumed the Human, and made it Divine; and also, unless the Lord had given here such a Word as might serve for a basis to the angelic heaven, and for its conjunction. That the conjunction of heaven with man is by the Word, may be seen in the work on Heaven and Hell. But that such is the case can be comprehended only by those who think spiritually, that is, by those who through the acknowledgment of the Divine in the Lord are conjoined with heaven, for they alone are able to think spiritually.

III. The extension of heaven, which is for angels, is so immense, that it cannot be filled to eternity, appears from what has been said in the work on Heaven and Hell. On the Immensity of Heaven ; and That they are, but few respectively of whom heaven is at present formed, in the little work on the Earths in the Universe.

IV. The perfection of heaven increases according to its numbers, is evident from its form, according to which its associations are disposed in order, and its communications flow, for it is the most perfect of all; and in proportion to the increase of numbers in that most perfect form, there is given a direction and consent of more and more to unity, and therefore a closer and a more unanimous conjunction; the consent and the conjunction derived from it increase from numbers, for everything is there inserted as a mediate relation between two or more, and what is inserted confirms and conjoins. The form of heaven is like the form of the human mind, the perfection of which increases according to the increase of truth and good, from whence are its intelligence and wisdom. The form of the human mind, which is in heavenly wisdom and intelligence, is like the form of heaven, because the mind is the least image of that form; hence it is, that on all sides there is a communication of the thoughts and affections of good and truth in such men, and in angels, with surrounding societies of heaven; and an extension according to the increase of wisdom, and thus according to the plurality of the knowledges of truth implanted in the intellect and according to the abundance of the affections of good implanted in the will; and therefore in the mind, for the mind consists of the intellect and the will. The human and angelic mind is such that it may be infilled to eternity, and as it is infilled, so it is perfected; and this is especially the case, when man is led by the Lord, for he is then introduced into genuine truths, which are implanted in his intellect, and into genuine goods, which are implanted in his will, for the Lord then disposes all things of such a mind into the form of heaven, until at length it is a heaven in the least form. From this comparison, which is a true parallel, it is evident, that the increasing number of the angels perfects heaven. Moreover, every form consists of various parts; a form which does not consist of various parts, is not a form, for it has no quality, and no changes of state; the quality of every form results from the arrangement of various things within it, from their mutual relation, and from their consent to unity, from which every form is considered as one; such a form, in proportion to the multitude of the various things arranged within it, is the more perfect, for every one of them, as was said above, confirms, corroborates, conjoins, and so perfects. But this is still more evident from what has been shown in the work on Heaven and Hell, especially where it treats of this: That every Society of Heaven is a Heaven in a lesser form, and every Angel a heaven in the least form ; and also in the article, On the Form of Heaven, according to which Consociations and Communications have place there ; and On the Wisdom of the Angels of Heaven.

V. Every Divine work has respect to infinity and eternity, is evident from many things which exist both in heaven and in the world: in neither of them is there ever given one thing exactly similar to, or the same as, another: no two faces are either alike or identical, nor will be to eternity: in like manner the mind of one is never altogether like that of another; wherefore there are as many faces and as many minds as there are men and angels. There never exists in any one man (in whom yet there are innumerable parts which constitute his body, and innumerable affections which constitute his mind) any one thing quite alike, or identical with any one thing in another man; hence it is that every one leads a life distinct from the life of another. The same order exists in the whole and in every part of nature. That such infinite variety is in each and in all, is because they all originate from the Divine, which is infinite; hence there is a certain image of infinity everywhere, to the end that the Divine may regard all things as His own work, and at the same time, that all things, as His work, may have respect to the Divine. A familiar instance may serve to illustrate the manner in which every thing in nature has respect to infinity and eternity. Any seed, be it the produce of a tree, or of grain, or of a flower, is so created, that it may be multiplied to infinity, and endure to eternity. For from one seed are produced many, five, ten, twenty, a hundred, and from each of these again as many more; such fructification from one seed continuing but for a century, would cover the surface not only of one, but of myriads of earths, the same seeds are so created, that their durations may be eternal. Hence it is evident, how the idea of infinity and eternity is in them; and the like is true in all other cases. The angelic heaven is the end for which all things in the universe were created, for it is the end on account of which the human race exists, and the human race is the end regarded in the creation of the visible heaven, and the earths included in it. Wherefore that Divine work, namely, the angelic heaven, primarily has respect to infinity and eternity, and therefore to its multiplication without end, for the Divine Himself dwells therein. Hence also it is clear, that the human race will never cease, for were it to cease, the Divine work would be limited to a certain number, and thus its looking to infinity would perish.

III. HEAVEN AND HELL ARE FROM THE HUMAN RACE. It is altogether unknown in the Christian world that heaven and hell are from the human race; for it is believed that angels were created at the beginning, and that heaven was formed of them; and that the Devil or Satan was an angel of light, who, becoming rebellions, was cast down with his crew, and that this was the origin of hell. The angels are greatly astonished at such a faith in the Christian world, and still more, that nothing at all is there known of heaven, when yet it is a primary doctrine in the church; and since such ignorance prevails, they are rejoiced in heart that it has now pleased the Lord to reveal to men many things concerning heaven, and also concerning hell; and by this means, as far as possible, to dissipate the darkness which daily increases, because the church has come to its end. Wherefore they wish me to declare from them, that there is in the universal heaven not one who was created an angel from the first, nor any devil in hell who was created an angel of light, and cast down, but that all both in heaven and in hell are from the human race; in heaven those who had lived in the world in heavenly love and faith, and in hell those who had lived in infernal love and faith; and that hell in the whole complex is called the Devil and Satan; that the hell behind, where those are who are called evil genii, is the Devil, and the hell in front, which is the abode of evil spirits, is Satan. What the nature of one hell is, and what the other, may be seen in the work on Heaven and Hell, towards the end. The angels said, that the Christian world have conceived such a belief about those in heaven and hell, from certain passages in the Word no otherwise understood than according to the sense of the letter, and not illustrated and explained by genuine doctrine from the Word; when yet the sense of the letter, if the genuine doctrine of the church does not shine before it, draws the mind away into various opinions; whence come ignorance, heresies, and errors. The hells, or the infernals, taken together, are called the Devil and Satan. They who have been devils in the world, become devils after death. The doctrine of the church must be from the Word. The Word is not understood without doctrine. True doctrine is a lamp to those who read the Word. Genuine doctrine must be from those who are in illustration from the Lord. They who are in the sense of the letter of the Word without doctrine, can come into no understanding of Divine truths. And they are led into many errors. The difference between those who teach and learn from the doctrine of the church from the Word, and those who teach and learn only from the sense of the letter of the word.

Another cause of such a belief in the man of the church is, that he believes that no one can go to heaven or hell before the time of the Last Judgment; of which he has conceived this opinion that the visible world is then to perish, and a new one will come into existence, and that then the soul will return into its body, and from their conjunction man will again live a man. This belief involves another about the angels, that they were created from the beginning; for it is impossible to believe that heaven and hell are from the human race, when it is believed that no man goes there till the end of the world. But in order that man may be convinced that it is not so, it has been granted me to have fellowship with angels, and also to speak with those who are in hell, and this now for many years, sometimes continuously from morning even to evening, and thus to be informed concerning heaven and hell; to the end that the man of the church may no longer remain in his erroneous belief, about a resurrection at the day of judgment, about a state of the soul in the interval, as well as about angels, and about the Devil; which belief, since it is a belief in falsity, induces darkness; and with those who think of such things from their own intelligence, brings on doubt, and at length denial; for they say in heart, how can so vast a heaven, and so many stars, with sun and moon, be destroyed and dissipated? and how can the stars fall from heaven upon the earth, which yet are larger than the earth? and how can bodies, eaten up by worms, consumed by putrefaction, and scattered to all the winds, be collected again for its own soul? in the meantime, where is the soul, and what is it without the senses which it had in the body? with such like sayings on matters, which being incomprehensible, fall not within belief, and destroy in many the faith in man's eternal life, in heaven and hell, and with them, in all the remaining things of the faith of the church. That faith has thus been destroyed is evident from those who say, Who ever came from heaven and told us that it exists? What is hell? Is it anything at all? What is the meaning of man's being tormented with fire to eternity? What is the day of judgment? Has it not been expected for ages in vain? and many more questions which involve a denial of all things. Lest therefore, they who think thus (as do many who, from their knowledge in worldly matters are reputed skilful and learned), should any longer disturb and seduce the simple in faith and heart, and induce infernal darkness concerning God, heaven, eternal life, and other subjects dependent upon these, the interiors of my spirit have been opened by the Lord, and thus it has been granted one to speak with all those of the deceased whom I ever knew in the life of the body, with some for days, with some for months, and with some for a year, and also with so many others, that I should come short if I reckoned them at an hundred thousand, of whom many were in the heavens, and many in the hells. I have also spoken with some two days after their decease, and told them that solemn preparations were then making for their funerals; to which they said, that it was well to reject that which had served them for a body and its functions in the world: and they desired me to say that they are not dead, but alive and equally men as before, and that they had only passed out of one world into another; and they did not know that they had lost anything, since they are in a body and its senses as before, and in intellect and will as before, and have like thoughts and affections, like sensations, pleasures, and desires, as in the world. Most of those newly deceased, when they saw that they were living men as before, and in a similar state (for after death the state of every one's life is at first similar to what it was in the world, but is successively changed with him either into heaven or into hell), were affected with new joy at being alive, and said that they had not believed this. But they greatly wondered that they had been in such ignorance and blindness concerning the state of their own lives after death; and more especially, that the man of the church is in such a state, when yet he of all in the world can be in light concerning them. Then for the first time they saw the cause of this blindness and ignorance, which is, that external things, which are worldly and corporeal, had occupied and filled their minds to such an extent, that they could not be elevated into the light of heaven and behold the things of the church, which are beyond its doctrinals. For mere darkness inflows from corporeal and worldly things, when they are so much loved as they are at the present day, when man wishes to think of the things of heaven, beyond the dictate of the doctrine of faith of his church. At this day few in Christendom believe that man rises again immediately after death, Pref. to chap. 16 of Gen. and. But at the time of the Last judgment, when the visible world is to perish. The cause of such belief. Nevertheless man does rise again immediately after death, and that then he is a man as to each and all things. The soul, which lives after death, is man's spirit, which is the real man in the man, and which also in the other life is in a perfect human form. The same from experience. And from the word. What in meant by the dead being seen in the holy city (Matt. xxvii. 53) is explained (. How man is raised from the dead; by experience. Of his state after resuscitation. False opinions about the soul and the resurrection.

Very many of the learned from the Christian world are amazed when they see themselves after death in a body, in garments, and in houses as they were in the world; and when they recall to memory what they had thought of the life after death, of the soul, of spirits, of heaven and of hell, they are affected with shame, declare that they have thought foolishly, and that the simple in faith are much wiser than they. The learned were explored, who had confirmed themselves in such things, and who had attributed all things to nature, and it was found, that the interiors of their minds were closed, and the exteriors opened, so that they had not looked to heaven, but to the world, and hence also to hell; for so far as the interiors of the mind are opened, so far man looks to heaven; but so far as the interiors are closed, and the exteriors opened, so far he looks to hell; for the interiors of man are formed for the reception of all things of heaven, and his exteriors for the reception of all things of the world, and they who receive the world, and not at the same time heaven, receive hell. In man the spiritual and the natural worlds are conjoined. Man's internal is formed in the image of heaven, but his external in the image of the world.

That the spirit of man, after its release from the body, is a man, and in a similar form, has been attested to me by the daily experience of many years; for I have seen, heard, and spoken with spirits a thousand times; and even on this very subject; that men in the world do not believe them to be such, that they who do believe it, are accounted as simple by the learned. The spirits were grieved in heart, that such ignorance should still prevail in the world, and most of all in the church; but this, they said, proceeded principally from the learned, who thought of the soul from the sensual corporeal; wherefore they have conceived no other idea of it, than as of mere thought; which, when it is regarded without any subject in which and from which it is viewed, is like some volatile form of pure ether, which is necessarily dispersed when the body dies. But since the church from the Word believes in the immortality of the soul, they were obliged to ascribe it to some vital quality, such as belongs to thought, though not the sensation which man has, till it is again conjoined to its body. On this opinion is founded the doctrine of the resurrection at the time of the Last Judgment, and a belief in the conjunction of the soul and the body then; for from this hypothesis about the soul, coupled with the belief of the church in man's eternal life, no other conclusion can be reached: hence it is, that when any one thinks of the soul, from the doctrine and the hypothesis together, he does not at all comprehend that it is a spirit, and that this is in the human form. Add to this, that scarcely any one at this day knows what the spiritual is, and still less that they who are spiritual, as all spirits and angels are, have any human form. Hence it is, that almost all who come from the world are greatly amazed that they are alive, and are equally men as before, with no difference whatever. But when they cease to be amazed at themselves, they then wonder that the church knows nothing of this state of men after death, when yet all who have ever lived in the world, are in the other life, and live as men. And because they have also wondered why this was not manifested to man by visions, it was told them from heaven, that this could be done, for nothing is easier, when the Lord pleases, but that still they who had confirmed themselves in falsities against it, would not believe, even though they themselves were to see it; and moreover that it is perilous to manifest anything from heaven to those who are in worldly and corporeal things, for in this case they would first believe and afterwards deny, and thus profane the very truth itself; for to believe and afterwards to deny, is to profane; and they who profane, are thrust down into the lowest and most grievous of all the hells. It is this danger which is meant by these words of the Lord: He hath blinded their eyes, and hardened their hearts, lest they should see with the eyes and understand with the heart; and convert themselves, and I should heal them (John 12:40). Also that they who are in worldly and corporeal loves, still would not believe, is meant by these words: Abraham said to the rich man in hell, They have Moses and the prophets, let them hear them; but he said, Nay, father Abraham, but if one from the dead come to them, they will be converted; but Abraham said to him, if they hear not Moses and the prophets, neither will they believe even if one rose from the dead (Luke 16:29-31).

    That heaven is from the human race, is evident from this, that angelic and human minds are similar; both enjoying the faculty of understanding, of perceiving, and of willing; both being formed for receiving heaven. For the human mind possesses wisdom as well as the angelic; but it is not so wise in the world, because it is in a terrestrial body, in which its spiritual mind thinks naturally, for its spiritual thought, which it has in common with an angel, then flows down into the natural ideas corresponding with the spiritual, and is thus perceived in them. But it is otherwise when the mind of man is freed from its connection with the body; then it no longer thinks naturally but spiritually; and when spiritually it then thinks what is incomprehensible and ineffable to the natural man, as an angel does. Hence it is evident, that man's internal, which is called his spirit, in its essence is an angel. That an angel is in a perfect human form, may be seen in the work on Heaven and Hell: but when man's internal is not opened above, but only below, then still, after its removal from the body, it is in a human form, but a direful and diabolical one, for it cannot look upwards to heaven, but only downwards to hell. There are as many degrees of life in man, as there are heavens, and they are opened after death according to his life. Heaven is in man. The men who are living a life of love and charity, have angelic wisdom in them, but that it is then latent, and that they come into it after death. In the Word, the man who receives the good of love and of faith from the Lord, is called an angel.

That heaven and hell are from the human race, the church moreover might have known from the Word, and made it a part of its doctrine, if it had admitted enlightenment from heaven, and had attended to the Lord's words to the robber, that: Today he should be with Him in paradise (Luke 23:43); and to those which the Lord spake concerning the rich man and Lazarus, that: The one went to hell, and spoke thence with Abraham, and that the other went to heaven (Luke 16:19-31). Also to what the Lord told the Sadducees respecting the resurrection, that: God is not the God of the dead, but of the living (Matt. 22:32). And furthermore they might have known it from the common faith of all who live well, especially from their faith in the hour of death, when they are no longer in worldly and corporeal things, in that they believe they will go to heaven, as soon as the life of their body departs. This faith prevails with all, so long as they do not think, from the doctrine of the church, of a resurrection at the time of the Last Judgment. Inquire into the subject and you will be confirmed that it is so.

He who has been instructed concerning Divine order, may moreover understand, that man was created to become an angel, because in him is the ultimate of order, in which ultimate, whatever belongs to celestial and angelic wisdom may be formed, renewed, and multiplied. Divine order never subsists in the mediate, so as to form anything there without an ultimate, for it is not in its own fullness and perfection, but it proceeds to the ultimate. But when it is in its ultimate, it then forms, and also by mediates there collated, renews and produces itself farther, which is effected by procreations; wherefore the seminary of heaven is there. This also is meant by the things related of man, and of his creation in the first chapter of Genesis: God said, Let us make man in our image, according to our likeness; and God created man in His image, in the image of God created He him; male and female created He them; and God blessed them, and God said unto them, be fruitful and multiply. "To create in the image of God, and in the likeness of God," is to confer upon man all things of Divine order from firsts to ultimates, and thus to make him an angel as to the interiors of his mind.

That the Lord rose again not only as to the Spirit, but also as to the Body, is because the Lord, when He was in the world, glorified His whole Human, that is, made it Divine. For the soul, which He had from the Father, was the Divine Itself from Himself, and the body was made a similitude of the soul, that is of the Father, and therefore also Divine. Hence it is that He Himself, unlike any man, rose again as to both; which He also manifested to His disciples, who believed they saw a spirit when they saw Him; for he said: Behold My hands and My feet, that it is I Myself: feel Me and see, for a spirit has not flesh and bones, as ye see Me have (Luke 24:36-39). By which He pointed out that He was not only Man as to the Spirit, but also as to the body. Man rises again as to the spirit only. The Lord alone rose as to the body also.

Moreover that heaven and hell are from the human race, has been shown in many articles in the work on Heaven and Hell as in the following: Of the Nations and People in Heaven who are out of the Church. Of Infants in Heaven. Of the Wise and the Simple in Heaven. Of the Rich and the Poor in Heaven. Every Man is a Spirit, as regards his own interiors. Man after Death is in a perfect human Form. Man after Death is in all the sense, memory, thought, and affection, which he had in the world, and leaves nothing but his terrestrial body. Of the First state of man after Death. Of the Second State of man after Death. Of his Third state. See moreover what is said of the Hells. From all these articles it may be seen, that heaven does not consist of any angels created in the beginning, nor hell of any devil and his crew, but solely of those who have been born men.

IV. ALL WHO HAVE BEEN BORN MEN FROM THE BEGINNING OF CREATION, AND ARE DECEASED, ARE EITHER IN HEAVEN OR IN HELL. I. This follows from what has been said and shown in the preceding article, namely, that heaven and hell are from the human race. II. And from this, that every man after the life in the world, lives to eternity. III. Thus all who have ever been born men from the creation of the world, and are deceased, are either in heaven or in hell. IV. Since all who will be born hereafter, will also come into the spiritual world, that world is so vast, and is such that the natural world, in which are men on earth, cannot be compared with it. But in order that all these things may be the more distinctly perceived, and more plainly evident, I will expound and describe them one by one.

I. That all who have ever been born men from the beginning of creation, and are deceased, are either in heaven or in hell, follows from those things which have been said and shown in the preceding article, namely, that heaven and hell are from the human race. This is clear without explanation. It has been the common belief hitherto, that men will not come into heaven or into hell before the day of the Last Judgment, when souls will return into their own bodies, and thus to enjoy such things as are believed to belong only to the body. The simple have been led into this belief by men professing wisdom, who have investigated the interior state of man. Because these have thought nothing concerning the spiritual world, but only of the natural world, nor therefore of the spiritual man, they have not known that the spiritual man which is in every natural man, is in the human form, as well as the natural man. Hence it never entered their minds that the natural man draws his own human form from his spiritual man; although they might have seen that the spiritual man acts at will upon the whole, and upon every part of the natural man, and that the natural man of himself does nothing at all. It is the spiritual man who thinks and wills, for this the natural man of himself cannot do; and thought and will are the all in all of the natural man; for the natural man acts as the spiritual man wills, and also speaks as the spiritual thinks, and that so entirely, that action is nothing but will, and speech is nothing but thought, for on the removal of thought and will, speech and action cease in a moment. From this it is evident that the spiritual man is truly a man, and that he is in the whole, and in every part of the natural man, and that therefore their effigies are alike, for the part or particle of the natural man, in which the spiritual does not act, does not live. But the spiritual man cannot appear to the natural man, for the natural cannot see the spiritual, but the spiritual can see the natural; for this is according to order, but the converse is contrary to order; since there is given an influx, and therefore also a sight, of the spiritual into the natural, for sight too is influx, but not the reverse. It is the spiritual man who is called the spirit of man, and who appears in the spiritual world in a perfect human form, and lives after death. Because they who are intelligent have not known anything of the spiritual world, and therefore nothing of the spirit of man, as was said above, they have conceived therefore an idea that man cannot live a man, before his soul returns into the body, and again puts on the senses. Hence have arisen such vain ideas about man's resurrection, namely, that bodies, though eaten up by worms and fish, or entirely fallen to dust, are to be collected again by the Divine omnipotence, and re-united to souls; and that this is not to happen till the end of the world, when the visible universe is to perish; with many more like ideas, which are every one of them inconceivable, and at the first glance of the mind, strike it as impossible, and contrary to Divine order, tending thus to weaken the faith of many; for those who think wisely, cannot believe what they do not in some measure comprehend; and belief in impossibilities is not given, that is, a belief in such things as man thinks to be impossible. Hence also those who disbelieve the life after death, derive an argument in support of their denial. But that man rises again immediately after his decease, and that then he is in a perfect human form, may be seen in the work on Heaven and Hell, in many of its articles. These things have been said, that it may be still more confirmed that heaven and hell are from the human race, from which it follows, that all who were ever born men from the beginning of creation, and are deceased, are either in heaven or in hell.

II. That every man after the life in the world lives to eternity, is evident from this, that man is then spiritual, and no longer natural, and that the spiritual man, separated from the natural, remains such as he is to eternity, for man's state cannot be changed after death. Moreover, the spiritual of every man is in conjunction with the Divine, since it can think of the Divine, and also love the Divine, and be affected with all things which are from the Divine, such as those which the church teaches, and therefore it can be conjoined to the Divine by thought and will, which are the two faculties of the spiritual man, and constitute his life; and that which can thus be conjoined to the Divine, can never die, for the Divine is with it, and conjoins it to Himself. Man is also created to the form of heaven as to his mind, and the form of heaven is from the Divine itself, as may be seen in the work on Heaven and Hell, where it has been shown, That the Divine of the Lord makes and forms Heaven. That Man is created to be a Heaven in the least form. That Heaven in the whole complex, has reference to one Man. That hence an Angel is in a perfect human Form ; an angel is a man as to his spiritual. On this subject moreover, I have often spoken with the angels, who wondered exceedingly, that of those who are called intelligent in the Christian world, and who also are believed by others to be intelligent, there are very many who utterly reject the belief in their own immortality, believing that the soul of man is dissipated at death, just as the soul of a beast is; not perceiving the distinction between the life of a man and the life of a beast; that man has the power of thinking above himself, of God, of heaven, of love, of faith, of good, spiritual and moral, of truths, and the like, and that thus he may be elevated to the Divine itself, and he conjoined by all those things to Him; but that beasts cannot be elevated above their own natural, to think of such things, and consequently that their spiritual cannot be separated from their natural after death, so as to live by itself, as man's spiritual can: whence also it is, that the life of a beast ceases on the dissipation of its natural life. The reason why many of the stalled intelligent in the Christian world, have no belief in the immortality of their own lives, the angels declared to be this, that in heart they deny the Divine, and acknowledge nature instead of the Divine; and they who think from such principles, are not able to think of any eternity by conjunction with the Divine, nor consequently, of the state of man as dissimilar to that of beasts, for in rejecting the Divine from thought, they also reject eternity. They declared moreover, that with every man there is an inmost or supreme degree of life, or an inmost or supreme something into which the Divine of the Lord proximately inflows, and from which He disposes all the remaining interiors belonging to the spiritual and natural man, which are successive in both according to the degrees of order. This inmost or supreme they called the Lord's entrance into man, and His veriest dwelling place with him; and they said, that by this inmost or supreme, man is man, and is distinguished from brute animals which do not have it; and that hence it is, that men, as regards the interiors which are of the mind and disposition, unlike animals, can be elevated by the Lord to Himself, can have faith in Him, be affected by love to Him, and can receive intelligence and wisdom, and speak from reason. When I asked them concerning those who day the Divine, and the Divine truths, by which the conjunction of the life of man with the Divine itself is effected, and who yet live to eternity, they replied, that these also have the faculty of thinking and of willing, and therefore of believing and loving the things which are from the Divine, as well as those who acknowledge the Divine, and that by this faculty, they too live to eternity; they added, that this faculty is from that inmost or supreme which is in every man, of which mention was made above; that even those who are in hell have that faculty, and that they derive from it the power of reasoning and speaking against Divine truths, has been shown in many places. Hence it is, that every man lives to eternity, whatever be his quality. Because every man after death lives to eternity, no angel or spirit ever thinks of death; indeed they do not at all know what it is to die; wherefore, when "death" is mentioned in the Word, the angels understand by it either damnation, which is death in the spiritual sense, or the continuation of life and the resurrection. These things have been said in confirmation that all the men who have ever been born, and have died, from the beginning of creation, are alive, some in heaven, and some in hell. There is also an influx from the spiritual world into the lives of beasts, but that it is general, and not special as with man. The distinction between men and beasts is, that men can be elevated above themselves to the Lord, can think of the Divine, love it, and may thus be conjoined to the Lord, whence they have eternal life; but it is otherwise with beasts, which cannot be elevated to such things. When "death" is mentioned in the word, and spoken of the wicked, in heaven are understood damnation, which is spiritual death, and also hell. They who are in goods and truths are called "living," but they who are in evils and falsities "dead". By "death," when spoken of the good who die, resurrection and continuation of life are understood in heaven, for at death man rises again, continues his own life, and advances in it to eternity.

III. In order that I might know that all who have ever been born men from the beginning of creation, and are deceased, are either in heaven or in hell, it has been granted me to speak with some who lived before the flood; and also with some who lived after the flood; and with certain of the Jewish nation, who are made known to us from the Word of the Old Testament; with some who lived in the Lord's time; with many who lived in the ages succeeding, even down to the present day; and moreover with all those of the dead, whom I had known during their lives in the body; and likewise with infants; and with many of the Gentiles. From this experience I have been fully convinced, that there is not even one, who was ever born a man, from the first creation of this earth, who is not in heaven or in hell.

IV. Because all, who are to be born hereafter, must also come into the spiritual world, that world is so vast and such, that the natural world, in which men are on earth, cannot be compared with it; this is evident from the immense multitude of men who have passed into the spiritual world since the first creation, and who are together there; as well as from the continual increase hereafter from the human race, which will be added to them, and this without end, according to what has been shown above, in an article for the purpose , namely, that the procreations of the human race on the earths will never cease. When my eyes have been opened, it has sometimes been granted me to see how immense, even now, is the multitude of men who are there; it is so great that it can scarcely be numbered, such myriads are there, and this only in one place, towards one quarter; what then must the numbers be in the other quarters? For all are there collected into societies, and the societies exist in vast numbers, and each society, in its own place, forms three heavens, and three hells under them; wherefore there are some who are on high, some who are in the middle, and some who are below them; and underneath, there are those who are in the lowest places, or in the hells; and those who are above dwell among themselves as men dwell in cities, in which hundreds of thousands are together. Whence it is evident, that the natural world, the abode of men on earth, cannot be compared with that world, as regards the multitude of the human race; so that when man passes from the natural world into the spiritual, it is like going from a village into a great city. That the natural world cannot be compared with the spiritual world as to quality, may appear from this, that not only have all the things which are in the natural world an existence there, but innumerable others besides, which never were seen in this world, nor can be presented to the sight, for spiritual things there are effigied each to its own type by appearances, as if natural, each with an infinite variety; for the spiritual so far exceeds the natural in excellence, that the things are few which can be produced to the natural sense; the natural sense not receiving one of the thousands which the spiritual mind receives; and all things which belong to the spiritual mind, are presented, even in forms to their sight. This is the reason why it is impossible to describe what the spiritual world is, as regards its magnificent and stupendous things. These moreover increase in proportion to the multiplication of the human race in the heavens, for all things are there presented in forms which correspond to the state of each as to love and faith, and thence as to intelligence and wisdom; thus with a variety which increases continually, as the multitude increases. Whence it has been said by those who have been elevated into heaven, that they saw and heard things there, which no eye has ever seen, and no ear has ever heard. From these things, it may appear that the spiritual world is such, that the natural world can not be compared with it. Moreover, what it is, may be seen in the work on Heaven and Hell, where it treats of the two Kingdoms of Heaven. Of the Societies of Heaven Of representatives and Appearances in Heaven. Of the Wisdom of the Angels of Heaven. The things there described, however, are very few.

V. THE LAST JUDGMENT MUST BE WHERE ALL ARE TOGETHER, THUS IN THE SPIRITUAL WORLD, AND NOT ON EARTH. Concerning the Last Judgment, it is believed that the Lord will then appear in the clouds of heaven with the angels in glory, and awaken from the sepulchers all who have ever lived since the beginning of creation, clothing their souls with their bodies; and thus summoned together He will judge them, those who have done well, to eternal life or heaven, those who have done ill, to eternal death or hell. The churches derive this belief from the sense of the letter of the Word, nor could it be removed, so long as men did not know that there is a spiritual sense within each thing which is said in the Word, and that this sense is the Word itself, to which the sense of the letter serves for a foundation or basis, and that without such a letter, the Word could not have been Divine, or have served in heaven, as in the world, for the doctrine of life and faith, and for conjunction. He therefore who knows the spiritual things corresponding to the natural things in the Word, can know that by "the Lord's coming in the clouds of heaven," is not meant such an appearance of Him, but His appearance in the Word; for "the Lord" is the Word, because He is the Divine truth; "the clouds of heaven" in which He is to come, are the sense of the letter of the Word, and "the glory" is its spiritual sense; "the angels" are the heaven from which He will appear, and they also are the Lord as to Divine truths. Hence the meaning of these words is now evident, namely, that when the end of the church is, the Lord will open the spiritual sense of the Word, and thus the Divine truth, such as it is in itself; therefore that this is the sign that the Last Judgment is at hand. That there is a spiritual sense within each thing and expression in the Word, and what it is may be seen in the Arcana Coelestia, in which each and all things of Genesis and Exodus are explained according to that sense; and a collection of passages extracted from it, concerning the Word and its spiritual sense, may be seen in the little work on The White Horse, Mentioned in the Apocalypse. The Lord is the Word, because He is the Divine truth in heaven. The Lord is the Word, also because it is from Him, and treats of Him ; and because it treats of the Lord alone, and primarily of the glorification of His Human in its inmost sense, so that the Lord Himself is therein. The coming of the Lord is His presence in the Word, and revelation. "Clouds" in the Word signify the Word in the letter, or the sense of its letter. "Glory in the Word signifies Divine truth, such as it is in heaven, and such as it is in the spiritual sense. "Angels" in the Word signify Divine truths from the Lord, since angels are receptions of them, and do not speak them from themselves, but from the Lord. "Trumpets" or "cornets," which the angels then have, signify Divine truths in heaven and revealed from heaven).

That the Last Judgment must be in the spiritual world, and not in the natural world, or on the earth, is evident from the two preceding articles, and also from those that follow. In the two preceding articles it has been shown, that heaven and hell are from the human race; and that all who were ever born men since the beginning of creation, and are deceased, are either in heaven or in hell, thus that all are there together; but in the articles which follow it shall be shown that the Last Judgment has already been accomplished.

Moreover, no one is judged from the natural man, thus not so long as he lives in the natural world, for man is then in a natural body; but every one is judged in the spiritual man, and therefore when he comes into the spiritual world, for man is then in a spiritual body. It is the spiritual in man which is judged, but not the natural, for this cannot be held guilty of any fault or crime, since it does not live of itself, but is only the servant, and instrument by which the spiritual man acts. Hence also it is, that judgment is effected upon men when they have put off their natural, and put on their spiritual bodies. In the spiritual body moreover, man appears such as he is with respect to love and faith, for every one in the spiritual world is the effigy of his own love, not only as to the face and the body, but also as to the speech and the actions (see the work on Heaven and Hell,. Hence it is, that the qualities of all are known, and they are immediately separated, whenever the Lord pleases. From what has been said it is plain, that judgment is effected in the spiritual world, but not in the natural world, or on the earth.

That the natural life in man effects nothing, but his spiritual life in the natural, since what is natural of itself is void of life; and that the life which appears in it, is from the life of the spiritual man, thus that this is what is judged; and moreover that being "judged according to deeds," means that man's spiritual is judged, may be seen in the work on Heaven and Hell, in the article headed, That Man after Death is such as his Life in the World was.

To these things I will add a certain heavenly arcanum, which is indeed mentioned in the work on Heaven and Hell, but has not yet been described. Every one after death is bound to some society, even when first he comes into the spiritual world. But a spirit in his first state is ignorant of it, for he is then in his externals and not yet in his internals. When he is in this state, he goes hither and thither, wherever the desires of his mind impel him; but still actually, he is where his love is, that is, in a society where those are who are in a love like his own. When a spirit is in such a state he then appears in many other places, in all of them also present as it were with the body, but this is only an appearance. Wherefore as soon as he is led by the Lord into his own ruling love, he vanishes instantly from the eyes of others, and is among his own, in the society to which he was bound. This peculiarity exists in the spiritual world, and is wonderful to those who are ignorant of its cause. Hence now it is, that as soon as spirits are gathered together, and separated, they are also judged, and every one is presently in his own place, the good in heaven, and in a society there among their own, and the evil in hell, and in a society there among their own. From these things it is moreover evident, that the Last Judgment can exist nowhere but in the spiritual world, both because every one there is in the likeness of his own life, and because he is with those who are in similar life, and thus everyone is with his own. But it is otherwise in the natural world; the good and the evil can dwell together there, the one ignorant of what the other is, nor are they separated from each other according to the love of their life. Indeed it is impossible for any one in the natural body, to be either in heaven or in hell; wherefore in order that man may come into one or the other, it is necessary that he put off his natural body, and be judged the spiritual body. Hence it is, as was said above, that the spiritual man is judged, and not the natural.

VI. THE LAST JUDGMENT EXISTS, WHEN THE END OF THE CHURCH IS; AND THE END OF THE CHURCH IS, WHEN THERE IS NO FAITH, BECAUSE THERE IS NO CHARITY. There are many reasons why the Last Judgment exists when the end of the church is. The principal reason is, that then the equilibrium between heaven and hell begins to perish, and with the equilibrium man's freedom itself; and when man's freedom perishes, he can no longer be saved, for he cannot then be led to heaven in freedom, but from freedom is borne to hell; for no man can be reformed without freedom, and all man's freedom is from the equilibrium between heaven and hell. That it is so, may appear from two articles in the work on Heaven and Hell, where it treats, Of the Equilibrium between Heaven and Hell : and, That Man is in that Freedom by means of that Equilibrium between Heaven and Hell ; and further, that no man can be reformed except in freedom.

That the equilibrium between heaven and hell begins to perish at the end of the church, may appear from this, that heaven and hell are from the human race, as shown above in its own article, and that when few men come into heaven, and many into hell, evil on the one part increases over good on the other; for evil increases in proportion as hell increases, and all man's evil is from hell, and all his good is from heaven. Now since evil increases over good at the end of the church, all are then judged by the Lord, the evil are separated from the good, all things are reduced into order, and a new heaven is established, and also a new church upon earth, and thus the equilibrium is restored. It is this then which is called the Last Judgment, of which more will be said in the following articles.

It is known from the Word, that the end of the church is, when faith no longer exists within it, but it is not yet known, that there is no faith, if there is no charity; therefore something shall now be said upon this subject. It is predicted by the Lord that there is no faith at the end of the church: When the Son of Man comes shall He find faith on the earth (Luke 18:8); and also that there is no charity then: In the consummation of the age iniquity will be multiplied, the charity of many will grow cold, and this gospel will be preached in all the world, and then shall the end come (Matt. 24:12, 14). "The consummation of the age" is the last time of the church. The state of the church successively decreasing as to love and faith, is described by the Lord in this chapter, but it is described there by mere correspondences, and therefore the things therein predicted by the Lord cannot be understood, unless the spiritual sense corresponding to each expression there is known; on which account it has been granted me by the Lord to explain in the Arcana Coelestia the whole of that chapter and a part of the next, concerning the consummation of the age, His advent, the successive vastation of the church, and the Last Judgment; see in the Arcana Coelestia.

Something shall now be said concerning this, that there is no faith, if there is no charity. It is supposed that faith exists, so long as the doctrinals of the church are believed; or that they who believe, have faith; and yet mere believing is not faith, but willing and doing what is believed, is faith. When the doctrinals of the church are merely believed, they are not in man's life, but only in his memory, and thence in the thought of his external man; nor do they enter into his life, before they enter into his will, and thence into his actions: then for the first time does faith exist in man's spirit; for man's spirit, the life of which is his life itself, is formed from his will, and from so much of his thought as proceeds from his will; the memory of man, and the thought derived from it, being only the outer court by which introduction is effected. Whether you say the will, or the love, it is the same, since every one wills what he loves, and loves what he wills; and the will is the receptacle of love, and the intellect, the function of which is to think, is the receptacle of faith. A man may know, think, and understand many things, but those which do not accord with his will or love, he rejects from him when he is left to himself, to meditate from his own will or love, and therefore he also rejects them after the life of the body, when he lives in the spirit; for that alone remains in man's spirit which has entered into his will or love, as was said above. Other things after death are viewed as foreign, which he casts out of doors, and regards with aversion, because they are not of his love. But it is another thing when man not only believes the doctrinals of the church which are from the Word, but wills them, and does them; then he has faith; for faith is the affection of truth from willing truth because it is truth; for to will truth itself because it is truth is the spiritual man, for it is withdrawn from the natural, which consists in willing truth, not for truth's sake, but for the sake of self-glory, fame and gain. Truth regarded apart from such things is spiritual, because in its essence it is Divine; wherefore, to will truth because it is truth, is also to acknowledge, and to love the Divine. These two are altogether conjoined, and are also regarded as one in heaven, for the Divine which proceeds from the Lord in heaven is Divine truth, as may be seen in the work on Heaven and Hell , and they are angels in the heavens, who receive it, and make it of their life. These things are said, in order that it may be known, that faith is not only to believe, but to will and do, therefore there is no faith if there is no charity. Charity or love is to will and to do.

That within the church at this day, faith is so rare, that it can scarcely be said to exist at all, was made evident, from many both learned and simple, whose spirits were explored after death, as to what their faith had been in the world; and it was found, that every one of them supposed faith to be merely to believe, and to persuade himself that it is so; and that the more learned of them placed it entirely in believing, with trust or confidence that they are saved by the Lord's passion and His intercession, and that scarcely one among them knew that there is no faith, if there is no charity, or love yea, they did not know what charity to the neighbor is, nor the difference between thinking and willing. For the most part they turned their backs upon charity, saying that charity effects nothing, but faith only. When it was said to them, that charity and faith are one, like the will and the understanding, and that charity has its seat in the will, and faith in the understanding, and that to separate the one from the other, is like separating the will from the understanding, this they did not understand. Whence it was made evident to me that scarcely any faith exists at the present day. This also was shown them to the life. They who were in the persuasion that they had faith, were led to an angelic society, where genuine faith existed, and when they were made to communicate with it, they clearly perceived that they had no faith, which afterwards moreover, they confessed in the presence of many. The same thing was also shown by other means to those who had made a profession of faith, and had thought they believed, without having lived the life of faith, which is charity; and every one of them confessed that they had no faith, because they had nothing of it in the life of their spirits, but only in some thought extrinsic to it, whilst they lived in the natural world.

Such is the state of the church at this day, namely, that in it there is no faith because there is no charity; and where there is no charity, there is no spiritual good, for that good exists from charity alone. It was said from heaven that there is still good with some, but that it cannot be called spiritual, but natural good, because Divine truths themselves are in obscurity, and Divine truths introduce to charity, for they teach it, and regard it as their end and aim; whence no other charity can exist than such as the truths are which form it. The Divine truths from which the doctrines of the churches are derived, respect faith alone, on which account they are called the doctrines of faith, and do not look to life; and truths which only regard faith and not life, cannot make man spiritual; for so long as they are out of the life they are only natural, being merely known and thought of like other things. Hence it is that spiritual good is not given at the present day, but only natural good with some. Moreover every church in the beginning is spiritual, for it begins from charity; but in the course of time it turns aside from charity to faith, and then from being an internal church it becomes an external one, and when it becomes external its end is, since it then places everything in knowledge, and little or nothing in life. Thus also as far as man from being internal becomes external, spiritual light is darkened within him, until he no longer sees Divine truth from truth itself, that is from the light of heaven, for Divine truth is the light of heaven, but only from natural light; which is of such a nature, that when it is alone, and not illumined by spiritual light, it sees Divine truth as it were in night, and recognizes it as truth for no other reason than that it is so called by the leader, and is received as such by the common assembly. Hence it is, that their intellectual faculty cannot be illustrated by the Lord, for as far as natural light shines in the intellectual faculty, in so far spiritual light is obscured. Natural light shines in the intellectual faculty, when worldly, corporeal, and earthly things are loved in preference to spiritual, celestial, and Divine things; so far also man is external.

But since it is not known in the Christian world that there is no faith if there is no charity, nor what charity towards the neighbor is, nor even that the will constitutes the man himself, and the thought only in as far as it is derived from the will, therefore, in order that these subjects may come into the light of the understanding, I will adjoin a collection of passages concerning them from the Arcana Coelestia, which may serve for illustration. FROM THE ARCANA COELESTIA. FAITH. They who do not know that all things in the universe refer themselves to truth and good, and to the conjunction of both, in order to the production of anything, do not know that all things of the church refer themselves to faith and love, and to the conjunction of both. All things in the universe refer themselves to truth and good, and to their conjunction. Truths belong to faith, and goods to love. They who do not know that each and all things in man have relation to the understanding and the will, and to the conjunction of both, in order that man may be man, also do not know that all things of the church have relation to faith and love, and to their conjunction, in order that the church may be in man. Man has two faculties, one of which is called the understanding, and the other the will. The understanding is dedicated to the reception of truths, or of those things which belong to faith; and the will to the reception of goods, or of those things which belong to love. Hence it follows, that love or charity makes the church, and not faith alone, or faith separated from them. Faith separated from charity is no faith. Such faith perishes in the other life. Doctrinals concerning faith alone, destroy charity. They who separate faith from charity are represented in the Word by Cain, by Ham, by Reuben, by the firstborn of the Egyptians, and by the Philistines. As far as charity departs, in so far prevails a religion respecting faith alone. The church in process of time turns aside from charity to faith, and at length to faith alone. In the last time of the church there is no faith, because there is no charity. They who make faith alone saving, excuse a life of evil; and they who are in a life of evil, have no faith, because they have no charity. They are inwardly in the falsities of their own evil, although they do not know it. Therefore good cannot be conjoined to them. Also in the other life they are opposed to good, and to those who are in good. The simple in heart know better than the learned what the good of life is, and thus what charity is, but not what separated faith is. Good is the esse, and truth the existere derived from it, and thus the truth of faith has its own esse of life from the good of charity. Hence the truth of faith lives from the good of charity, or charity is the life of faith. Faith is not alive in man, when he only knows and thinks of the things of faith, but when he wills them, and from willing, does them. The conjunction of the Lord with man is not by faith, but by the life of faith, which is charity. Worship from the good of charity is true worship, but worship from the truth of faith, without the good of charity, is merely an external act. Faith alone, or faith separated from charity, is as the light of winter, in which all things of the earth are torpid, and nothing is produced; but faith with charity is as the light of spring and of summer, in which they all bloom and are made productive. The wintry light, which is that of separated faith, in the other life is turned into dense darkness, when the light of heaven inflows; and they who are in that faith, then come into blindness and stupidity. They who separate faith from charity, are in darkness, and thus in ignorance of truth, and thence in falsities, for falsities are darkness. They cast themselves into falsities, and hence into evils. The errors and falsities into which they cast themselves. The Word is closed against them. They do not see and attend to all the things which the Lord so often spoke concerning love and charity, which see. They neither know what good is, what heavenly love is, nor what charity is. Charity makes the church, and not faith separated from charity. How much of good would exist in the church, if charity were regarded as primary. The church would he one, and not divided into many, if charity were its essential; and then it would be unimportant if men did differ on the doctrines of faith and of external worship. All in heaven are regarded from charity, and none from faith without it. The twelve disciples of the Lord represented the church, as to the all of faith and charity, in one complex, as in like manner did the twelve tribes of Israel. Peter, James and John, represented faith, charity, and the goods of charity, in their order. Peter represented faith and John the goods of charity (Pref. to chap. 18 and 22 of Genesis). In the last times, there would be no faith in the Lord, because no charity, was represented by Peter's denying the Lord three times, before the cock crew twice; for Peter there in a representative sense is faith. "Cockcrowing," as well as "twilight," signifies in the Word the last time of the church. And "three" or "thrice," signify what is complete to the end. The like is signified by what the Lord said to Peter, when Peter saw John following the Lord: What is it to thee, Peter? Follow thou Me, John; for Peter said of John: What is he (John 21:21, 22;)? John rested on the breast of the Lord, because he represented the goods or charity. All the names of persons and places in the Word signify things abstracted from them. CHARITY. That heaven is distinguished into two kingdoms, one of which is called the celestial kingdom, and the other the spiritual; love in the celestial kingdom is love to the Lord, and is called celestial love; and love in the spiritual kingdom is charity towards the neighbor, and is called spiritual love. Heaven is distinguished into those two kingdoms, may be seen in the work on Heaven and Hell. And the Divine of the Lord in the heavens is love to Him, and charity towards the neighbor , in the same work. It is not known what good and truth are, unless it he known what love to the Lord and charity towards the neighbor are, because all good is of love and charity, and all truth is of good. To know truths, to will truths, and to be affected by truths for truth's sake, that is, because they are truths, is charity. Charity consists in an internal affection of doing truth, and not in an external affection without it. Therefore charity consists in performing uses for the sake of uses, and its kind is according to the uses. Charity is man's spiritual life. The whole Word is the doctrine of love and charity. Men at this day do not know what charity is. Still it may be known from the light of reason, that love and charity constitute man. Also that good and truth agree together, and one belongs to the other; therefore charity and faith do the like. In the supreme sense the Lord is the neighbor, because He is to be loved above all things; hence all that is the neighbor which is from Him, and in which He is; therefore good and truth are the neighbor. The distinction of neighbor is according to the quality of good; thus according to the presence of the Lord. Every man, and every society, also our country, and the church, and in the universal sense the kingdom of the Lord, are the neighbor; and to do well by them, from the good of love, according to their several states, is to love the neighbor; thus the neighbor is their good, which we ought to consult. Civil good, which is justice, and moral good, which is the good of life in society, are also the neighbor. To love the neighbor is not to love the person, but that in him which makes him the neighbor, that is, good and truth. They who love the person, and not that which makes the neighbor in him, love the evil as well as the good. And they do service to the evil as well as to the good, when yet to serve the evil is to injure the good, and this is not to love the neighbor. The judge who punishes the evil to amend them, and lest they should corrupt the good, loves the neighbor. To love the neighbor is to do what is good, just, and upright in every work, and in every function. Hence charity towards the neighbor extends itself, both in general and in particular, to all that a man thinks, wills, and does. To do good and truth for the sake of good and truth, is to love the neighbor. They who do this, love the Lord, who in the supreme sense, is the neighbor. A life of charity is a life according to the Lord's precepts; so that to live according to Divine truths, is to love the Lord. Genuine charity is not meritorious. Because it is from an internal affection, thus from the delight of doing good. They who separate faith from charity, in the other life make a merit of faith, and of the good works they did, as matters of external form. The doctrine of the Ancient Church was the doctrine of life, which is the doctrine of charity. The ancients, who were of the church, arranged the goods of charity in order, and distinguished them into classes, giving names to each, and this was the source of their wisdom. Wisdom and intelligence increase immensely in the other life, with those who have lived a life of charity in the world. The Lord inflows with Divine truths into charity, because into the very life of man. Man is as a garden, when charity and faith are conjoined in him, but as a desert when they are not conjoined. Man recedes from wisdom in proportion as he recedes from charity. They who are not in charity, are in ignorance of Divine truths, howsoever wise they may think themselves. The angelic life consists in performing the goods of charity, which are uses. The spiritual angels are forms of charity. THE WILL AND THE UNDERSTANDING. Man has two faculties, one of which is called the understanding, and the other the will. Those two faculties make the man himself. The man is such, as those two faculties are in him. By them also man is distinguished from the beasts, because the understanding of man may be elevated by the Lord, and see Divine truths, and his will may be elevated equally, and perceive Divine goods; and thus man may be conjoined to the Lord by those two faculties, which make him man; but that it is not so with beasts. And since man, in that faculty, is above the beasts, he cannot die as to his interiors, which belong to his spirit, but he lives to eternity (n. 5302). All things in the universe refer themselves to good and truth; thus in man to the will and the understanding. For the understanding is the recipient of truth, and the will of good. It amounts to the same whether you say truth, or faith, for faith is of truth, and truth is of faith; and also whether you say good, or love, for love is of good, and good is of love; for what a man believes, he calls truth; and what he loves, he calls good. Hence it follows, that the understanding is the recipient of faith, and the will is the recipient of love. And since man's understanding may be receptive of faith towards God, and his will of love towards God, that he may be conjoined to God by faith and love, and whoso can be conjoined to God by faith and love, can never die. The will of man is the very esse of his life, since it is the receptacle of love or good, and the understanding is the existere of his life derived form it, since it is the receptacle of faith or truth. Thus the life of the will is the principle life of man, and the life of the understanding proceeds from it. Just as light proceeds form fire or flame. The things which enter the understanding and the will at the same time, are appropriated to man, but not those which enter the understanding alone. Those things become properties of man's life, which are received by the will. Hence if follows, that man is man from the will, and form the understanding thence. Every man moreover is loved and esteemed by others, according to the good of his will and the understanding thence; for he who wills well, and understands well, is loved and esteemed, but he who understands well, and does not will well, is rejected and despised. Man also after death remains as his will, and the understanding thence. And those things which belong to the understanding, and not at the same time to the will, then vanish away, because they are not in man. Or, what amounts to the same, man remains after death as his love, and its derivative faith are, or as his good and its derivative truth are; and the things which belong to faith, and not at the same time to love, or the things which belong to truth, and not at the same time to good, then vanish away, because they are not in man, and thus not of man. Man may receive in the understanding what he does not do from the will, or he may understand what he cannot will, because it is against his love. The reason why man scarcely knows the distinction between thinking and willing. How perverted is the state of those whose understanding and will do not act in unity. Such is the state of hypocrites, of deceivers, of flatterers, and of dissemblers. All the will of good, and all the derivative understanding of truth are from the Lord; not so the understanding of truth, separated from the will of good. It is the understanding which is enlightened by the Lord. The understanding is enlightened as far as man receives truth in the will, that is, as far as he wills to do according to it (n. 3619). The understanding has light from heaven, as the sight has light from the world. The understanding is such, as are the truths from good of which it is formed. The understanding is that which is from truths from good, but not that which is from falsities from evil. The understanding is the seeing, from matters of experience and science, truths, the causes of things, connections, and consequences, in series. The understanding is the seeing and perceiving whether a thing be truth, before it is confirmed, but not the being able to confirm every thing. The seeing and perceiving whether a thing be truth before it is confirmed, is given to those only who are affected with truth for the sake of truth, and are thus in spiritual light. The light of confirmation is natural light, communicable even to the evil. That all dogmas, even false ones, may be confirmed, until they appear like truths.

VII. ALL THE THINGS WHICH ARE PREDICTED IN THE APOCALYPSE, ARE AT THIS DAY FULFILLED. No one can know what all the things which are contained in the Apocalypse signify and involve, unless he knows the internal or spiritual sense of the Word; for everything there is written in a style similar to that of the prophecies of the Old Testament, in which each Word signifies some spiritual thing, which does not appear in the sense of the letter. Besides, the contents of the Apocalypse cannot be explained as to their spiritual sense, except by one who also knows how it went with the church, even to its end, which can only be known in heaven, and is the thing contained in the Apocalypse. For the spiritual sense of the Word treats everywhere of the spiritual world, that is, of the state of the church in the heavens, as well as in the earth; hence the Word is spiritual and Divine. It is this state which is there expounded in its own order. Hence it may appear, that the things contained in the Apocalypse can never be explained by any one but him to whom a revelation has been made concerning the successive states of the church in the heavens; for there is a church in the heavens as well as on the earth, of which something shall be said in the following articles.

The quality of the Lord's church on earth, cannot be seen by any man, so long as he lives in the world, still less how the church in process of time has turned aside from god to evil. The reason is, that man whilst he is living in the world, is in externals, and only sees those things which appear before his natural man; but the quality of the church as to spiritual things, which are its internals, does not appear in the world. Yet it does appear in heaven as in clear day, for the angels are in spiritual thought, and also in spiritual sight, and hence see nothing but spiritual things. Furthermore, all the men who have been born in this world from the beginning of creation are together in the spiritual world, as shown above, and are all there distinguished into societies according to the goods of love and faith, as may be seen in the work on Heaven and Hell; whence it is that the state of the church, and its progressions, are manifest in heaven before the angels. Now since the state of the church as to love and faith is described in the spiritual sense of the Apocalypse, therefore no one can know what all the things in its series involve, but he to whom it has been revealed from heaven, and to whom at the same time it has been granted to know the internal or spiritual sense of the Word. This I can assert, that each thing there, nay, that every word, contains within it a spiritual sense, and all things of the church, as to its spiritual state, from the beginning to the end, are fully described in that sense; and because every word there signifies some spiritual thing, therefore not a word can be wanting without the series of things in the internal sense thereby suffering a change; on which account, at the end of that book, it is said: If any one shall take away from the words of the book of this prophecy, God will take away his part out of the book of life, and from that holy city, and from those things which are written in that book (Apoc. 22:19). It is the same with the books of the Old Testament; in them also every thing, and every word, contains an internal or spiritual sense, wherefore not one word can be taken away from them either. Hence it is that, of the Lord's Divine providence, those books have been preserved entire to an iota since the time in which they were written, and by the care of many who have enumerated their minutest particulars; this was provided by the Lord on account of the sanctity which is within each iota, letter, word, and thing they contain.

Since in like manner there is an internal or spiritual sense in every word in the Apocalypse, and since that sense contains the arcana of the state of the church in the heavens, and on the earth; and since those arcana can be revealed to no one, but to him who knows that sense, and to whom at the same time it has been granted to have consort with the angels, and to speak spiritually with them, therefore, lest the things which are therein written should be hidden to men, and should hereafter be disregarded, because they are not understood, its contents have been disclosed to me; but because they are many they cannot be described in this little work. On which account I will explain the whole book from beginning to end, and disclose the arcana which are within it. This explanation shall be published in less than two years, together with certain things in Daniel, which have hitherto lain hidden, because their spiritual sense was unknown.

He who does not know the internal or spiritual sense, never can divine what is meant in the Apocalypse by "the dragon," and by "the battle" of Michael and his angels with it; what by "the tail" with which the dragon drew down the third part of the stars from heaven; what by "the woman" who brought forth the son a male, which was caught up to God, and whom the dragon persecuted; what by "the beast ascending from the sea," and "the beast ascending from the earth," which had so many horns; what by "the harlot," with whom the kings of the earth committed whoredom; what by the first and second "resurrection," and by "the thousand years"; what by "the lake of sulphur and of fire," into which the dragon, the beast, and the false prophet were cast; what by "the white horse"; also what by "the former heaven, and the former earth" which passed away; and what by "the new heaven and the new earth," in the place of the former; and by "the sea," which was no more; also what by "the city New Jerusalem descending from heaven," and by its "measures," "wall," "gates," and "foundation of precious stones"; what by the various "numbers"; besides other things, which are the deepest mysteries to those who know nothing of the spiritual sense of the Word. But the meaning of all these things shall be unfolded in the promised explanation of that book.

It has been remarked before, that all the things which are contained in that book, in the heavenly sense, are now fulfilled. In this little work I will deliver some general account of the Last Judgment, the Babylon destroyed, the first heaven and the first earth which passed away, the new heaven, the new earth, and the New Jerusalem; in order that it may be known, that all things are now accomplished. But the details can only be delivered, where all these things are explained according to the description of them in the Book of Revelation

VIII. THE LAST JUDGMENT HAS BEEN ACCOMPLISHED. It was shown above, in an article for the purpose, that the Last Judgment does not exist on the earth, but in the spiritual world, where all from the beginning of creation are together; and since it is so, it is impossible for any man to know when the Last Judgment is accomplished, for every one expects it to exist on earth, accompanied by a change of all things in the visible heaven, and on the earth and in the human race there. Lest therefore the man of the church from ignorance should live in such a belief, and lest they who think of the Last Judgment should expect it forever, whence at length the belief in those things which are said of it in the literal sense of the Word must perish, and lest perchance therefore many should recede from a belief in the Word, it has been granted me to see with my own eyes that the Last Judgment is now accomplished; that the evil are cast into the hells, and the good elevated into heaven, and thus that all things are reduced into order, the spiritual equilibrium between good and evil, or between heaven and hell, being thence restored. It was granted me to see from beginning to end how the Last Judgment was accomplished; and also how Babylon was destroyed, also how those who are meant by "the dragon" were cast into the abyss, and how the New Heaven was formed, and the New Church instituted in the heavens, which is meant by "the New Jerusalem." It was granted me to see all these things with my own eyes, in order that I might be able to testify of them. This Last Judgment was commenced in the beginning of the year 1757, and was fully accomplished at the end of that year.

But it is to be known that the Last Judgment was effected upon those who had lived from the Lord's time to this day, but not upon those who had lived before. For a Last Judgment had twice before existed on this earth; one which is described in the Word by "the flood," the other was effected by the Lord Himself when He was in the world, which is also meant by the Lord's words: Now is the judgment of this world, now is the prince of this world cast out (John 12:31); and in another place: These things I have spoken unto you that in Me ye may have peace; be of good cheer, I have overcome the world (John 16:33); and also by these words in Isaiah: Who is this that cometh from Edom, walking in the multitude of His strength, great to save? I have trodden the wine-press alone, therefore I have trodden them in My anger; whence their victory is sprinkled upon My garments, for the day of vengeance is in My heart, and the year of My redeemed has come; therefore He became a Savior (Isa. 63:1-8); and in many other places. A Last Judgment has twice before existed on this earth, because every judgment exists at the end of a church, as shown above in an article for the purpose, and there have been two churches on this earth, one before the flood, and one after it. The church before the flood is described in the first chapters of Genesis by the new creation of the heaven and the earth, and by paradise; its end, by the eating of the tree of science, and the subsequent particulars; and its Last Judgment by the flood; the whole by mere correspondences, according to the style of the Word; in the internal or spiritual sense of which, by "the creation of the heaven and the earth," the institution of a new church is meant, see the first article; by "the paradise in Eden," its celestial wisdom; by "the tree of science," and by "the serpent," the scientific which destroyed it; and by "the flood," the Last Judgment upon the men of whom it consisted. But the other church, which was after the flood, is also described in certain passages in the Word (as in Deut. 32:7-14), and elsewhere. This church was extended through much of the Asiatic world, and was continued with the posterity of Jacob. Its end was, when the Lord came into the world. A Last Judgment was then effected by Him upon all who belonged to that church from its first institution; and, at the same time, upon the residue from the first church, The Lord came into the world for that end, to reduce all things in the heavens into order, and through the heavens all things on earth, and at the same time to make His Human Divine; for if this had not been done, no one could have been saved. That there were two churches on this earth before the Lord's coming is shown in various passages in the Arcana Coelestia, a collection of which may be seen below; and that the Lord came into the world to reduce all things in the heavens into order, and through them all things on earth, and to make His Human Divine. The third church on this earth is the Christian. Upon this church, and, at the same time, upon all those who had been in the first heaven since the Lord's time, the Last Judgment of which I now treat, was effected. The first and Most Ancient Church on this earth was that which is described in the first chapters of Genesis, and it was a celestial church, the chief of all the churches. Their quality they who were of that church are in heaven. They are in the greatest light there. There were various churches after the flood, which are called in one word, the Ancient Church. Through what kingdoms of Asia the Ancient Church was extended. The quality of the men of the Ancient Church. The Ancient Church was a representative church. What the quality of the Ancient Church was, when it began to decline. The distinction between the Most Ancient and Ancient Church. Of the church that commenced from Eber, which was called the Hebrew church. The distinction between the Ancient and the Hebrew church. Of the church instituted among the posterity of Jacob, or sons of Israel. The statutes, judgments and laws, which were commanded among the sons of Israel, were in part like those which existed in the Ancient Church. In what manner the representative rites of the church which was instituted among the sons of Israel, differed from the representative rites of the Ancient Church. In the Most Ancient Church there was immediate revelation from heaven; in the Ancient Church revelation by correspondences; in the church among the sons of Israel, by a living voice; and in the Christian church by the Word. The Lord was the God of the Most Ancient Church, and also of the Ancient Church, and was called Jehovah. The Lord, when He was in the world, reduced all things in the heavens and in the hells into order. The Lord then freed the spiritual world from the antediluvian. Their quality. The Lord by temptations and victories subjugated the hells, and reduced all things into order, and at the same time glorified His Human. The Lord effected this by Himself, or by His own Power. The Lord alone fought. Hence the Lord alone became righteousness and merit. Thus the Lord united His Human with the Divine. The passion of the cross was the last temptation, and plenary victory, by which He glorified Himself, that is, made His Human Divine, and subjugated the hells. The Lord could not be tempted as to the Divine Itself. Therefore He assumed a human from the mother, into which He admitted temptations. He expelled whatever was hereditary from the mother, and put off the human He received from her, even until He was her son no longer, and He put on the Human Divine. The Lord saved men by the subjugation of the hells, and the glorification of His Human.

How this Last Judgment was effected cannot be described in all its details in this little work, for they are many, but shall be described in the Explanation of the Apocalypse. For the judgment was accomplished not only upon all the men of the Christian church, but also upon all who are called Mohammedans, and, moreover, upon all the Gentiles in the whole world. And it was effected in this order: first upon those of the Papal religion; then upon the Mohammedans; afterwards upon the Gentiles; and lastly upon the Reformed. The judgment upon those who were of the Papal religion shall be shown in the following article, on Babylon which has been destroyed; the judgment upon the Reformed in the article, on the first heaven which passed away; but something shall be said in this article, on the judgment upon the Mohammedans and Gentiles.

The following was seen to be the arrangement in the spiritual world of all the nations and people to be judged Collected in the middle, appeared those who are called the Reformed, where they were also distinct according to their countries; the Germans there towards the north; the Swedes there towards the west; the Danes in the west; the Dutch towards the east and the south; the English in the center. Surrounding this whole mid-region in which were the Reformed, appeared collected those of the Papal religion, the greater part of them in the western, some part in the southern quarter. Beyond them were the Mohammedans, also distinct according to their countries, who all appeared in the south-west. Beyond these, the Gentiles were congregated in vast numbers, constituting the very circumference. Beyond these appeared as it were a sea, which was the boundary. This arrangement of the nations in the various quarters, was an arrangement according to each nation's common faculty of receiving Divine truths; for in the spiritual world every one is known from the quarter, and the part of it, in which he dwells; and, moreover, in a society with many, he is known from his tarryings with reference to the quarters; concerning which, see the work on Heaven and Hell. It is the same when he goes from place to place; all advance to the quarters is then effected according to the successive states of the thoughts from the affections which belong to his own life; in accordance with which all those who are spoken of in what follows were led to their own places. In a word, the ways in which every one walks in the spiritual world are actual determinations of the thoughts of the mind; whence it is, that "ways," "walking," and the like, in the spiritual sense of the Word, signify the determinations and progressions of spiritual life.

In the Word, the four quarters are called "the four winds," and a gathering is called "a gathering from the four winds"; as where the Last Judgment is the subject treated of in Matthew: He shall send His angels, and they shall gather together the elect from the four winds, from one end of the heavens to the other ; and elsewhere: All nations shall be gathered together before the Son of man, and He shall separate them one from another, as a shepherd separates the sheep from the goats, and He shall set the sheep on the right and the goats on the left (Matt. 25:31, 32). This signifies that the Lord will then separate those who are in truths and at the same time in good, from those who are in truths and not in good; for in the spiritual sense of the Word, "the right" signifies good, and "the left" truth, and "sheep" and "goats" the same. The judgment was effected upon these alone; the evil who were in no truths being in the hells already; for all the evil in heart who have denied the Divine, and have rejected the truths of the church from their belief are cast thither alter death, and therefore before the judgment. "The first heaven" which passed away, consisted of those who were in truths, and not in good, and "the new heaven" was formed of those who were in truths, and at the same time in good.

As regards the judgment upon the Mohammedans and Gentiles, which is treated of in this article, it was thus effected. The Mohammedans were led forth from their places, where they were gathered together in the south-west, by a way round the Christians, from the west, through the north, to the east, as far as its southern boundary; and the good were separated from the evil in the way. The evil were cast into marshes and lakes, many too being scattered about in a certain far desert. But the good were led through the east to a land of great extent near the south, and habitations were there given them. They who were led thither had in the world acknowledged the Lord as the greatest Prophet, and as the Son of God, and had believed that He was sent by the Father to instruct the human race, and at the same time had lived a moral spiritual life according to their religious principles. Most of these, when instructed, receive faith in the Lord, and acknowledge Him to be one with the Father. Communication is also granted them with the Christian heaven, by influx from the Lord; but they are not commingled with it, because religion separates them. All of that religion, as soon as they come into the other life among their own, first seek Mohammed, yet he does not appear, but in his place there are two others, who call themselves Mohammeds, and who have obtained seats in the middle, under the Christian heaven, towards the left part of it. These two are in the place of Mohammed, because all after death, whatever be their religion, are first led to those they had worshiped in the world, for every one's religion adheres to him, but they recede on perceiving that these can render them no assistance. They are thus yielded up into their own religion at first, as the only possible means of effecting their withdrawal from it. Where Mohammed himself is, and what he is, and whence come those two who fill his place, shall be told in the book in which the Apocalypse is explained.

The judgment was effected upon the Gentiles in nearly the same manner as upon the Mohammedans; but they were not led like them in a circuit, but only a short way in the west, where the evil were separated from the good, the evil being there cast into two great gulfs, which stretched obliquely into the deep, but the good were conducted above the middle, where the Christians were, towards the land of the Mohammedans in the eastern quarter, and dwellings were given them behind, and beyond the Mohammedans, to a great extent in the southern quarter. But those of the Gentiles who in the world had worshiped God under the Human form, and bad led lives of charity according to their religious principles, were conjoined with Christians in heaven, for they acknowledge and adore the Lord more than others; the most intelligent of them are from Africa The multitude of the Gentiles and Mohammedans who appeared, was so great, that it could be numbered only by myriads. The judgment on this vast multitude was effected in a few days, for every one after being yielded up into his own love and into his own faith, is immediately assigned and carried to his like.

From all these particulars appears the truth of the Lord's prediction concerning the Last Judgment, that: They shall come from the east and west, and from the north and south, and shall sit down in the kingdom of God (Luke 13:29).

IX. BABYLON AND ITS DESTRUCTION. That all the things which are predicted in the Apocalypse are at this day fulfilled, may be seen above ; and that the Last Judgment has already been accomplished, may be seen in the preceding article; where it is also shown how the judgment was effected upon the Mohammedans and Gentiles. Now follows an account of the manner in which it was effected upon the Papists, who are meant by "Babylon," which is treated of in many parts of the Apocalypse, and its destruction especially in chapter 18, where it is thus described: An angel cried vehemently with a great voice, Babylon hath fallen, hath fallen, and has become the habitation of demons, and the hold of every foul spirit, and the cage of every unclean and hateful bird. But before it is told how that destruction was effected, I shall premise: I. What is meant by "Babylon," and what its quality is. II. The quality of those in the other life who are of Babylon. III. Where their habitations have hitherto been. IV. Why they were there tolerated until the day of the Last Judgment. V. How they were destroyed, and their habitations made a desert. VI. Those of them who were in the affection of truth from good were preserved.

VII. The state of those hereafter who come thence from the earth.

I. What is meant by Babylon, and what its quality is. By Babylon are meant all who wish to have dominion by religion. To have dominion by religion, is to have dominion over men's souls, thus over their very spiritual life, and to use the Divine things, which are in their religion, as the means. All those who have dominion for an end, and religion for the means are in general Babylon. They are called Babylon because such dominion began in ancient times; but it was destroyed in its beginning. Its commencement is described by the city and the tower, the head of which was to be in heaven; and its destruction, by the confusion of lips, whence its name Babel was derived (Gen. 11:1-9). What the particulars there related mean in the internal or spiritual sense of the Word, may be seen explained in the Arcana Coelestia. Moreover that this dominion began and was instituted in Babel, appears in Daniel, where it is said of Nebuchadnezzar, that he set up an image which all were to adore. And it is also meant by Belshazzar and his peers drinking out of the golden and silver vessels, which Nebuchadnezzar had carried away from the temple of Jerusalem, at the same time they worshiped gods of gold, silver, copper, and iron; wherefore it was written on the wall: He hath numbered, he hath weighed, he hath divided; and on the same night the king himself was slain. "The vessels of gold and silver" of the temple of Jerusalem, signify the goods and truths of the church; "drinking out of them," and at the same time worshiping gods of gold, silver, copper, and iron, signify profanation; and "the writing upon the wall," and "the death of the king" signify visitation, and destruction denounced against those who make use of Divine goods and truths as means. What their quality is who are called Babylon, is also described sometimes in the prophets; as in Isaiah: Thou mayest take up this parable concerning the king of Babylonia. Jehovah hath broken the staff of the wicked, the scepter of those having dominion; thou, Lucifer, hast fallen from heaven; thou art cut down even to the earth; thou hast said in thy mind, I will ascend into the heavens; I will exalt my throne over the stars of God, and I sit on the mountain of the assembly, in the sides of the north, I will become like the Most High. Nevertheless thou shalt be cast down into hell, to the sides of the pit; I will cut off the name and residue of Babylon and will cause her to become an hereditary possession of the bittern (14:4, 5, 12, 13, 14, 15, 22, 23). And again it is said in the same: The lion said, Babylon is fallen, is fallen, and all the graven images of her god are cast down. See also (47 and 48 14-20; and Jer. 50:1-3). From these passages it is now evident what Babylonia is. It should be known that the church becomes Babylonia, when charity and faith cease, and the love of self begins to rule in their place; for this love in proportion as it is unchecked, rushes on, aiming to dominate not merely over all whom it can subject to itself on earth, but even over heaven; nor does it rest there, but it climbs the very throne of God, and transfers to itself His Divine power. That it did this, even before the Lord's coming, appears from the passages of the Word adduced above. But that Babylonia was destroyed by the Lord when He was in the world, both by their becoming altogether idolatrous, and by the Last Judgment upon them in the spiritual world. This is meant by the prophetic sayings, that "Lucifer," who there is Babylon, was cast into hell, and that "Babylon has fallen"; and moreover by "the writing on the wall," and "the death of Belshazzar"; and also by "the stone, hewn from the rock," which destroyed the statue, of which Nebuchadnezzar dreamed.

But Babylon treated of in the Apocalypse, is the Babylon of this day, which arose after the Lord's coming, and is known to be with the Papists. This Babylon is more pernicious and more heinous than that which existed before the Lord's coming, because it profanes the interior goods and truths of the church, which the Lord revealed to the world, when He revealed Himself. How pernicious, how inwardly heinous it is: may appear from the following summary. They acknowledge and adore the Lord apart from all power of saving: they entirely separate His Divine from His Human, and transfer to themselves His Divine power, which belonged to His Human; for they remit sins; they send to heaven; they cast into hell; they save whom they will; they sell salvation; thus they arrogate to themselves what belongs to the Divine power alone: and since they exercise this power, it follows that thee make gods of themselves, each one according to his station, by transference from the highest of them, whom they call Christ's vicar, down to the lowest; thus they regard themselves as the Lord, and adore Him, not for His own sake, but for theirs. They not only adulterate and falsify the Word, but even take it away from the people, lest they should enter into the smallest light of truth; and not satisfied with this, they moreover annihilate it, acknowledging the Divine in the decrees of Rome, superior to the Divine in the Word; so that they exclude all from the way to heaven; for the acknowledgment of the Lord, faith in Him, and love to Him, are the way to heaven; and the Word is what teaches the way: whence it is, that without the Lord, by means of the Word, there is no salvation. They strive with all diligence to extinguish the light of heaven, which is from Divine truth, in order that ignorance may exist in the place of it, and the denser the ignorance, the more acceptable it is to them. They extinguish the light of heaven, by prohibiting the reading of the Word, and of books which contain doctrines from the Word; instituting worship by masses in a language not understood by the simple, and in which there is no Divine truth; and besides, they fill their world with falsities which are darkness itself, and which remove and dissipate the light. They likewise persuade the common people, that they have life in the faith of their priests, thus in the faith of another and not in their own. They also place all worship in a holy external, without the internal, making the internal empty, because it is without the knowledges of good and truth; and yet Divine worship is external, only so far as it is internal, since the external proceeds from the internal. Besides this, they introduce idolatries of various kinds, They make and multiply saints; they see and tolerate the adoration of these saints, and even the prayers offered to them almost as to gods; they set up their idols everywhere; boast of the great abundance of miracles done by them; set them over cities, temples, and monasteries; their bones taken out of their tombs they account holy, which yet are most vile; thus turning the minds of all from the worship of God, to the worship of men, Moreover, they use much artful precaution lest any one should come out of that thick darkness into light, from idolatrous worship to Divine worship; for they multiply monasteries, from which they send out spies and guards in all directions; they extort the confessions of the heart, which are also confessions of the thoughts and intentions, and if any one will not confess, they threaten him with infernal fire and torments in purgatory; and those who dare to speak against the Papal throne, and their dominion, they shut up in a horrible prison, which is called the inquisition. All these things they do for the sole end that they may possess the world and its treasures, and live in luxury and be the greatest, while the rest are slaves. But domination such as this, is not that of heaven over hell, but of hell over heaven, for as far as the love of having dominion is with man, especially with the man of the church, so far hell reigns. That this love reigns in hell, and makes hell, may be seen in the work on Heaven and Hell. From this summary it may appear that they have no church there, but Babylon; for the church is where the Lord Himself is worshiped, and where the Word is read. The attribution by the church, of two natures to the Lord, and thus the separation of His Divine from His Human, was effected in a council, for the sake of the Pope, that the Pope might he acknowledged as the Lord's vicar, disclosed from heaven in the Arcana Coelestia.

II. The quality of those in the other life who are Babylon can appear only to one to whom it has been given by the Lord to be together with those who are in the spiritual world. Since this has been granted to me, I am able to speak from experience, for I have seen them, I have heard them, and I have spoken with them. Every man after death is in a life similar to his life in the world; this cannot be changed, save only as regards the delights of the love, which are turned into correspondences, as may appear from the two articles in the work on Heaven and Hell. It is the same with the life of those now treated of, which is altogether such as it was in the world, with this difference, that the hidden things of their hearts are there uncovered, for they are in the spirit, in which reside the interior things of the thoughts and intentions, which they had concealed in the world, and had covered over with a holy external. And since these hidden things were then laid open, it was perceived that more than half of those who had usurped the power of opening and shutting heaven, were altogether atheists; but since dominion resides in their minds as in the world, and is based on this principle that all power was given by the Father to the Lord Himself, and that it was transferred to Peter, and by order of succession to the primates of the church, therefore an oral confession about the Lord remains adjoined to their atheism; but even this remains only so long as they enjoy some dominion by means of it. But the rest of them, who are not atheists, are so empty, as to be entirely ignorant of man's spiritual life, of the means of salvation, of the Divine truths which lead to heaven; and they know nothing at all of heavenly faith and love, believing that heaven may be granted of the Pope's favor to any one, whatever he be. Now since every one is in a life in the spiritual world, similar to his life in the natural world, without any difference, so long as he is neither in heaven nor in hell (as is shown, and may be seen in the work on Heaven and Hell,), and since the spiritual world, as regards its external appearance, is altogether like the natural world , therefore they also live a similar moral and civil life, and above all have similar worship, for this is inrooted, and inheres to man in his inmost, nor can any one after death be withdrawn from it, except he be in good from truths, and in truths from good. But it is more difficult to withdraw the nation now treated of from its worship, than other nations, because it is not in good from truths, and still less in truths from good; for its truths are not from the Word, with the exception of some few, which they have falsified by applying them to dominion; and hence it has none other than spurious good, for such as the truths are, such does the good become. These things are said, in order that it may be known, that the worship of this nation, in the spiritual world, is altogether similar to its worship in the natural world. These things premised, I will now relate some particulars of the worship and life of the Papists in the spiritual world. They have a certain council, in place of the council or consistory at Rome, in which their primates meet, and consult on various matters of their religion, especially on the means of holding the common people in blind obedience, and of enlarging their dominion. This council is situated in the southern quarter, near the east; but no one who has been a Pope or a cardinal in the world dares to enter it, because the semblance of Divine authority possesses their minds, from their having in the world arrogated the Lord's power to themselves; wherefore, as soon as they present themselves there, they are carried out, and cast to their like in a desert. But those among them, who have been upright in mind, and have not from confirmed belief usurped such power, are in a certain obscure chamber behind this council. There is another assembly in the western quarter, near the north; the business there, is the intromission of the credulous common people into heaven. They there dispose around them a number of societies which live in various external delights; in some of the societies they play, in some they dance, in some they compose the face into the various expressions of hilarity and mirthfulness; in some they converse in a friendly manner; in some they discuss civil affairs, in others religious matters; in other societies again, they talk obscenities; and so on, They admit their dependents into one of these societies such as each may desire, and call it heaven; but all of them, after being there a few hours, are wearied and depart, because those joys are external, and not eternal. In this way, moreover, many are withdrawn from a belief in their doctrinal concerning intromission into heaven. As regards their worship in particular, it is almost like their worship in the world; as in the world, it consists in masses, not performed in the common language of spirits, but in one composed of lofty-sounding words, which induce an external holiness and awe, and are utterly unintelligible. In like manner they adore saints, and expose idols to view; but their saints are nowhere to be seen, for all those who have sought to be worshiped as deities, are in hell; the rest who did not seek to be worshiped, are among common spirits. This their prelates know, for they seek and find them, and when found they despise them; yet they conceal it from the people, that the saints may still be worshiped as tutelar deities, but that the primates themselves, who are set over the people, may be worshiped as the lords of heaven. In like manner, moreover, they multiply temples and monasteries as they did in the world; they scrape together riches, and accumulate costly things, which they hide in cellars; for costly things exist in the spiritual, as well as in the natural world, and far more abundantly. In like manner they send forth monks, to allure the Gentiles to their religious persuasion, in order that they may subject them to their rule. They commonly have watch towers erected in the middle of their assemblies, from which they are enabled to enjoy an extended view into all the surrounding region. And moreover, by various means and arts they establish for themselves communications with persons far and near, joining in league with them, and drawing them over to their own party. Such is their state in general; but as to particulars, many prelates of that religion take away all power from the Lord, and claim it for themselves, and because they do this, they do not acknowledge any Divine. They still counterfeit holiness in externals; yet this holiness in itself is profane, because in their internals there is no acknowledgment of the Divine. Hence it is that they communicate with certain societies of the lowest heaven by a holy external, and with the hells by a profane internal, so that they are in both; on which account, moreover, they allure simple good spirits, and give them habitations near themselves, and also congregate wicked spirits, and dispose them around the society in all directions, by the simple good conjoining themselves with heaven, and by the wicked with hell. Hence they are enabled to accomplish heinous things which they perpetrate from hell. For the simple good who are in the lowest heavens look only to their holy external, and their very holy adoration of the Lord in externals, but they do not see their wickedness, and therefore they favor them, and this is their greatest protection; yet in process of time they all recede from their holy external, and then, being separated from heaven, they are cast into hell. From these things it may be known in some degree, what is the quality of those in the other life who are from Babylon. But I am aware that they who are in this world, and have no idea of man's state after death, of heaven, or of hell, but an inane and empty one, will wonder at the existence of such things in the spiritual world. But, that man is equally a man after death, that he lives in fellowships as he did in the world, that he dwells in houses, hears preaching in temples, discharges duties, and sees things in that world, similar to those in the former world he has left, may appear from all that has been said and shown of the things I have heard and seen, in the work on Heaven and Hell.

I have spoken with some from that nation, concerning the keys given to Peter; whether they believe that the power of the Lord over heaven and earth was transferred to him, and because this was the fundamental of their religion, they vehemently insisted on it, saying, that there was no doubt about it, because it was said manifestly. But when I asked them whether they knew that in each expression of the Word there is a spiritual sense, which is the sense of the Word in heaven, they said at first, that they did not know it, but afterwards they said they would inquire; and on inquiring, they were instructed that there is a spiritual sense within each expression of the Word, which differs from the sense of the letter, as the spiritual differs from the natural; and they were also instructed that no person named in the Word is named in heaven, but that some spiritual thing is there understood in place of him. Finally, they were informed, that instead of "Peter" in the Word is meant the truth of the faith of the church, from the good of charity, and that the same is meant by "a rock," which is there named with Peter, for it is said: Thou art Peter, and upon this rock will I build My church (Matt. 16:18, seq.). By this is not meant that any power was given to Peter, but that it is given to truth from good, for in the heavens all power belongs to truth from good, or to good through truth; and since all good, and all truth, are from the Lord, and nothing from man, that all power is the Lord's. When they heard this they replied indignantly, that they wished to know whether there is a spiritual sense in those words, wherefore the Word which is in heaven was given them, in which Word there is not the natural sense, but the spiritual, because it is for the angels, who are spiritual; that there is such a Word in heaven, may be seen in the work on Heaven and Hell. And when they read it, they saw manifestly that Peter is not named there, but truth from good, which is from the Lord, instead of him. Seeing this they rejected it with anger, and would almost have torn it in pieces with their teeth, had it not at that moment been taken away. Hence they were convinced, although unwilling to be convinced, that the Lord alone has that power, and by no means can it belong to any man, because it is the Divine power. The twelve disciples of the Lord represented the church as to the all of truth and good, or of faith and love, as in like manner did the twelve tribes of Israel. Peter, James, and John, represented faith, charity, and the goods of charity. Peter represented faith. The keys of the kingdom of heaven being given to Peter, signifies that all power is given to truth from good, or to faith from charity, proceeding from the Lord; thus that all power belongs to the Lord. "A key" signifies the power of opening and shutting. All power is in good by truths, or in truths from good, proceeding from the Lord. "A rock" in the Word signifies the Lord as to Divine truth. All names of persons and places in the Word signify things and states. Their names do not enter heaven, but are turned into the things they signify, and they cannot be pronounced in heaven. How elegant is the internal sense of the word, where mere names occur, is illustrated by examples.

III. Where their habitations in the spiritual world have hitherto been. It was said above), that all the nations and peoples in the spiritual world were seen to be as follows: collected in the middle appeared those who are called the Reformed; around this middle, those of the Papal religion; the Mohammedans, beyond them; and lastly the various Gentiles. Hence it may appear that the Papists formed the nearest circumference around the Reformed in the center. The reason of this is that they who are in the light of truth from the Word are in the center, and they who are in the light of truth from the Word are also in the light of heaven, for the light of heaven is from the Divine truth, and the Word is that in which this is. That the light of heaven is from the Divine truth, may be seen in the work on Heaven and Hell ; and that it is the Divine truth , Light, moreover, proceeds from the center towards the circumferences, and illuminates. Hence it is that the Papists proximately surround the center, for they have the Word, and it is also read by those of the ecclesiastical order, though not by the people. This is the reason why the Papal nation in the spiritual world have obtained habitations around those who are in the light of truth from the Word. Their manner of dwelling, before their habitations were utterly destroyed, and made into a desert, shall now be told. The greatest part of them dwelt in the south and in the west; but some in the north and in the east. In the south dwelt those who had excelled others in talent in the world, and had confirmed themselves in their own religion. Great numbers of the nobility and the rich also dwelt there. They did not dwell upon the earth there, but under it, from dread of robbers, guards being placed at the entrances. In that quarter, moreover, there was a great city, extending nearly from east to west, and somewhat into the west, situated very near the center where the Reformed were. Myriads of men or spirits tarried in that city. It was full of temples and monasteries. The ecclesiastics also carried into it all precious things which they were enabled by their various artifices to scrape together, and they hid them in its cells and subterranean crypts, which were so elaborately formed, that no one besides themselves could enter, for they were disposed around in the form of a labyrinth. On the treasures there amassed, in the full confidence that they could never be destroyed, they had set their hearts. When I saw those crypts I was amazed at the art displayed in constructing them, and enlarging them without end. The most of those who call themselves of the society of Jesus were there, and cultivated amicable relations with the rich who dwelt round about. Towards the east in that quarter was the council where they consulted on the enlargement of their dominion, and on the means of keeping the people in blind obedience. This concerning their habitations in the southern quarter. In the north, dwelt those who less excelled in ability, and had less confirmed themselves in their own religion, because they were in an obscure faculty of discerning and thence in blind faith. The multitude was not so great there as in the south. Most of them were in a great city extending lengthwise from the angle of the east to the west, and also a little into the west. It also was full of temples and monasteries. On its outmost side which was near the east there were many of various religions, and also some of the Reformed. A few places, moreover, beyond the city in that quarter, were occupied by the Papists. In the east dwelt those who had been in the greatest delight of ruling in the world, and at the same time in somewhat of natural light. They appeared there on mountains, but only in the quarter which faces the north; there were none in the other part which faces the south. In the angle towards the north, there was a mountain, on the top of which they had placed a certain one of unsound mind, whom, by communications of the thoughts, which are known in the spiritual, but unknown in the natural world, they were enabled to inspire to command anything they chose. And they gave out that he was the very God of heaven, appearing under a human form, and thus paid him Divine worship. They did this, because the people were desirous of receding from their idolatrous worship, wherefore, they devised it as a means of keeping them in obedience. That mountain is meant in Isaiah by "the mountain of assembly in the sides of the north," and those on the mountains are there meant by "Lucifer" (ver. 12); for such of the Babylonish crew as dwelt in the east, were in greater light than others, which light also, they had prepared for themselves by artifice. There also appeared some who were building a tower: which should reach even to heaven where the angels are, but this was only representative of their machinations; for machinations are presented in the spiritual world, before the eyes of those who stand at a distance, by many things which yet do not exist actually with those who are in the machinations: this is a common thing there. By this appearance it was given me to know what was signified by: The tower whose head should be in heaven, whence the place was called Babel (Gen. 11:1-10). These things are concerning their habitations in the east. In the west, in front, dwelt those of that religion who lived in the dark ages, for the most part underground, one posterity beneath another. The whole tract in front which looked to the north, was, as it were, excavated, and filled with monasteries. The entrances to them lay through caverns covered by roofs, through which they went out and in, They rarely spoke with those who lived in the following ages, being of a different disposition, and not so malicious; for as, in their times, there was no contention with the Reformed, there was there fore less of the craft and malice from hatred and revenge. In the western quarter beyond that tract, were many mountains, on which dwelt the wickedest of that nation, who in heart denied the Divine and yet orally professed their belief in Him, and adored Him with gestures more devoutly than others. They who were there, devised nefarious arts to keep the common people under the yoke of their sway, and also to force others to submit to that yoke: these arts it is not allowed to describe, they are so heinous. In general they are such as are mentioned in the work on Heaven and Hell, The mountains on which they dwelt, are meant in the Apocalypse by "the seven mountains," and those who were there are described by the woman sitting upon the scarlet beast: I saw a woman sitting upon a scarlet beast, full of names of blasphemy, having seven heads, and ten horns: she had on the forehead a name written, mystery, Babylon the great, mother of the whoredoms and abominations of the earth: the seven heads are seven mountains, on which the woman sitteth (Apoc. 17:3, 5, 9). By "a woman" in the internal sense, is meant the church, here in the opposite sense, a profane religion; by "the scarlet beast," the profanation of celestial love; by "the seven mountains," the profane lobe of ruling. These are concerning their habitations in the west. The reason why they dwell distinct according to quarters is, because all in the spiritual world are carried into that quarter, and into that part of it, which corresponds to their affections and loves, and no one to any other place; concerning which see the work on Heaven and Hell, where it treats of the four quarters of heaven. In general, all the consultations of the Babylonish race tend to this, that they may dominate, not only over heaven, but over the whole earth, and thus that they may possess heaven and earth, obtaining each by means of the other, To effect this, they continually devise and batch new statutes and new doctrinals. They make the same endeavor also in the other life as they made in the world, for every one after death is such as he was in the world, especially as to his religion. It was granted me to hear certain of the primates consulting about a doctrine, which was to be a rule for the people: it consisted of many articles, but they all tended to this; that they might obtain dominion over the heavens, and the earth, and that they might have all power for themselves, and the Lord none. These doctrinals were after. wards read before the bystanders, and thereupon a voice was heard from heaven, declaring, that they were dictated from the deepest hell, though the hearers did not know it; which was further confirmed by this; that a crowd of devils from that hell, of the blackest and direst appearance, ascended, and tore those doctrinals from them, not with their hands, but with their teeth, and carried them down to their hell. The people who saw it were astounded.

IV. Why they were there tolerated, until the day of the Last Judgment. The reason was, because it is from Divine order that all who can be preserved, shall be preserved, even until they can no longer be among the good. Therefore all those are preserved, who can emulate spiritual life in externals, and present it in a moral life, as if it were therein, whatever they may be as to faith and love in Internals; so also those are preserved who are in external holiness, though not in internal. Such were many of that nation, for they could speak piously with the common people, and adore the Lord in a holy manner to implant religion in their minds, and lead them to think of heaven and hell, and could hold them in doing goods by preaching works. Thus they were able to lead many to a life of good, and therefore into the way to heaven; on which account also, many of that religion were saved, although few of their leaders. For these are such as the Lord means by: False prophets, who come in sheep's clothing, but inwardly are ravening wolves (Matt. 7:15). By "prophets," in the internal sense of the Word, are meant those who teach truth, and by it lead to good; and by "false prophets," those who teach falsity, and seduce by it. They are also like the scribes and Pharisees, who are described by the Lord in these words: They sit in Moses' seat; all things that they bid you observe, observe and do, but do not according to their word; for they say and do not; all their works they do to be seen of men; they shut up the kingdom of the heavens against men, but go not in themselves: they eat widows' houses, for a pretence pouring forth long prayers. Woe unto you, hypocrites, ye make clean the outside of the cup and platter, but within they are full of rapine and iniquity; cleanse first the inside of the cup and platter, that the outside may be clean also; ye are like whited sepulchres, which appear outwardly beautiful, but within are full of the bones of the dead: thus ye outwardly appear just before men, but within ye are full of hypocrisy and iniquity (Matt. 23:1-34). Another reason moreover why they were tolerated was, because every man after death retains his religious principles that he has acquired in the world; into which therefore he is introduced, when first he comes into the other life. Now with this nation, the religious principle was implanted by those who gave an oral preference to sanctity, and feigned holy gestures, and moreover, impressed the people with a belief that they could be saved through them; hence also they were removed, but were preserved among their own. But the principal reason was, that all are preserved from one judgment to another, who live a life similar to a spiritual life in externals, and emulate as it were a pious and holy internal; by whom the simple may receive instruction and guidance: for the simple in faith and heart look no farther than to see what is external, and apparent before the eyes. Hence all such were tolerated from the commencement of the Christian church, until the day of the judgment. That a Last Judgment has existed twice before, and now exists for the third time, was shown above. Of all these "the former heaven" consisted, and they are meant in the Apocalypse (20:5, 6) by "those who are not of the first resurrection." But since they were such as above described, that heaven was destroyed, and they of the second resurrection were cast out. But it ought to be known that they only were preserved who suffered themselves to be held in bonds by laws both civil and spiritual, they being capable of living together in society; nevertheless they who could not be held in bonds by those laws were not preserved, but were cast into hell long before the day of the Last Judgment: for societies are continually purified and purged from such. Hence, they who led a wicked life, who enticed the common people to do evils, and entered on abominable arts, such as exist among spirits in the hells , were cast out of societies, and this in their turns. In like manner also those who are interiorly good are removed from societies, lest they should be contaminated by those who are interiorly evil; for the good perceive the interiors, and therefore pay no regard to the exteriors, except just so far as they agree with the interiors; they are sent in their turns to places of instruction , and are carried thence into heaven; for "the new heaven" is formed of them, and they are meant by "those who are of the first resurrection." These things are said that it may be known, why so many of the Papal religion were tolerated and preserved until the day of the Last Judgment; but more will be said on the same subject in the following article, where "the first heaven" which passed away is to be treated of.

V. How they were destroyed, and their habitations made a desert. This I will here describe in a few words; more fully in the Explanation of the Apocalypse. That Babylonia there treated of has been destroyed, no one but he who saw it can know, and it was given me to see how the Last Judgment was brought about and accomplished upon all, especially upon those of Babylon. I, therefore, will describe it This was granted me, principally, in order to reveal to the world, that all things predicted in the Apocalypse are Divinely inspired, and that the Apocalypse is a prophetic book of the Word. For if this were not revealed to the world, and at the same time the internal sense which is in each expression there, as in each expression of the Prophets of the Old Testament, that book might be rejected, on account of not being understood; which would produce such incredulity, that the things there said would not be held worthy of belief, nor that any such Last Judgment would come; in which unbelief those of the Babylon would confirm themselves more than others. Lest this should be, it pleased the Lord to make me an eye-witness. But all that I saw of the Last Judgment upon those of the Babylon, or of the destruction of Babylon, cannot be here adduced, being in itself sufficient to fill a volume. In this place I shall merely relate certain general things, reserving the particulars for the Explanation of the Apocalypse. Inasmuch as the Babylonish nation was settled in and extended over many tracts in the spiritual world, and had formed to itself societies in all the quarters there , I will describe how they were destroyed separately in each quarter.

Destruction was effected after visitation, for visitation always precedes. The act of exploring what the men are, and moreover the separation of the good from the evil, is visitation; and the good are then removed, and the evil are left behind. This having been done, there were great earthquakes, from which they perceived that the Last Judgment was at hand, and trembling seized them all. Then those who dwelt in the southern quarter, and especially in the great city there , were seen running to and fro, some with the intention of betaking themselves to flight, some of hiding themselves in the crypts, others of hiding in the cells and caves where their treasures were, out of which others again carried anything they could lay their hands on. But after the earthquakes there burst up an ebullition from below, which overturned everything in the city and in the region round it. After this ebullition came a vehement wind from the east which laid bare, shook, and overthrew everything to its foundations, and then all who were there were led forth, from every part, and from all their hiding-places, and cast into a sea of black waters: those who were cast into it, were many myriads. Afterwards from that whole region a smoke ascended, as after a conflagration, and finally a thick dust, which was borne by the east wind to the sea, and strewn over it; for their treasures were turned into dust, with all those things they had called holy because they possessed them. This dust was strewn over the sea, because such dust signifies what is damned. At last there was seen as it were a blackness flying over that whole region, which when it was viewed narrowly appeared like a dragon; a sign that the whole of that great city and region was become a desert, This was seen, because "dragons" signify the falsities of such a religion, and "the abode of dragons" signifies the desert after their overthrow; as in Jeremiah (9:11; x. 22; 49:33; Mal. 1:3) It was also seen that some had as it were a millstone around the left arm, which was a representative of their having confirmed their abominable dogmas from the Word; a millstone signifies such things: hence it was plain what these words signify in the Apocalypse: The angel took up a stone like a great millstone, and cast it into the sea, saying, thus with violence shall that great city Babylon be thrown down, and shall no more be found (Apoc. 18:21). But they who were in the council, which also was in that region, but nearer to the east, in which they were consulting on the modes of enlarging their dominion, and of keeping the people in ignorance, and thence in blind obedience , were not cast into that black sea, but into a gulf which opened itself long and deep beneath and around them. Thus was the Last Judgment accomplished upon the Babylonians in the southern quarter. But the Last Judgment upon those in front in the western quarter, and upon those in the northern quarter, where the other great city stood, was thus effected. After great earthquakes, which rent everything in those quarters to the very foundations-these are the earthquakes which are meant in the Word (Matt. 24:7; Luke 21:11; likewise Apoc. 6:12; 8:5; 11:13; 16:18); and in the prophecies of the Old Testament, and not any earthquakes in this world-an east wind went forth from the south through the west into the north, and laid bare that whole region first that part of it in front in the western quarter, where the people of the dark ages dwelt underground, and afterwards the great city, which extended from that quarter even through the north to the east, and from these regions thus laid bare, all things were exposed to view. But because there were not such great riches there, no ebullition, and no sulphurous fire consuming treasures were seen, but only overturn and destruction, and at length exhalation of the whole into smoke; for the east wind went forth, blowing to and fro; it overthrew and destroyed and also swept away. The monks and common people were led forth to the number of many myriads; some were cast into the black sea, on that side of it which faces the west; some into the great southern gulf, mentioned above; some into the western gulf, and some into the hells of the Gentiles, for a part of those who lived in the dark ages were idolaters like the Gentiles, A smoke also was seen to ascend from that region, and to proceed as far as the sea; over which it hovered, depositing a black crust there; for that part of the sea into which they were cast, was encrusted over with the dust and smoke, into which their dwellings and their riches were reduced; wherefore that sea has no longer a visible existence, but in its place is seen, as it were a black soil, under which is their hell, The Last Judgment upon those who dwelt upon the mountains in the eastern quarter , was thus accomplished. Their mountains were seen to subside into the deep, and all those who were upon them to be swallowed up; and he whom they had placed upon one of the mountains, and whom they proclaimed to be god, was seen to become first black, then fiery, and with them to be cast headlong into hell. For the monks of the various orders who were upon those mountains, said that he was God and that they were Christ, and wherever they went, they took with them the abominable persuasion that themselves were Christ. Finally, judgment was effected upon those who dwelt more remotely in the western quarter, upon the mountains there, and who are meant by "the woman sitting upon the scarlet beast who had seven heads which are seven mountains," of whom also something is related above. Their mountains also were seen, some were open in the middle, where an immense chasm was made and whirled about in a spiral, into which those on the mountains were cast. Other mountains were torn up by their foundations and turned upside down, so that the summit became the base; those who were thence in the plains were inundated as with a deluge, and covered over, and those who were among them from other quarters were cast into gulfs. But the things now related are only a small part of all I saw; more will be given in the Explanation of the Apocalypse. They were effected and accomplished in the beginning of the year 1757. As regards the gulfs into which all were cast, except those who were cast into the black sea, they are many. Four of them were disclosed to me; one great gulf in the southern quarter, towards the east there; another in the western quarter, towards the south; a third in the western quarter, towards the north there; a fourth still further in the angle between the west and the north: the gulfs and the sea are their hells. These were seen, but in addition to these there are many more, which were not seen; for the hells of the Babylonish people are distinct according to the various profanations of spiritual things, which are of the good and truth of the church.

Thus now was the spiritual world freed from such spirits, and the angels rejoiced on account of its liberation from them, because they who were of Babylon infested and seduced all whomsoever they could, and there more than in the world; for their cunning is more malignant there, because they are spirits; for it is the spirit of each in which all his wickedness is hidden, since the spirit of the man is what thinks, wills, intends, and plots. Many of them were explored, and it was found that they believed nothing at all, and that the heinous lust of seducing, the rich for the sake of their riches, and the poor for the sake of dominion, was rooted in their minds, and that on account of that end they kept all in the densest ignorance, thus blocking up the way to light, thus to heaven: for the way to light and to heaven is obstructed, when the knowledges of spiritual things are overwhelmed by idolatries, and when the Word is adulterated, weakened, and taken away.

VI. Those of them who were in the affection of truth from good were preserved. Those of the Papal nation who lived piously, and were in good, although not in truths, and still from affection desired to know truths, were taken away and carried into a certain region, in front in the western quarter, near the north, and there habitations were given them, and societies of them were instituted, and then priests from the Reformed were sent to them, who instructed them from the Word, and as they are instructed, they are accepted in heaven.

The state of those hereafter who come thence from the earth. Since the Last Judgment has now been accomplished, and by means of it all things are reduced by the Lord into order, and since all who are interiorly good are taken into heaven, and all who are interiorly evil are cast into hell, it is not permitted them henceforth as heretofore, to form societies below heaven and above hell, nor to have anything in common with others, but as soon as they come thither, which is after the death of each, they are altogether separated, and after passing a certain time in the world of spirits, they are carried into their own places. They therefore who profane holy things, that is, who claim for themselves the power of opening and shutting heaven, and of remitting sins, which yet are powers belonging to the Lord alone, and who make Papal bulls equal to the Word, and have dominion for an end, are henceforth carried away immediately into that black sea, or into the gulfs, where the hells of profaners are. But it was said to me from heaven, that those of that religious persuasion who are such, do not look at all to the life after death, because they deny it in heart, but only to life in the world; and that hence they hold of no account this lot of theirs after death, which yet is to endure to eternity, but laugh at it, as a thing of nought.

X. THE FORMER HEAVEN AND ITS ABOLISHMENT. It is said in the Apocalypse: I saw a great throne, and One sitting upon it, from whose face the earth and the heaven fled away, and their place was not found (Rev. 20:11). And afterwards: I saw a new heaven and a new earth; the first heaven and the first earth had passed away (Rev. 21:1). That by "a new heaven and a new earth," and by the passing away of the former heaven and the former earth is not meant the visible heaven and our habitable earth, but an angelic heaven and a church, was shown above in the first article, and also in those which follow it. For the Word in itself is spiritual, and therefore treats of spiritual things; and spiritual things are the things of heaven and the church; these are expressed by natural things in the sense of the letter, because natural things serve as a basis to spiritual things, and without such a basis the Word would not be a Divine work, because it would not be complete; for the natural, which is the ultimate in Divine order, completes and makes the interiors, which are spiritual and celestial, to subsist upon it, as a house upon its foundation. Now because man has thought of the things of the Word from the natural and not from the spiritual, therefore, by "the heaven and the earth" which are mentioned here and elsewhere, they have understood none other than the heaven and earth which exist in the world of nature; hence it is that everyone expects the passing away and destruction of these, and then also the creation of new ones. But lest they should expect this everlastingly, from age to age in vain, the spiritual sense of the Word is opened, that thus it may be known what is meant by many things in the Word, which, when thought of naturally, do not enter the understanding, and, at the same time, what is meant by "the heaven and the earth" which will pass away.

But before showing what is meant by "the first heaven and the first earth," it should be known, that by "the first heaven" is not meant the heaven formed of those who have become angels from the first creation of this world to the present time, for that heaven is abiding, and endures to eternity; for all who enter heaven are under the Lord's protection, and he who has once been received by the Lord, can never be plucked away from Him. But by "the first heaven" is meant that which was composed of others than those who have become angels, and for the most part of those who could not become angels. Who they were, and their quality, shall be told in the following pages. This heaven it is, of which it is said, that it "passed away." It was called heaven, because they who were in it dwelt on high, forming societies upon rocks and mountains, and living in delights similar to natural ones, but still not in any that were spiritual; for very many who come from the earth into the spiritual world, believe themselves to be in heaven, when they are on high, and in heavenly joy, when they are in delights such as they had in the world. Hence it wasn't called heaven, but "the first heaven which passed away."

It is moreover to be known, that this heaven which is called "the first," did not consist of any who had lived before the Lord's coming into the world, but all were from those who lived after His coming, for as was shown above a Last Judgment is effected at the end of every church, and then the former heaven is abolished, and a new heaven is created or formed; for all who lived in an external moral life, and in external piety and sanctity, although not in any internal, were tolerated from the beginning to the end of the church provided the internals which belong to the thoughts and intentions could be held in bonds by the laws of society, civil and moral; but at the end of the church their internals are disclosed, and the judgment is then effected upon them, Hence it is that a Last Judgment has been effected upon the inhabitants of this planet twice before, and now for the third time ; thus also a heaven and an earth have twice passed away before, and a new heaven and a new earth have been created; for the heaven and the earth are the church in either world, as shown above. Hence it is plain, that "the new heaven and the new earth," mentioned in the prophets of the Old Testament, are not that "new heaven and new earth" mentioned in the Apocalypse, but that the former existed from the Lord when He was in the world, and that the latter exist from Him now. Concerning those in the prophets of the Old Testament, it is thus written: Behold, I am about to create a new heaven and a new earth, neither shall the former be remembered (Isa. 65:17). And in another place: I am about to make a new heaven and a new earth (Isa. 66:22). Besides what is said in Daniel.

Since the first heaven which passed away is the subject now treated of, and since no one knows anything concerning it, I will describe it in order. I. Of whom the first heaven consisted. II. What its quality was. III. How it passed away.

I. Of whom the first heaven consisted. The first heaven was composed of all those upon whom the Last Judgment was effected, for it was not effected upon those in hell, nor upon those in heaven, nor upon those in the world of spirits, concerning which world see the work on Heaven and Hell (n. 421-520), nor upon any man yet living, but solely upon those who had made to themselves the likeness of a heaven, of whom the greater part were on mountains and rocks; these also were they whom the Lord meant by "the goats," which He placed on the left (Matt. 25:32, 33, seq.). Hence it may appear, that the first heaven existed, not merely from Christians, but also from Mohammedans and Gentiles, who had all formed to themselves such heavens in their own places. What their quality was shall be told in a few words. They were those who had lived in the world in external and not in internal holiness; who were just and sincere for the sake of civil and moral laws, but not for the sake of Divine laws, therefore who were external or natural and not internal or spiritual men; who also were in the doctrinals of the church, and were able to teach them, although they were not in a life according to them; and who filled various offices, and did uses, but not for the sake of uses. These, and all throughout the whole world who were like them, and who lived after the Lord's coming, constituted "the first heaven." This heaven therefore was such as the world and church is upon earth, among those who do good not because it is good, but because they fear the laws, and the loss of fame, honor, and gain; they who do good for no other origin, do not fear God, but men, nor do they have any conscience. In the first heaven of the Reformed, there was a large part of them, who believed that man is saved by faith alone, and had not lived the life of faith, which is charity; and who loved much to be seen of men. In all these, so long as they were associated together, the interiors were closed that they might not appear, but when the Last Judgment was at hand they were opened; and it was then found that inwardly they were obsessed by falsities and evils of every kind, and that they were against the Divine, and were actually in hell For every one after death is immediately bound to his like, the good to their like in heaven, but the evil to their like in hell, yet they do not go to them before the interiors are disclosed; in the meantime they may be consociated with those who are like them in externals. But it is to be known that all who were interiorly good thus who were spiritual, were separated from them, and elevated into heaven, and that all who were exteriorly as well as interiorly evil, were also separated from them, and cast into hell; and this from the time immediately succeeding the Lord's advent, down to the last time, when the judgment was; and that those only were left, to form societies among themselves, who constituted the first heaven, and who were such as are described above,

There were many reasons why such societies, or such heavens were tolerated; the principal reason was, that by external holiness, and by external sincerity and justice, they were conjoined with the simple good, who were either in the lowest heaven, or were still in the world of spirits and not yet introduced into heaven. For in the spiritual world, there is a communication, and thence a conjunction, of all with their like; and the simple good, in the lowest heaven, and in the world of spirits, look principally to externals, yet are not interiorly evil; wherefore if these spirits had been forcibly removed from them before the appointed time, heaven would have suffered in its ultimates; and yet it is the ultimate, upon which the superior heaven subsists, as upon its own basis. That they were tolerated until the last time on this account, the Lord teaches in the following words: The servants of the householder came and said unto him, Didst thou not sow good seed in thy field, whence then are the tares? And they said, Wilt thou then that we go and gather them up? But he said, Nay, lest, whilst ye gather up the tares, ye root up at the same time the wheat with them; let both therefore grow together until the harvest, and at the time of harvest I will say to the reapers, gather ye together first the tares, and bind them in bundles to burn; but gather the wheat into barns. He that hath sowed the good seed, is the Son of man; the field is the world; the good seed are the sons of the kingdom, the tares are the sons of evil; the harvest is the consummation of the age: as therefore the tares are gathered together, and burnt with fire, so shall it be in the consummation of the age (Matt, 13:27-30, 37-40). "The consummation of this age," is the last time of the church; "the tares" are those who are interiorly evil; "the wheat" are those who are interiorly good; "the gathering the tares together, and binding them in bundles to burn," is the Last Judgment. The like is meant in the same chapter by the Lord's parable of the fishes of every kind, which were gathered together, and the good placed in vessels, but the bad cast away; concerning which it is also said: So shall it be in the consummation of the age; the angels shall go forth, and separate the evil from the midst of the just (vers. 47-49). They are compared to fishes, because "fishes" in the spiritual sense of the Word, signify natural and external men, both good and evil; what "the just" signify may be seen below. "Bundles" in the Word signify the arrangement of the truths and falsities with man into series, thus also the arrangement of men in whom truths and falsities are. "The Son of man" is the Lord as to Divine truths. "Sons" are the affections of truth from good ; therefore "the sons of the kingdom" are those who are in the affections of truth from good; and "the sons of evil," those who are in the affections of falsity from evil; whence the latter are called tares," and the former "good seed," for "tares" signify falsity from evil, and "good seed," truth from good; "the seed of the field" is truth from good, in man, from the Lord. "Seed" in the opposite sense is falsity from evil. "The seed of the field" is also the nutrition of the mind by Divine truth from the Word and "sowing" is instruction. "The consummation of the age" is the last time of the church."Fishes," in the spiritual sense of the Word, signify scientifics, which belong to the natural or external man, and hence also natural or external men, both evil and good. Animals of all kinds correspond with such things as are with man. In the Word, they to whom the Lord's justice and merit are attributed, are called "just"; they to whom their own justice and merit are attributed, are called "unjust".

II. What the quality of the first heaven was, may be concluded from the things already said of it; as also from this, that they who are not spiritual by acknowledgment of the Divine, by a life of good, and by the affection of truth, and still appear as spiritual by external holiness, by discoursing on Divine things, and by sincerities for the sake of themselves and the world, rush into the abominations which agree with their lusts, when they are left to their own internals; for nothing withholds them, neither fear of God, nor faith, nor conscience. Hence it was, that as soon as they who were in the first heaven were let into their interiors, they appeared conjoined with the hells.

III. How the first heaven passed away, was described before, in describing the Last Judgment upon the Mohammedans and Gentiles ; and upon the Papists , since they also in their own places were constituents of the first heaven, It remains that something be said of the Last Judgment upon the Reformed, who are also called Protestants and Evangelical, or how the first heaven composed of them passed away; for, as was said above, judgment was effected upon those only of whom the first heaven consisted, After being visited, and let into their own interiors, they were separated from each other, and divided into classes according to evils and falsities therefrom, and according to falsities and evils therefrom, and were cast into hells corresponding to their loves. Their hells surrounded the middle region on all sides, for the Reformed were in the middle, the Papists around them, the Mohammedans around the Papists, and the Gentiles in the outmost circuit. Those who were not cast into hells, were cast out into deserts; but there were some sent down to the plains in the southern and northern quarters, there to form societies, and be instructed and prepared for heaven; these are they who were preserved. But how all these things were accomplished, cannot be described in particular in this place, for the judgment upon the Reformed was of longer continuance than upon others, and was effected by successive changes. Now since much that is worthy of mention was then heard and seen, I will present the particulars in their own order in the Explanation of the Apocalypse.

XI. THE STATE OF THE WORLD AND OF THE CHURCH HEREAFTER. The state of the world hereafter will be altogether similar to what it has been heretofore, for the great change which has taken place in the spiritual world, does not induce any change in the natural world as to the external form; so that after this there will be civil affairs as before, there will be peace, treaties, and wars as before, with all other things which belong to societies in general and in particular, The Lord said that: In the last times there will be wars, and then nation will rise against nation, and kingdom against kingdom, and there will be famines, pestilences, and earthquakes in divers places (Matt. 24:6, 7). This does not signify that such things will exist in the natural world, but that the things corresponding with them will exist in the spiritual world: for the Word in its prophecies does not treat of the kingdoms on earth, nor of the nations there, thus neither concerning their wars, nor of famines, pestilences, and earthquakes there, but of such things as correspond to them in the spiritual world; what these things are, is explained in the Arcana Coelestia, and a collection of passages on the subject may be seen below. But as for the state of the church, this it is which will be dissimilar hereafter; it will be similar indeed as to the external appearance, but dissimilar as to the internal. As to the external appearance divided churches will exist as heretofore, their doctrines will be taught as heretofore; and the same religions as now will exist among the Gentiles. But henceforth the man of the church will be in a more free state of thinking on matters of faith, thus on the spiritual things which relate to heaven, because spiritual freedom has been restored to him. For all things in the heavens and in the hells are now reduced into order, and all thought concerning Divine things and against the Divine inflows from thence; from the heavens all thought which is in harmony with Divine things, and from the hells all which is against Divine things. But man does not observe this change of state in himself, because he does not reflect upon it, and because he knows nothing of spiritual freedom and of influx; nevertheless it is perceived in heaven, and also by man himself after his death. Because spiritual freedom has been restored to man, therefore the spiritual sense of the Word has now been disclosed, and by it interior Divine truths have been revealed; for man in his former state would not have understood them, and he who would have understood them, would have profaned them. That man has freedom by means of the equilibrium between heaven and hell, and, that man cannot be reformed except in freedom, may be seen in the work on Heaven and Hell. That "wars" in the Word signify spiritual combats. Hence all "the arms of war," as "the bow," "the sword," "the shield," signify something of spiritual combat. "Kingdoms" signify churches as to truths and as to falsities. "Nations" signify those in the church who are in goods and who are in evils. "Famine" signifies a defect of the knowledges of good and truth. It also signifies the desolation of the church. "Pestilence" signifies the vastation and consummation of good and truth. "Earthquakes" signify changes of the state of the church.

I have had various conversations with angels, concerning the state of the church hereafter. They said that they know not things to come, for the knowledge of things to come belongs to the Lord alone; but they know that the slavery and captivity in which the man of the church was formerly, has been taken away, and that now, from restored freedom, he can better perceive interior truths, if he wills to perceive them; and thus be made more internal, if he wills to become so; but that still they have slender hope of the men of the Christian church, but much of some nation far distant from the Christian world, and therefore removed from infesters, which nation is such that it is capable of receiving spiritual light, and of being made a celestial-spiritual man, and they said, that at this day interior Divine truths are revealed in that nation, and are also received in spiritual faith, that is, in life and heart, and that they adore the Lord.

Last Judgment Continued

I. THE LAST JUDGMENT HAS BEEN ACCOMPLISHED. In the former small work on The Last Judgment, the following subjects were treated of: The day of the Last Judgment does not mean the destruction of the world. The procreations of the human race will never cease. Heaven and hell are from the human race. All who have ever been born men from the beginning of creation, and are deceased, are either in heaven or in hell. The Last Judgment must be where all are together; therefore in the spiritual world, and not on the earth. The Last Judgment exists when the end of the church is; and the end of the church is when there is no faith, because there is no charity. All the things which are predicted in the Apocalypse are at this day fulfilled. The Last Judgment has been accomplished. Babylon and its destruction. The former heaven and its abolition. The state of the world and of the church hereafter.

The subject of the Last Judgment is continued, principally that it may be known what the state of the world and the church was before the Last Judgment, and what the state of the world and the church has become since; also, how the Last Judgment was accomplished upon the Reformed.

It is a common opinion in the Christian world, that the whole heaven we see, and the whole earth inhabited by men will perish at the day of the Last Judgment, and that a new heaven and a new earth will exist in their places; that the souls of men will then receive their bodies, and that man will thus again be man as before. This opinion has become a matter of faith, because the Word has not been understood otherwise than according to the sense of its letter; and it could not be understood otherwise, until its spiritual sense was disclosed, also, because by many the belief has been acquired that the soul is only a breath exhaled by man; and that spirits, as well as angels, are of the substance of wind. While there was such a deficiency of understanding concerning souls, and concerning spirits and angels, the Last Judgment could not be thought of in any other manner. But when it comes to be understood, that a man is a man after death, just as he was a man in the world, with the sole difference that then he is clothed with a spiritual body, and not as before with a natural body; and that the spiritual body appears before those who are spiritual, even as the natural body appears before those who are natural, it may then also be understood, that the Last Judgment will not be in the natural, but in the spiritual world; for all the men who were ever born and have died, are together there.

When this is understood, then may the paradoxes be dissipated, which man would otherwise think concerning the state of souls after death, and their reunion with putrid corpses, and concerning the destruction of the created universe, thus concerning the Last Judgment. The paradoxes concerning the state of souls after death that he would think are these: That man would then be like an exhalation, or like wind, or like ether; either that he would be floating in the air, or not abiding in any place, but in a somewhere, which they call Pu; and that he would see nothing, because he had no eyes; hear nothing, because he had no ears; speak nothing, because he had no mouth; and would therefore be blind, deaf, and dumb; and continually in the expectation, which could not but be sad, of receiving again at the day of the Last Judgment, those functions of the soul from which all the delight of life proceeds. Also that the souls of all who have lived since the first creation, must be in a like miserable state, and that the men who lived fifty or sixty centuries ago, were likewise still floating in the air, or remaining in Pu, and awaiting judgment; besides other lamentable things.

I pass over paradoxes, similar to, and equally numerous with these, which the man who does not know that he is a man after death as before, must think concerning the destruction of the universe. But when he knows that a man after death is not an exhalation or a wind, but a spirit, and if he has lived well, an angel in heaven, and that spirits and angels are men in a perfect form, can then think from his understanding concerning the state of man after death, and the Last Judgment, and not from faith separate from the understanding, from which mere traditions go forth: and he may also with certainty conclude from his understanding, that the Last Judgment, which is predicted in the Word, will not exist in the natural world, but in the spiritual world, where all are together: and furthermore, that whenever it does exist, it must be revealed, for the sake of belief in the Word.

Put away from you the idea that the soul is like an exhalation, and then think of your own state, or of the state of your friends, or of the state of your infants after death. Will you not think that you will live a man, and they likewise? And since there is no life which is life without the senses, you cannot think otherwise than that they also see, hear, and speak; thus also panegyrists write over the deceased, placing them in heaven among the angels, in white garments, and in paradises. But if afterwards you relapse into the idea, that the soul is an exhalation, and has no sensitive life until after the Last Judgment, can you help being distracted when you think, What and where shall I be in the meantime? Shall I float in the air, or remain in Pu? 6-1 Yet the preacher teaches me that after death I shall come among the happy, if I have believed well and lived well. You may believe then, as the truth is, that you are a man after death as well as before it, with only the difference that there is between the natural and the spiritual. Thus also all those think who believe in eternal life, and know nothing of this hypothetical tradition concerning the soul.

From what has been said already, it may appear that the Last Judgment cannot exist in the natural world, but in the spiritual world. That it also has existed there, may be seen from the things related of it from sight, in the former small work on The Last Judgment, and still further from the particulars about to be related from sight, of the Last Judgment upon the Reformed. He who attends may also see it from the new things which are now revealed concerning heaven, the Word, and the church. What man can draw such things from himself?

II. THE STATE OF THE WORLD AND OF THE CHURCH BEFORE THE LAST JUDGMENT, AND AFTER IT. That the Last Judgment has been accomplished in the spiritual world, may appear from what has just been said. Nevertheless, in order to know anything of the state of the world and the church before and after it, it is altogether necessary that the following things should be known: I. What is meant by "the former heaven" and "the former earth" which passed away (Apoc. 21:1). II. Who, and of what quality were those who were in the former heaven and in the former earth. III. Before the Last Judgment was effected upon them much of the communication between heaven and the world, thus also between the Lord and the church, was intercepted. IV. After the Last Judgment the communication was restored. V. Hence it is, that after the Last Judgment, and not before, revelations were made for the New Church. VI. The state of the world and of the church before the Last Judgment was like evening and night, but after it like morning and day.

I. What is meant by "the former heaven" and "the former earth" which passed away, mentioned in the Apocalypse (21:1) "The former heaven" and "the former earth" there mentioned, does not mean the heaven visible to the eyes of men in the world, nor the earth which is inhabited by men; nor the former heaven, in which all those are who have lived well since the first creation. But congregations of spirits are meant who had made seeming heavens between heaven and hell for themselves, and because all spirits and angels dwell upon lands, as well as men, therefore by "the former heaven" and "the former earth," these are meant. The passing away of that heaven and that earth was seen, and it has been described from sight in the work on The Last Judgment.

II. Who, and of what quality were those who were in "the former heaven," and "the former earth," was described in the small work on The Last Judgment; but because the understanding of what follows depends on the knowledge of who they were and their quality, something shall here be said concerning them. All those who gathered themselves together under heaven, and in various places formed seeming heavens for themselves, and also called them heavens, were conjoined with the angels of the lowest heaven, but only as to externals, not as to internals. For the most part they were the goats and those akin to them, who are named in Matthew (25:41-46); who indeed, in the world had not done evils, for they had lived well morally; but they had not done goods from a good origin, for they had separated faith from charity, and hence had not regarded evils as sins. Because they had lived as Christians in externals, they were conjoined with the angels of the lowest heaven, who were like them in externals, but not like them in internals; they being "the sheep," and in faith, yet in the faith of charity. On account of this conjunction they were necessarily tolerated; for to separate them, before the Last Judgment, would have brought injury upon those who were in the lowest heaven, who would have been drawn into destruction with them. This is what the Lord foretold in Matthew: Jesus spoke a parable; the kingdom of the heaven is like unto a man who sowed good seed in his field; but while men slept, his enemy came, and sowed tares, and went away; when the blade was sprung up, and brought forth fruit, then appeared the tares also; so the servants of the householder coming, said unto him, Lord, didst not thou sow good seed in thy field? Wilt thou then that we go and gather them up? But he said, Nay, lest, while ye gather up the tares, ye root up at the same time the wheat with them: let both grow together until the harvest; and in the time of harvest I will say to the reapers, Gather ye together first the tares, and bind them in bundles to burn them; but gather the wheat into my barn. He who hath sown the good seed, is the Son of man; the field is the world; the seed are the sons of the kingdom; the tares are the sons of evil; the harvest is the consummation of the age; as therefore the tares are gathered together, and burned, so shall it be in the consummation of the age (Matt. 13:24-30, 37-40). "The consummation of the age" is the last time of the church; "the tares" are those who are interiorly evil; "the wheat" are those who are interiorly good; "the gathering together in bundles to burn," is the Last Judgment upon them; that harm should not be done to the good by separation before the Last Judgment, is signified by "lest in gathering up the tares, ye root up at the same time the wheat with them: let both grow until the harvest."

III. Before the Last Judgment was effected upon them, much of the communication between heaven and the world, thus between the Lord and the church, was intercepted. All enlightenment comes to man from the Lord through heaven, and it enters by an internal way. So long as there were congregations of such spirits between heaven and the world, or between the Lord and the church, man could not be enlightened. It was as when a sunbeam is cut off by a black interposing cloud, or as when the sun is eclipsed, and its light arrested, by the interjacent moon. Wherefore, if anything had been then revealed by the Lord, either it would not have been understood, or if understood, still it would not have been received, or if received, still it would afterwards have been suffocated. Now since all these interposing congregations were dissipated by the Last Judgment, it is plain, IV. That the communication between heaven and the world, or between the Lord and the church, has been restored.

V. Hence it is, that after the Last Judgment has been accomplished, and not before, revelations were made for the New Church. For since communication has been restored by the Last Judgment, man can be enlightened and reformed; that is, can understand the Divine truth of the Word, receive it when understood, and retain it when received, for the interposing obstacles are removed; and therefore John, after the former heaven and the former earth passed away, said that: He saw a New Heaven and a New Earth, and then, the holy city Jerusalem, descending from God out of heaven, prepared as a Bride before her Husband; and he heard the One sitting upon the throne, say, Behold, I make all things new (Apoc. 21:1, 2, 5). That the church is meant by "Jerusalem" may be seen in The Doctrine Concerning the Lord. Concerning its new things.

VI. The state of the world and of the church before the Last Judgment was like evening and night, but after it, like morning and day. When the light of truth does not appear, and truth is not received, there is a state of the church in the world like evening and night; that there was a state before the Last Judgment, may appear from what is said above ; but when the light of truth appears, and the truth is received, there is a state of the church in the world like morning and day. Hence it is, that these two states of the church are called "evening and morning" and "night and day," in the Word; as in the following passages: The Holy One said unto me, Until the evening the morning two thousand three hundred; then shall the sanctuary be justified (Dan. 8:14). The vision of the evening and the morning is truth (Dan. 8:26). There shall be one day, which is known to Jehovah, neither day nor night, for about the time of evening there shall be light (Zech. 14:7). One crying unto me out of Seir, Watchman, what of the night? The watchman said, The morning cometh, and also the night (Isa. 21:11, 12). Concerning the last time of the church, Jesus said: Watch, for ye know not when the Lord of the house will come, whether at evening, at midnight, at cock-crowing, or in the morning (Mark 13:35). Jesus said, I must work while it is day; the night cometh, when no one can work (John 9:4); and elsewhere (as in Isa. 17:14; Jer. 6:4, 5; Ps. 30:6; 65:9; 90:6). Since such things are meant by "evening and night," therefore the Lord, in order to fulfil the Word, also was buried in the evening and afterward rose again in the morning.

III. THE LAST JUDGMENT UPON THE REFORMED. In the former small work on The Last Judgment it treated of the judgment upon those who are meant by Babylon; and something of the judgment upon the Mohammedans and upon the Gentiles; but not of the judgment upon the Reformed. It was said only, that the Reformed were in the middle, arranged there according to countries; the Papists around them; the Mohammedans around the Papists, and around these the Gentiles and peoples of various religions. The Reformed constituted the middle, or central region, because the Word is read by them and the Lord is worshiped, and hence with them there is the greatest light; and spiritual light, which is from the Lord as a sun, which in its essence is the Divine love, proceeds and extends itself on every side, and enlightens even those who are in the extreme circumferences, and opens the faculty of understanding truths, as far as from their religion they can receive them. For spiritual light in its essence is the Divine wisdom, and it enters the understanding in man, as far as, from knowledges received, he has the faculty of perceiving it; and it does not pass through spaces, like the light of the world, but through the affections and perceptions of truth, therefore, in an instant, to the last limits of the heavens. From these are the appearances of spaces in that world. Concerning these things more may be seen in The Doctrine Concerning the Sacred Scripture.

The Last Judgment upon the Reformed shall be described in the following order. I. Upon whom of the Reformed the Last Judgment was effected. II. The signs and visitations before the Last Judgment. III. How the universal judgment was effected. IV. The salvation of the sheep.

I. Upon whom among the Reformed the Last Judgment was effected. The Last Judgment was effected upon those only of the Reformed, who in the world confessed God, read the Word, heard preaching, partook of the sacrament of the Supper, and did not neglect the solemnities of the worship of the church; and yet thought that adulteries, various kinds of theft, lying, revenge, hatred, and the like, were allowable. These although they confessed God, still made no account of sins against Him; they read the Word, and still they made no account of the precepts of life in it; they heard preachings, and still they paid no attention to them; they went to the sacrament of the Supper, and still they did not desist from the evils of their former life; they did not neglect the solemnities of worship, and still they amended their lives in nothing. Thus they lived as if from religion, in their externals, yet in their internals they had nothing of it. These are they who are meant by "the dragon" in the Apocalypse (chap. 12); for it is there said of the dragon, that it was seen in heaven, that it fought with Michael in heaven, and that it drew down the third part of the stars from heaven; which things are said, because these, by means of the confession of God, by reading the Word, and by external worship, communicated with heaven. The same are meant by "the goats" in Matthew, chap. 25; to whom it is not said that they did evils, but that they omitted to do goods; and all such omit to do goods which are goods, because they do not shun evils as sins, and although they do not do them, still they think them allowable, and thus do them in spirit, and also in body, when permitted.

Upon all these from the Reformed the Last Judgment was effected, but not upon those who did not believe in God, who contemned the Word, and rejected from their hearts the holy things of the church; for all these, when they came from the natural world into the spiritual world, were cast into hell.

All who lived like Christians in externals, and made no account of the Christian life, made one exteriorly with the heavens, but interiorly with the hells, and since they could not be torn away in a moment from their conjunction with heaven, they were detained in the world of spirits, which is midway between heaven and hell, and it was permitted them to form societies, and to live together as in the world; and there by arts unknown to the world, to cause splendid appearances, and by this means to persuade themselves and others, that they were in heaven; therefore, from that external appearance they called their societies heavens. The heavens and the earths upon which they dwelt, are meant by "the former heaven, and the former earth which passed away" (Apoc. 21:1).

Meanwhile, so long as they remained there, the interiors of their minds were closed, and the exteriors were opened; by which means, their evils, by which they made one with the hells: did not appear. But when the Last Judgment was at hand, their interiors were disclosed, and they then appeared before all such as they really were; and since they then acted in unity with the hells, they were no longer able to simulate the Christian life, but from delight rushed into evils and crimes of every kind, and were turned into devils, and, moreover, were seen as such, some black, some fiery, and some livid like corpses; those who were in the pride of their own intelligence, appearing black; those who were in the insane love of ruling over all, appearing fiery; and those who were in the neglect and contempt of truth, appearing livid like corpses. Thus were the scenes of those theaters changed.

The Reformed constitute the inmost or middle part of the world of spirits, which is midway between heaven and hell, and are there arranged according to countries. In the center of this middle region are the English; towards the south and the east of it are the Dutch; towards the north, the Germans; towards the west and the north, the Swedes; and towards the west, the Danes. But those only who have lived the life of charity, and its faith, are in that middle region: many societies of them dwell there. Surrounding them are those of the Reformed, who have not lived the life of faith and charity: these are they who made as it were heavens to themselves. But there is a different arrangement of all in heaven, and also of all in hell. The reason why the Reformed constitute the middle there is, because with them the Word is read, and the Lord is also worshiped, from which the greatest light is there; and thence, as from a center, this light is propagated to all the circumferences and enlightens. For the light in which spirits and angels are, proceeds from the Lord as a sun, and this sun, in its essence, is the Divine love, and the light which proceeds from it in its essence is the Divine wisdom: all the spiritual of that world is derived from it.

Concerning the Lord as the sun in the spiritual world, and concerning the light and heat of that sun, see the work on Heaven and Hell.

Every arrangement of the societies in that world, is an arrangement according to the differences of love; the reason of which is, that love is the life of man, and the Lord, who is Divine love itself, arranges them according to its reception; and the differences of loves are innumerable, which no one knows but the Lord alone. He so conjoins the societies, that they all lead as it were one life of man; the societies of the heavens one life of celestial and spiritual love; the societies of the hells, one life of diabolical and infernal love; He conjoins the heavens and the hells by oppositions. Because there is such an arrangement, every man after death goes into the society of his own love, nor can he go into any other, for his love opposes it. Hence it is that they who are in spiritual love are in heaven, but they who are in natural love only, are in hell. Spiritual love is implanted solely by the life of charity, and natural love remains natural, if the life of charity is omitted; and natural love, if it is not subjected to spiritual love, is opposed to it.

From these things it may appear, upon whom of the Reformed the Last Judgment was effected; that it was not upon those who were in the center, but upon those who were around it; who from external morality, as was said, appeared exteriorly like Christians, but interiorly they were not Christians, because they had no spiritual life.

II. The signs and visitations before the Last Judgment. There was seen above those who had formed to themselves seeming heavens as it were a storm cloud, which appearance was from the presence of the Lord in the angelic heavens above them, especially from His presence in the lowest heaven, lest any of them on account of the conjunction should be carried away and perish with them. The higher heavens moreover were brought down nearer to them, by which the interiors of those upon whom the judgment was about to come were disclosed; on which disclosure, they appeared no longer like moral Christians, as before, but like demons. They were tumultuous and strove among themselves about God, the Lord, the Word, faith, and the church; and because their lusts for evils were then also set free, they rejected all these things with contempt and ridicule, and rushed into every kind of enormity. Thus the state of those heavenly inhabitants was changed. Then at the same time all their splendid appearances, which they had made for themselves by arts unknown in the world, vanished away; their palaces were turned into vile huts; their gardens into stagnant pools; their temples into heaps of rubbish; and the very hills upon which they dwelt, into gravel heaps, and into other similar things, which corresponded to their wicked minds and lusts. For all the visible things of the spiritual world are correspondences of the affections of spirits and angels. These were the signs of the coming judgment.

As the disclosure of the interiors increased, so the order among the inhabitants was changed and inverted. Those who were most powerful in reasonings against the holy things of the church, rushed into the middle, and assumed the dominion; and the rest, who were less powerful in reasonings, receded to the circumferences, and acknowledged those who were in the middle as their tutor-angels. Thus they collected themselves together into the form of hell.

These changes of their state were accompanied by various concussions of their dwellings and lands; which were followed by earthquakes, mighty according to their perversions. Here and there, too, chasms were made towards the hells which were under them, and a communication was thus opened with them. Exhalations were then seen ascending like smoke mingled with sparks of fire. These also were signs which preceded, which are also meant by the Lord's words concerning the consummation of the age, and then concerning the Last Judgment, in the Evangelists: Nation shall be stirred up against nation; there shall be great earthquakes in divers places; signs also from heaven, terrible and great. And there shall be distress of nations, the sea and the billows roaring (Luke 21:10, 11, 25; Matt. 24:7; Mark 13:8).

Visitations also were made by angels; for before any ill conditioned society perishes, visitation always precedes. The angels exhorted them to desist, and denounced destruction upon them if they did not. Then they also sought out and separated any good spirits who were intermingled with them. But the multitude, excited by their leaders, reviled the angels, and rushed in upon them, for the purpose of dragging them into the forum, and treating them in an abominable manner; just as was done in Sodom. Most of them were in faith separated from charity; and there were also some who professed charity, and yet lived shamefully.

III. How the universal judgment was effected. After the visitations and premonitory signs of the coming judgment could not turn their minds from criminal acts, and from seditious plottings against those who acknowledged the Lord as the God of heaven and earth, held the Word holy, and led a life of charity, the Last Judgment came upon them. It was thus effected.

The Lord was seen in a bright cloud with angels, and a sound as of trumpets was heard from it; which was a sign representative of the protection of the angels of heaven by the Lord, and of the gathering of the good from every side. For the Lord does not bring destruction upon anyone, but only protects His own, and draws them away from communication with the evil; and when they are withdrawn, the evil come into their own lusts, and from them rush into every kind of abomination. Then all who were about to perish, were seen together like a great dragon, with its tail extended in a curve, and elevated towards heaven, bending itself about on high in various directions, as though it would destroy heaven, and draw it down. But the effort was vain, for the tail was cast down, and the dragon, which had also appeared elevated, sank down. It was granted me to see this representation, that I might know and make known who are meant by "the dragon" in the Apocalypse; namely, that "the dragon" means all who read the Word, hear preachings, and perform the holy things of the church, making no account of the lusts of evil by which they are enticed, and interiorly they meditate thefts and frauds, adulteries and obscenities, hatred and revenge, lies and blasphemies; and who thus live in spirit like devils, and in body like angels. These constituted the body of the dragon, but the tail was constituted of those who, when in the world, were in faith separated from charity, and were like the former as to thoughts and intentions.

Then I saw some of the rocks upon which they were, subsiding even to the lowest depths; some carried far away; some opening in the middle, and those who were on them cast down through the chasm; and some inundated as with a flood. And I saw many collected into companies, as into bundles, according to the genera and species of evil, and cast hither and thither into whirlpools, marshes, stagnant pools, and deserts, which were so many hells. The rest who were not on rocks, but scattered here and there, and who yet were in similar evils, fled amazed to the Papists, Mohammedans, and Gentiles, and professed their religions, which they could do without any disturbance of mind, because they had no religion; but still lest they should seduce these also, they were driven away, and thrust down to their companions in the hells. This is a general description of their destruction; the particulars which I saw, are more than can be here described.

The salvation of the sheep. After the Last Judgment was accomplished, there was then joy in heaven, and also light in the world of spirits, such as was not before. The joy in heaven and its quality, after the dragon was cast down, is described in the Apocalypse (12:10-12); and there was light in the world of spirits, because those infernal societies had been interposed like clouds which darken the earth. A similar light also then arose with men in the world, from which they had new enlightenment.

I then saw angelic spirits in great numbers rising from below, and elevated into heaven, who were the sheep, there reserved and guarded by the Lord for ages back, lest they should come into the malignant sphere flowing forth from dragonists, and their charity be suffocated. These are they, who are meant in the Word, by "those who went forth from the sepulchers"; also, by "the souls of those slain for the testimony of Jesus," who were watching; and by those "who are of the first resurrection."

CONTINUATION CONCERNING THE SPIRITUAL WORLD. IV. THE SPIRITUAL WORLD. The spiritual world has been treated of in a special work on Heaven and Hell, in which many particulars of that world are described; and since every man enters that world after death, his state then is also described there. Who does not know that man will live after death, because he is born a man, and created in the image of God, and because the Lord, in His Word, teaches it? But what his future life will be has hitherto been unknown. It has been believed that he would then be a soul, of which no other idea was conceived than as of air or ether, in which some capacity of thought would reside, without such sight as belongs to the eye, without such hearing as belongs to the ear, and without speech such as belongs to the mouth. And yet man is equally a man after death; and such a man that he does not know otherwise than that he is still in the former world; he sees, hears, and speaks as in the former world; he walks, runs, and sits as in the former world; he eats and drinks as in the former world; he sleeps and wakes as in the former world; he enjoys conjugial delight as in the former world; in a word he is a man as to each and all things. From which it is plain, that death is but a continuation of life, and is only transition.

There are many causes why man has not known of this state of his after death; one of which is, that he could not be enlightened, so little faith had he in the immortality of the soul; as may appear from many even of the learned, who believe that they are like beasts, only more perfect than they, in being able to speak; and therefore in their heart they deny the life after death, although they profess it with the mouth. From this thought of theirs they have become so sensual, that they could not believe that a man is a man after death, because they do not see him with their eyes, for they say, how can a soul be such a man? It is otherwise with those who believe they will live after death; these think interiorly in themselves, that they will come into heaven, enjoy delights with the angels, see heavenly paradises, and stand before the Lord in white garments, besides other things. This is their interior thought; their exterior thought may wander from it, when they think of the soul from the hypothesis of the learned.

That a man is equally a man after death, although he does not appear before the eyes, may appear from the angels seen by Abraham, Gideon, Daniel, and other prophets; from the angels seen in the Lord's sepulchre, and afterwards, oftentimes, by John in the Apocalypse; especially from the Lord Himself, who showed His disciples that He was a Man, by touch, and by eating, and yet became invisible before their eyes. The reason why they saw Him was, because the eyes of their spirits were then opened; and when these are opened, the things in the spiritual world appear as clearly as the things in the natural world.

Because it has pleased the Lord to open for me the eyes of my spirit, and to keep them open now for nineteen years, it has been given me to see the things which are in the spiritual world, and also to describe them. I can affirm that they are not visions, but things seen in all wakefulness.

The difference between a man in the natural world, and a man in the spiritual world, is, that the one man is clothed with a spiritual body, but the other with a natural body; and the spiritual man sees the spiritual man, as clearly as the natural man sees the natural man; but the natural man cannot see the spiritual man, and the spiritual man cannot see the natural man, on account of the difference between the natural and the spiritual; what kind of difference this is, can be described, but not in a few words.

From the things seen during so many years, I am enabled to relate the following: that there are lands in the spiritual world, just as in the natural world; and that there are hills and mountains, plains and valleys, and also fountains and rivers, lakes and seas; there are paradises and gardens, groves and woods, and palaces and houses; also that there are writings and books, offices and trades; and that there are precious stones, gold and silver; in a word, there are each and all things that exist in the natural world, and they are infinitely more perfect in the heavens.

But the difference in general is this; that all things in the spiritual world are from a spiritual origin, and hence, as to their essence, are spiritual, they are from the sun there which is pure love; and all things in the natural world are from a natural origin, and hence as to their essence are natural, for they are from the sun there which is pure fire. Hence it is, that the spiritual man must be nourished with food from a spiritual origin, as the natural man is with food from a natural origin. More may be seen in the work on Heaven and Hell.

V. THE ENGLISH IN THE SPIRITUAL WORLD. There are two states of thought with man, an external and an internal state; man is in the external state in the natural world, in the internal state in the spiritual world: these states make one with the good, but not with the evil. What a man is as to his internal, is rarely manifest in the natural world, because from his infancy, he has wished to be moral, and has learned to seem so. But what he is, clearly appears in the spiritual world, for spiritual light discloses it, and also man is then a spirit, and the spirit is the internal man. Now, since it has been given me to be in that light, and from it, to see what the internal is in the men of various kingdoms, by an interaction of many years with angels and spirits, it behooves me to manifest it, because of its importance. Here I will say something of the noble English nation only.

The more excellent of the English nation are in the center of all Christians. The reason why they are in the center is, because they have interior intellectual light. This is not apparent to any one in the natural world, but it is conspicuous in the spiritual world. This light they derive from the liberty of thinking, and thence of speaking and of writing, in which they are. With others, who are not in such liberty, intellectual light is darkened because it has no outlet. But this light is not active of itself, but is rendered active by others, especially by men of reputation and authority among them. As soon as anything is said by these men, or as soon as anything they approve is read, that light shines forth, and seldom before. On this account governors are placed over them in the spiritual world, and priests of great reputation for learning and distinguished ability are given them, whose commands and monitions, from this their natural disposition, they cheerfully obey.

They rarely go out of their own society, because they love it as in the world they love their country. There is also a similarity of minds among them, from which they contract intimacy with friends of their own country, and rarely with others. They also mutually aid each other; and they love sincerity.

There are two great cities similar to London, into which most of the English come after death; these cities it was given me to see, as well as to walk through. The middle of the one city answers to that part of the English London where there is a meeting of merchants, called the Exchange; there the governors dwell. Above that middle is the east; below it is the west; on the right side of it is the south; on the left side of it is the north. They who have led a life of charity more than the rest, dwell in the eastern quarter, where there are magnificent palaces. The wise, with whom there are many splendid things, dwell in the southern quarter. They who more than others love the liberty of speaking and of writing, dwell in the northern quarter. They who make profession of faith, dwell in the western quarter; to the right in this quarter, there is an entrance into the city, and an exit from it; they who live wickedly are there sent out of it. The presbyters, who are in the west, and who, as was said, profess faith, dare not enter the city through the broad streets, but only through the narrower ways, because they who are in the faith of charity, are the only inhabitants who are tolerated in the city. I have heard them complaining of the preachers in the west, that they prepare their discourses with such art and at the same time eloquence, interweaving justification by faith to them unknown, that they do not know whether good is to be done or not; they preach intrinsic good, and separate it from extrinsic good, which they sometimes call meritorious, and therefore not acceptable to God; yet still they call it good, because it is useful. But when those who dwell in the eastern and southern quarters of the city hear such mystical discourses, they walk out of the temples, and the preachers are afterwards deprived of the priesthood.

The other great city similar to London, is not in the Christian center , but lies beyond it in the north. They who are interiorly evil come into it after death. In the middle of it there is an open communication with hell, by which they are swallowed up in turn.

I once heard presbyters from England conversing together concerning faith alone, and I saw a certain image made by them which represented faith alone. It appeared in obscure light like a great giant, and in their eyes like a beautiful man; but when the light of heaven was let in, the upper part of it appeared like a monster, and the lower like a serpent, not unlike the description which is given of Dagon, the idol of the Philistines. When they saw this they left it, and the bystanders cast it into a stagnant pool.

It was perceived from those of the English who are in the spiritual world, that they have as it were a twofold theology, one from the doctrine of faith, and the other from the doctrine of life; from the doctrine of faith for those who are initiated into the priesthood: from the doctrine of life for those who are not initiated into the priesthood, and who are commonly called the laity. This doctrine of life is set forth in the exhortation which is read in the temples on any Sabbath day, to those who go to the Sacrament of the Supper; in which it is openly said that if they do not shun evils as sins, they cast themselves into eternal damnation, and that if they then approach the holy communion the devil will enter into them, as he entered into Judas. I have sometimes spoken with the priests concerning this doctrine of life, that it does not agree with their doctrine of faith. They made no reply, but thought what they did not dare to utter. You may see that exhortation in The Doctrine of Life for the New Jerusalem.

I have often seen a certain Englishman, who became celebrated by a book he published some years ago, in which he attempted to establish the conjunction of faith and charity by an influx and interior operation of the Holy Spirit. He gave out that this influx affected man in an inexpressible manner, and without his being conscious of it, but did not touch, much less manifestly move his will or excite his thought to do anything as of himself, except permissively; the reason being, that nothing of the man might enter into the Divine Providence as one with it; also that thus evils might not appear before God. He thus excluded the external exercises of charity for the sake of any salvation, but favoring them for the sake of the public good. Since his arguments were ingenious, and the snake in the grass was not seen, his book was received as most orthodox. This author retained the same dogma after his departure from the world, nor could he recede from it, because it was confirmed in him. The angels spoke with him, and said that this was not the truth, but mere ingenuity with eloquence; and that the truth is, that man ought to shun evil and do good as from himself, yet with the acknowledgment that it is from the Lord, and that there is no faith before this, still less is that thought which he calls faith. And since this was opposed to his dogma, it was permitted him of his own sagacity to inquire further, whether such unknown influx and internal operation apart from the external operation of man is given. He was then seen to strain his mind, and to wander about in thought in various ways, always in the persuasion that man is no otherwise renewed and saved. But as often as he came to the end of his way, his eyes were opened, and he saw that he was wandering, and even confessed it to those who were present. I saw him wandering thus for two years, and in the end of his ways confessing that no such influx is given, unless evil in the external man be removed, which is effected by shunning evils as sirs, as if from himself; and I heard him at length saying, that all who confirm themselves in that heresy, will be insane from the pride of their own intelligence.

I have spoken with Melancthon, and then asked him concerning his state; but he was not willing to reply. Wherefore I was informed of his lot by others, which is that he is alternately in a fretted stone chamber, and alternately in hell, and that in his chamber he appears clothed in a bear's skin on account of the cold, and because of the uncleanness there he does not admit newcomers from the world, who wish to visit him on account of the reputation of his name. He still speaks of faith alone, which in the world he established more than others.

VI. THE DUTCH IN THE SPIRITUAL WORLD. It was said above , that Christians with whom the Word is read and the Lord is worshiped, are in the middle of the nations and people of the whole spiritual world, because the greatest spiritual light is with them, and the light is radiated thence as from a center into all the circumference even to the last boundary; and it enlightens, according to what is said in The Doctrine of the New Jerusalem Concerning the Sacred Scripture. In this middle, the Reformed Christians have places allotted to them according to their reception of spiritual light from the Lord; and since the English have that light stored up in the intellectual part, therefore they are in the inmost of that middle region; and because the Dutch keep that light more nearly conjoined to natural light, and hence there is no such brightness of light apparent among them, but in its place something not transparent which is receptive of rationality from spiritual light, and at the same time from spiritual heat, they, in the Christian middle region, have obtained dwellings in the east and south; in the east from the faculty of receiving spiritual heat, which in them is charity, and in the south from the faculty of receiving spiritual light, which in them is faith. That the quarters in the spiritual world are not like the quarters in the natural world, and that dwellings according to quarters, are dwellings according to the reception of faith and love, and that they who excel in love and charity, are in the east, and they who excel in intelligence and faith, are in the south, may be seen in the work on Heaven and Hell. Another reason why they are in these quarters of the Christian middle region is, that trade is their final love, and money is the mediate subservient love, and that love is spiritual; but where money is the final love, and trade the mediate subservient love, the love is natural, and partakes of avarice. In the before-mentioned spiritual love, which regarded in itself is the common good, in which and from which is the good of the country, the Dutch excel others.

The Dutch adhere more firmly than others to the principles of their religion, nor are they drawn away from them; and if they are convinced that one or another of them is not in agreement, still they do not admit it, but turn themselves back, and remain unmoved. Thus they remove themselves from an interior intuition of truth, for they keep their rational under obedience, in spiritual things. Because they are such, when they enter the spiritual world after death, they are prepared for receiving the spiritual of heaven, which is

Divine truth, quite differently from others. They are not taught, because they do not receive; but what heaven is, is described to them, and afterwards it is granted them to ascend there, and to see it; and then whatever agrees with their genius is infused into them, which being done, they are sent down, and return to their companions with a full desire for heaven. If then they do not receive this truth, that God is One in Person and in essence, and that this God is the Lord, and that in Him is the Trinity; and also this truth, that faith and charity as matters of knowledge and discourse, are of no avail apart from the life of faith and charity, and that faith and charity are given by the Lord when evils are shunned as sins; if when they are taught these truths, they turn themselves away, and still think of God as existing in three Persons, and of religion, merely that there is such a thing, they are reduced to misery, and their trade is taken away, until they are brought to the greatest extremities. And they are then led to those who have abundance of everything, and a flourishing trade, and when there, the thought is insinuated into them from heaven, whence it is that they are such, and at the same time to reflect on the faith of these persons concerning the Lord, and upon their life, in that they shun evils as sins. In a little time they make inquiries, and perceive an agreement with their own thought and reflection; this is done repeatedly. At length, they think of themselves, that in order to be relieved from their miseries, they must believe and do the same. Then, as they receive that faith, and live that life of charity, opulence and enjoyment of life are given them. In this manner, those of them who have led anything of a life of charity in the world, are amended by themselves, and not by others, and are prepared for heaven. They afterwards became more constant than others, so that they may be called constancies; and they do not allow themselves to be led away by any reasoning, fallacy, or obscurity brought on by sophistries, or by any preposterous view from confirmations alone.

The Dutch are easily distinguished from others in the spiritual world, because they appear in like garments as in the natural world, with the difference that those are in more shining ones who have received faith and that spiritual life. They appear in similar garments, because they remain constant in the principles of their religion; and in the spiritual world all are clothed according to their religious principles; whence it is, that they who are in Divine truths, have garments of white and of fine linen.

The cities in which the Dutch dwell, are guarded in a peculiar manner, all the streets in them are covered, and in the streets are gates, in order that they may not be viewed from the surrounding rocks and hills. This they do from their inherent prudence in concealing their designs, and not divulging their intentions; for these things in the spiritual world are brought forth by inspection. When anyone enters a city with the purpose of exploring their state, when he is about to depart, he is led to the closed gates of the streets, back and forth to many, and this to extreme weariness, and he is then let out; this is done to the end that he may not return. Wives who claim dominion over their husbands, dwell on one side of the city, and only meet them by invitation, given formally; and the husbands then lead them to houses, where married pairs are living, without there being any dominion of the one over the other, and show them how neat and clean their houses are, and how delightful their life is, and that these are the results of mutual and conjugial love. Those who attend to, and are affected with these things, desist from dominion, and they live together, and they then obtain a dwelling nearer to the middle, and are called angels. The reason is, that conjugial love is a celestial love, which is without dominion.

In the days of the Last Judgment, I saw many thousands of that nation cast out of the cities there, and out of the villages and surrounding lands. They were those who when in the world had done nothing of good from any religion or conscience, but only on account of reputation, that they might appear sincere for the sake of gain; for such when the prospect of fame and gain is taken away, as is the case in the spiritual world, then rush into every abomination; and when they are in the fields, and outside the cities, they rob every one they encounter. I saw them cast into a fiery gulf stretching under the eastern tract, and into a dark cavern stretching under the southern tract. This casting out I saw on the 9th day of January, 1757. Those only were left, among whom there was religion, and a conscience from religion.

I have spoken, but only once, with Calvin; he was in a society of heaven, which appears in front, above the head; and he said that he did not agree with Luther and Melancthon about faith alone, because works are so often named in the Word, and the doing of them commanded, and that therefore, faith and works ought to be conjoined. I heard from one of the governors of that society, that Calvin was accepted in his society, because he was upright and made no disturbance.

What Luther's lot is, shall be told elsewhere, for I have often heard and seen him. Here, I shall only say, that he has often wished to recede from his faith alone, but in vain; and that therefore, he is still in the world of spirits, which is midway between heaven and hell; where he sometimes suffers hard things.

VII. THE PAPISTS IN THE SPIRITUAL WORLD. The Papists, and the Last Judgment upon them, were treated of in the small work on The Last Judgment. The Papists in the spiritual world appear around the Reformed, and are separated from them by an interval, which they are not permitted to pass. Nevertheless, those who are of the order of Jesuits, by clandestine arts procure for themselves communications, and also send out emissaries, by unknown paths, for the purpose of seducing them. But they are discovered, and after being punished, they are either sent back to their companions, or are cast into hell.

After the Last Judgment, their state was so changed, that they were not allowed to gather together in companies, as before; but ways were appointed to every love, both good and evil, which those who come from the world immediately enter, and go to a society corresponding to their love. Thus the wicked are borne away to a society which is in conjunction with the hells, and the good to a society which is in conjunction with the heavens; thus precaution is taken that they may not form artificial heavens for themselves as before. Such societies in the world of spirits, which is midway between heaven and hell, are innumerable; being as many as there are genera and species of good and evil affections. And in the meantime, before spirits are either elevated into heaven, or cast down into hell, they are in spiritual conjunction with men in the world, because they too are in the midst between heaven and hell.

All those of the Papists, who have not been wholly idolaters, and who, from their religious persuasion, have done goods out of a sincere heart, and have also looked to the Lord, are led to societies which are instituted in the confines nearest to the Reformed, and are instructed there, the Word being read, and the Lord preached to them; and they who receive truths and apply them to life, are elevated into heaven and become angels. There are many such societies of them in every quarter, and they are guarded on all sides from the treacheries and cunning devices of the monks, and from the Babylonish leaven. Moreover, all their infants are in heaven, because, being educated by the angels under the guidance of the Lord, they know nothing of the falsities of the religion of their parents.

All who come from the earth into the spiritual world, are at first kept in the confession of faith, and in the religion of their country; and so therefore are the Papists. On this account, they always have some representative Pontiff set over them, whom they also adore with the same ceremony as in the world. Rarely does any Pope from the world act the Pontiff there; yet he who was Pope at Rome twenty years ago, was appointed over the Papists, because he cherished in heart that the Word is more holy than is believed, and that the Lord ought to be worshiped. But, after filling the office of Pope for some years, he abdicated it, and betook himself to the Reformed Christians, among whom he still is, and enjoys a happy life. It was granted me to speak with him, and he said, that he adored the Lord alone, because He is God, who has power over heaven and earth, and that the invocations of saints, and also their masses, are trifles; and that when he was in the world, he intended to restore that church, but that for reasons, which he mentioned, he found it impossible to do so. When the great northern city of the Papists was destroyed, on the day of the Last Judgment, I saw him carried out of it on a couch, and taken to a place of safety. Quite a different thing happened to his successor.

Here I am allowed to add something memorable. It was granted me to speak with Louis XIV., grandfather of the reigning king of France, who while he was in the world, worshiped the Lord, read the Word, and acknowledged the Pope only as the highest one of the church; in consequence of which, he has great dignity in the spiritual world, and rules the best society of the French nation. Once I saw him as it were descending by ladders, and after he descended I heard him saying, that he seemed to himself as if at Versailles, and then there was silence round about for half an hour; at the end of that time, he said, that he had spoken with the king of France, his grandson, concerning the Bull Unigenitus, advising him to desist from his former design, and not to accept it, because it was detrimental to the French nation, he said that he insinuated this into his thought profoundly. This took place in the year 1759, on the 13th day of December, about eight o'clock in the evening.

VIII. THE POPISH SAINTS IN THE SPIRITUAL WORLD. It is known that man has from his parents implanted or hereditary evil, but in what it consists is known to few. It consists in the love of ruling, which is such, that as far as the reins are given it, so far it bursts forth, until it even burns with the lust of ruling over all, and at length of wishing to be invoked and worshiped as God. This love is the serpent, which deceived Eve and Adam, for it said to the woman: God knows, that in the day ye eat of the fruit of the tree, your eyes shall be opened, and then ye shall be as God (Gen. 3:4, 5). As far therefore as man rushes with loosened reins into this love, so far he turns himself away from God, and turns towards himself, and becomes an atheist; and then the Divine truths which are of the Word, may serve as means, but because dominion is the end, the means are in the heart only as they serve him. This is the reason why those who are in the mediate and in the ultimate degree of the love of ruling, are all in hell, for that love is the devil there; and in hell there are some of such a nature, that they cannot bear to hear any one speaking of God.

Those of the Papal nation have this love who have had dominion from the frenzy of its delight, and have despised the Word, and preferred the dictates of the Pope to it. They are utterly devastated as to externals, until they no longer know anything of the church, and then they are cast down into hell and become devils. There is a certain separate hell for those who wish to be invoked as gods, where such is their fantasy, that they do not see what is, but what is not. Their delirium is such as affects persons in a malignant fever, who see things floating in the air and in the chamber, and on the covering of the bed, which do not exist. This worst of evils is meant by: The head of the serpent, which is bruised by the Seed of the woman, and which wounds His heel (Gen. 3:15). "The heel" of the Lord, who is "the Seed of the woman," is the Divine proceeding in ultimates, which is the Word in the sense of the letter.

Because man from heredity is such, that he wishes to rule, and as the reins are loosened, successively over more, and at length over all, and because the wish to be invoked and worshiped as God, is the inmost of this love of ruling, therefore all who have been made saints by the Papal bulls, are removed from the sight of others and hidden, and are deprived of all interaction with their worshipers. This is done, lest that worst root of evils should be excited in them, and they should be hurried into such fantastic deliriums as prevail in the above mentioned hell. In such deliriums are those who, when they lived in the world, have eagerly sought to be made saints after death, for the purpose of being invoked.

Many of the Papal nation, especially the monks, when they come into the spiritual world, seek the saints, each the saint of his own order; yet they do not find them, and therefore they wonder. But afterwards they are instructed by others, that they are either intermingled with those who are in the heavens, or with those who are in the hells, every one according to his life in the world; and that in whichsoever they are, they know nothing of the worship and invocation of themselves; and that they who know it, and wished to be invoked, are in that separate and delirious hell. The worship of saints is such an abomination in heaven, that whenever they hear of it they are horrified, because as far as worship is paid to any man, in so far it is withheld from the Lord, for thus He alone cannot be worshiped; and if the Lord is not alone worshiped, a discrimination is made, which destroys communion, and the felicity of life which flows from it.

That I might know, for the sake of informing others, what kind of men the Popish saints are, as many as a hundred of them, who knew of their canonization, were brought up from the lower earth. The greater part ascended from behind, and only a few in front, and I spoke with one of them, who they said was Xavier. While he talked with me, he was quite foolish, yet he was able to tell me, that in his place, where he remains confined, he is not so; but that he becomes foolish as often as he thinks that he is a saint. I heard a like murmur from those who were behind.

It is otherwise with the so-called saints who are in heaven; they know nothing at all of what is doing upon earth, nor have I spoken with them, lest any idea of this should enter their minds. Only once Mary, the mother of the Lord, passed by, and appeared over head in white raiment, and then, stopping awhile, she said that she had been the mother of the Lord, and that He was indeed born of her, but that He became God, and put off all the human from her, and that therefore she now adores Him as her God, and is unwilling that any one should acknowledge Him as her Son, because in Him all is Divine.

I will here add this Relation. A certain woman in splendid raiment and with saint-like countenance, occasionally appears in a middle altitude, to the Parisians who are in a society in the spiritual world, and tells them she is Genevieve. But as soon as any of them begin to adore her, then instantly her countenance is changed, and her raiment too, and she becomes like an ordinary woman, and chides them for wishing to adore a woman, who, among her companions, is in no more repute than a maid servant; wondering that men in the world are caught by such trifles. The angels said that she appears for the purpose of separating those there who worship man from those who worship the Lord.

IX. THE MOHAMMEDANS IN THE SPIRITUAL WORLD; AND MOHAMMED. The Mohammedans in the spiritual world appear behind the Papists in the west, and form as it were a circle around them. The principal reason why they appear there is, because they acknowledge the Lord as the Greatest Prophet, the Son of God, the Wisest of all, who was sent into the world to teach men. Every one in that world dwells at a distance from the Christian center where the Reformed are, according to his confession of the Lord and of one God; for that confession conjoins minds with heaven, and determines distance from the east, above which the Lord is. They who, from the life of evil, are not in that confession in heart, are in the hells beneath them.

Since religion makes man's inmost, and all the rest proceeds from the inmost, and since Mohammed is closely connected with their religion, therefore some Mohammed is always placed in their sight; and in order that they may turn their faces to the east, above which the Lord is, he is placed beneath in the Christian center. It is not the Mohammed himself who wrote the Koran, but another who fills his office; nor is it always the same, but he is changed. Once it was one from Saxony, who had been taken by the Algerians, and became a Mohammedan; and who, having been also a Christian, was actuated to speak to them concerning the Lord, that He was not the Son of Joseph, as they believed in the world, but the Son of God Himself, by which he insinuated into them an idea of the unity of the Lord's Person and Essence with the Father. To this Mohammed, others afterwards succeeded, who were actuated to declare the same. By this means, many of them accede to a truly Christian faith concerning the Lord, and they who do so accede, are carried to a society nearer to the east, where communication is granted them from heaven, into which they are afterwards elevated. In the place where the seat of that Mohammed is, there appears a fire like a torch, that he may be known, but it is invisible to all but

Mohammedans.

Mohammed himself, who wrote the Koran, is not to be seen at the present day. I was told, that in early times he presided over the Mohammedans, but because be wished to domineer over all things of their religion as a God, he was cast out of his seat which he held beneath the Papists, and was sent downwards, to the right side near the south. Once some societies of Mohammedans were excited by the malicious to acknowledge Mohammed as God. To quell the sedition, Mohammed was raised up from below and shown to them, and then I also saw him. He appeared like corporeal spirits, who have no interior perception, his face approaching to black; and I heard him saying these words only, "I am your Mohammed;" and soon sinking down, as it were, he returned to his place.

As regards their religion, it was permitted such as it is, because of its agreement with the genius of the Orientals, on which account, too, it was received in so many kingdoms; and because, at the same time, it made the precepts of the Decalogue a matter of religion, and it had something from the Word, and especially because it acknowledged the Lord as the Son of God, and the wisest of all. And besides it dissipated the idolatries of many nations. The reason why Mohammed was not made the means of opening to his followers a more interior religion, was on account of polygamy, which exhales uncleanness towards heaven; for the marriage of a husband with one wife, corresponds to the marriage of the Lord and the Church.

Many of them are receptive of truth, and they see justice in reasons, as I was enabled to observe from conversations with them in the spiritual world. I spoke with them concerning the One God, the resurrection, and marriage. Of the One God they said, that they do not comprehend the Christians when speaking of the Trinity, and saying that there are three Persons, and that each Person is God, and still saying that God is one. But I replied, that the angels in the heaven which is from Christians, do not speak thus, but say, that God is one in essence and in Person, and in whom is a Trine, and that men on earth call this Trine three Persons; and that this Trine is in the Lord. In confirmation, I read before them out of Matthew and Luke, all that is said there of the conception of the Lord from God the Father, as well as the passages in which He Himself teaches, that He and the Father are one. On hearing this they perceived it, saying that thus the Divine essence is in Him. Of the Resurrection they said, that they do not comprehend Christians when they speak of the state of man after death, making the soul like wind or air, and hence is deprived of all delight before its reunion with the body at the day of the Last Judgment. But I replied, that only some talk thus, but that they who are not of that class, believe they will come into heaven after death, will speak with the angels, and enter upon heavenly joy, which they do not conceive to be dissimilar to their joy in the world, although they do not describe it; and I told them, that at the present day, many particulars of the state after death are revealed to them, which they did not know before. Of Marriage, I have had many conversations with them, and have told them, among other things, that conjugial love is a celestial love, which can exist only between two, and that conjunction with many wives does not admit the celestial of that love. They heard my reasons, and perceived their justice; as also this, that polygamy was permitted them, because they are Orientals, who without this permission would have burned for foul adulteries more than Europeans, and would have perished.

X. THE AFRICANS AND THE GENTILES IN THE SPIRITUAL WORLD. The Gentiles who know nothing concerning the Lord, appear around those who know of Him; so that no others make the extreme circumferences but those who are altogether idolatrous, and have adored the sun and moon. But they who acknowledge one God, and make precepts like those of the Decalogue a part of religion and of life, are seen in a higher region, and thus communicate more immediately with the Christians in the center; for thus the communication is not intercepted by the Mohammedans and Papists. The Gentiles are also distinguished according to their genius and faculty of receiving light through the heavens from the Lord; for there are some of them who are more interior, and some who are more exterior; and these diversities are not derived from their place of birth, but from their religion. The Africans are more interior than the rest.

All who acknowledge and worship one God, the Creator of the universe, have concerning Him the idea of Man: they say, that concerning God, no one can have any other idea. When they hear that many cherish the idea of Him as of a small cloud, they inquire where they are, and on being told that they are among Christians, they deny the possibility of it. But it is replied, that Christians have this idea, because God in the Word is called Spirit, and of a spirit, they are accustomed to think that it is like a particle of cloud, not knowing that every spirit and every angel is a man. Yet when they were explored, to discover whether their spiritual and natural ideas were alike, it was found that they were not alike with those who interiorly acknowledge the Lord as the God of heaven and earth. I heard a certain presbyter of the Christians saying, that no one can have an idea of the Divine Human; and I saw him led about to various Gentiles, in succession to those who were more and more interior, and from them to their heavens, and at length to the Christian heaven, and the interior perception of all concerning God was communicated to him, and he perceived that their idea of God was no other than the idea of Man, which is the same as the idea of the Divine Human.

There are many societies of Gentiles, especially from the Africans, who, on being instructed by the angels concerning the Lord, say that it cannot be otherwise than that God the Creator of the universe should appear in the world, because He created them and loves them; and that the appearance must be made before the very eyes in the Human form. When they are told, that He did not appear as the angels are wont to appear, but that He was born Man, and thus became visible, they hesitate awhile, and inquire whether He was born from a human father; and on hearing that he was conceived by the God of the universe, and born of a virgin, they say that thus He has the Divine essence itself, which because it is infinite and life itself, He was not such a man as others are. They are afterwards informed by the angels, that in aspect He was like another man, but that when He was in the world, His Divine essence, which in itself is infinite and life itself, rejected the finite nature and its life from the mother, and thus made His Human, which was conceived and born in the world, Divine. The Africans comprehended and received these things, because they think more interiorly and spiritually than others.

Such being the character of the Africans even in the world, there is, at the present day, a revelation with them, which commencing in the center, is communicated around, but does not reach the seas. They acknowledge our Lord as the God of heaven and earth, and laugh at the monks in those parts they visit, and at the Christians who talk of a three-fold Divinity, and of salvation by mere thinking, saying, that there is no man who has any worship, who does not live according to his religion, and that whosoever does not, must become stupid and wicked, because then he receives nothing from heaven. Ingenious wickedness they also call stupidity, because in it there is not life but death. I have heard the angels rejoicing over this revelation, because, by means of it, a communication is opened for them with the human rational, hitherto closed up by the blindness which has been drawn over the things of faith. It was told me from heaven, that the truths now published in The Doctrine of the New Jerusalem Concerning the Lord, Concerning the Word, and in The Doctrine of Life for the New Jerusalem, are orally dictated by angelic spirits to the inhabitants of that country.

When I spoke with the Africans in the spiritual world, they appeared in striped garments of linen: they said that such garments correspond to them, and that their women have striped garments of silk. Of their little children, they related, that they frequently ask their nurses for food, saying that they are hungry, and when food is set before them, they examine and taste whether it agrees with them, and eat but little; whence it is evident, that spiritual hunger, which is a desire of knowing genuine truths, produces this effect; for it is a correspondence When the Africans wish to know their state as to the affection and perception of truth, they draw their swords; and if these shine, they know that they are in genuine truths, in a degree according to the shining; this, too, is from correspondence. Of marriage they said, that it is indeed allowed them by law to have several wives, but that still they take but one, because love truly conjugial is not divided; and that if it is divided, its essence which is heavenly perishes, and it becomes external and thence lascivious, and in a short time grows vile, as its potency diminishes, and at length is loathed when the potency is lost; but love truly conjugial, which is internal, and derives nothing from lasciviousness, remains to eternity, and increases in potency, and in the same degree in delight.

Strangers from Europe they said, are not admitted, and when any penetrate into their country, especially monks, they ask them what they know, and when they relate any particulars of their religious persuasion, they call them trifles which offend their very ears, and they then send them out of the way to work, in order that they may do something useful; and if they refuse to work, they sell them for slaves, whom their law allows them to chastise at will; and if they cannot drive them to do anything useful, they are at last sold for a small sum to the lowest class.

XI. THE JEWS IN THE SPIRITUAL WORLD. Before the Last Judgment the Jews appeared in a valley in the spiritual world, at the left side of the Christian center; but after it, they were transferred into the north, and forbidden to hold interaction with Christians, except with those who wandered outside the cities. In that quarter, there are two great cities into which the Jews are led after death, and which before the judgment, were called Jerusalems, but after it by another name, because after the judgment by "Jerusalem" is meant the church in which the Lord alone is adored. In these cities, converted Jews are appointed over them, who admonish them not to speak scoffingly of Christ; and punish those who still do so. The streets of their cities are filled with mire up to the ankles, and their houses are full of uncleanness, from which they smell, so that they cannot be approached.

An angel sometimes appears to them in a middle altitude above them, with a rod in his hand, and gives them to believe that he is Moses, and exhorts them to desist from the madness of expecting the Messiah even there, because Christ, who governs them and all other men, is the Messiah: he says, that he knows it to be so, and also, that when he was in the world, he knew something concerning Him. On hearing this, they retire; the chief part of them forgetting, and only a few retaining it. They who do retain it are sent to synagogues, which are composed of the converted, and are there instructed; and if they receive instruction, they have new garments given them in place of their old tattered ones, and are presented with the Word neatly written, and with a dwelling in a not unsightly city. But they who do not receive, are cast down into the hells, beneath their great tract; many also are cast into forests and into deserts, where they commit robberies among themselves.

In that world, as in the former, they traffic in various things, especially in precious stones, which, by unknown ways, they procure for themselves from heaven, where there are precious stones in abundance. The reason of their trading in precious stones is, that they read the Word in its original language, and regard the sense of its letter as holy, and precious stones correspond to the sense of the letter of the Word. On the subject of this correspondence, see The Doctrine of the New Jerusalem Concerning the Sacred Scripture. They sell their precious stones to the Gentiles who encircle them in the northern quarter. They also have the art of producing imitations, and of inducing the fancy that they are genuine; but they who do so are heavily fined by their governors.

The Jews are more ignorant than others as to their being in the spiritual world, believing that they are still in the natural world. The reason is, that they are wholly external men, and do not think at all of their religion from the interior. On this account also they speak of the Messiah just as they did before, as that He will come with David, and will go before them glittering with diadems, and introduce them into the land of Canaan; and that in the way, by lifting His rod, He will dry up the rivers which they will pass over; and that Christians, whom among themselves they call Gentiles, will then lay hold of the skirts of their garments, and humbly entreat to be allowed to accompany them, and that they will receive the rich according to their wealth, and that even the rich are to serve them. For they are unwilling to know, that "the land of Canaan" in the Word, means the church, and "Jerusalem," the church as to doctrine; and hence that "Jews" mean all those who will be of the Lord's church. That such is the meaning of "Jews" in the Word, may be seen in The Doctrine Concerning the Sacred Scripture. When they are asked, whether they believe that they also are to enter the land of Canaan, they reply, that they will then descend into it. When it is said, that this land cannot possibly hold them all, they reply that it will then be enlarged. When it is said that they do not know where Bethlehem is nor who is of the stock of David, they say, that it is known to the Messiah who is to come. When asked, how the Messiah the Son of Jehovah, can dwell with those who are so evil, they reply that they are not evil. When it is said that still Moses describes them in his song (Deut. 32) as the worst of nations, they answer, that Moses at that time was angry, because he was to die. But when they are told, that Moses wrote it by the command of Jehovah, they are silent, and go away to consult about the matter. When it is said, that they took their origin from a Canaanite, and from the whoredom of Judah with his daughter-in-law (Gen. 38), they are enraged, and say, that it suffices them to be descended from Abraham. When they are told that interiorly in the Word there is a spiritual sense, which treats of Christ alone, they reply, that it is not so, but that interiorly in the Word there is nothing but gold; besides many such things.

XII. THE QUAKERS IN THE SPIRITUAL WORLD. There are enthusiastic spirits, separated from all others, of such gross perception, that they believe themselves to be the Holy Spirit. When Quakerism commenced, these spirits, being drawn out as it were from encircling forests where they were wandering, obsessed many; infusing the persuasion that they were moved by the Holy Spirit; and because they perceived the influx sensibly, they became so completely filled with this kind of religious persuasion, that they believed themselves more enlightened and holier than the rest; therefore also they could not be withdrawn from their religious persuasion. They who have confirmed themselves therein, come into a similar enthusiasm after death, and are separated from the rest, and sent away to their like in forests, where, at a distance, they appear like wild swine. But they who have not confirmed themselves, being separated from the others, are remanded to a place like a desert, in the extreme borders of the southern quarter, where they have caves for their temples.

After the former enthusiastic spirits were removed from them, the trembling which from these spirits had seized their bodies ceased, and they now feel a motion in their left side. It was shown, that from the first time they have gone successively into worse things, and at length, by command of their holy spirit, into heinous things, which they divulge to no one. I conversed with the founder of their religious persuasion, and with Penn, who said that they had no part in such things. But they who have perpetrated such things, are sent down after death into a dark place, where they sit in corners, appearing like the dregs of oil.

Since they have rejected the two sacraments, Baptism and the Holy Supper, and still read the Word, and preach the Lord, and speak obsessed by enthusiastic spirits, and thus commix the holy things of the Word with truths profaned, therefore no society is formed of them in the spiritual world, but after being dissociated they wander hither and thither, and are dispersed, and gathered into the above mentioned desert.

XIII. THE MORAVIANS IN THE SPIRITUAL WORLD. I have conversed much with the Moravians, who are also called Herrnhuters. They appeared, at first, in a valley not far from the Jews; but after being examined and detected, were conveyed away into uninhabited places. When they were being examined, they knew how with cunning to captivate minds, saying, that they were the remains of the Apostolic Church, and that therefore they salute each other as brethren, and those who receive their interior mysteries as mothers; also that they teach faith better than others and love the Lord because He suffered the cross, calling Him the Lamb, and the Throne of grace; with other like expressions, by which they induce the belief that the Christian church itself is with them. Those who are captivated by their smooth speeches and draw near to them, are examined by them to see whether they are such that they dare disclose to them their mysteries; if not they conceal them; if they can they reveal them; and then they warn and also threaten those who divulge their mystery concerning the Lord.

Since they did the same in the spiritual world, when yet it was perceived that interiorly they did not think so, in order that this might be disclosed, they were admitted into the lowest heaven; but they did not endure the sphere of the charity and faith of the angels there, and they fled away. Afterwards, because in the world they believed that they alone would be alive, and would enter the third heaven, they were also carried up into this heaven, but on perceiving the sphere of love to the Lord there, they were seized with anguish of heart, and began to suffer interior tortures, and to move convulsively, like those who are in the agony of death, therefore they cast themselves down headlong thence. In this manner it was first made manifest that inwardly they had cherished nothing of charity toward the neighbor, and nothing of love to the Lord. They were afterwards sent to those whose function it is to examine the interiors of the thoughts, and these said of them, that they hold the Lord in little estimation, that they reject the life of charity so as to abhor it, and that they make the Word of the Old Testament useless, and despise the Word of the Evangelists; only of their good pleasure selecting from Paul, where anything is said of faith alone; and that these are their mysteries, which they conceal from the world.

After it was made manifest that they acknowledge the Lord only as the Arians do, that they despise the Word of the Prophets and Evangelists, and hold a life of charity in hatred, when yet upon these three things as on pillars the whole heaven depends; then they who were in the knowledge and at the came time in the belief of their mysteries, were adjudged Anti-Christs, who reject the three essentials of the Christian church, namely, the Divine of the Lord, the Word, and charity, and were cast outside the Christian world into a desert, which is in the end of the southern quarter near the Quakers.

When Zinzendorf first came into the spiritual world after death, and was permitted to speak as before in the world, I heard him asserting, that he knew the mysteries of heaven, and that no one enters heaven who is not of his doctrine; and also, that they who do good works for the sake of salvation, are utterly damned, and that he would rather admit atheists into his congregation than them. The Lord, he said, was adopted by God the Father as His Son, because He endured the cross, and that still He was simply a man. When it was said to him, that the Lord was conceived by God the Father, he replied, that he thought of that matter as he chose, not daring to speak out as the Jews do. Moreover, I have perceived many scandals from his followers, when I have been reading the Evangelists.

They say, that they have a sensation, and thence an interior confirmation of their dogmas. But it was shown to them, that their sensation was from visionary spirits, who confirm a man in all his religious persuasions, and enter more closely with those, who like the Moravians, love their religious persuasion, and think much concerning it. These spirits also talked with them, and they mutually recognized each other.

Last Judgment Posthumous

THE ENGLISH. The English appear a little to the right, in front, in a plane just above the head. The light with them appears more interior than with others in the Christian world, by which light the spiritual is received which flows in from above. They see clearly in a moment what flows in, and at once receive it; nor do they let it down into their natural so grossly as others. Hence it is that the spiritual appears clear also in the natural; but with others more obscure. But they who are such, are those who have loved what is right and sincere, and have acted from truth and sincerity, and who at the same time have thought of God from religion.

When the Last Judgment was being executed, the Protestants were then led into the middle, and they then appeared in this order: The English in the middle, the Dutch towards the east and south, the Germans more towards the north, the Swedes to the north and west in the middle. All then appeared according to their general genius as to the reception of good and truth.

Few of the English become genii, whose quality may be described, since they do not depend much on their own thought, but on the mouth of authority: for they easily receive if only they are persuaded that the man is learned and sincere, and of their own nation; their thought then appears lucid and interior.

It was perceived that many of the English will receive the Heavenly Doctrine, and thereby come into the New Jerusalem; because they are such that they receive the truths of faith more easily than others, and see them in interior light.

I have spoken with the English concerning their natural disposition; whence it is with them, that when they hear truths from one among them worthy of belief, they then see them, and thus easily conform to them; and whence it is that with them there is a snowy appearance above their natural, that it is from heavenly light, from which is intelligence: in like manner with the Dutch. But as to the Dutch, with them there is not that snowy appearance, but something firm in the confines of their spiritual and natural minds; and that therefore they are slower. The cause of the appearance of the light with the English was told, namely, that it is from their life, which differs from the life of all other nations. That the cause might be perceived, a comparison was made with the Italians of this day; that their governments are altogether opposite. In England there is freedom to speak and write both on civil and spiritual things; but no freedom at all to use deceit and cunning to deceive others, nor to lie in wait to murder, rob and kill; and if they do it, there is no remission. But it is the opposite with the Italians at this day. In Italy there is freedom to deceive by cunning and guile, and also to kill; which freedom they have from so many asylums, and from the dispensations: but there is no freedom at all to speak and write on ecclesiastical and civil affairs there, on account of the inquisition. Hence it is that the Italian nation retains such things within, and thus a fire, which is a slow hatred, revenge, and cruelty; which fire is like that which, after a conflagration, lies hid long under the ashes, and consumes. But with the English nation it is otherwise, because it is allowed to speak and write freely.

There such a fire is not laid up, but immediately burns out; and they are kept in what is sincere and just by the fact that they are not permitted to deceive, to rob, and to kill; since there is then no dispensation, nor anywhere an asylum.

The English have quite an exquisite perception that a thing is so, when it is said from reason. They have an interior sight as to religion; but this sight which they have is a receptive sight, but not so active that they can see before it has been confirmed by some celebrated leader among them. Their interior sight is called the intuitive and affirmative sight of reception, and likewise confirmative; but chiefly by means of elegant things composed in a spiritual manner; and this descends and proceeds from that snowy appearance of theirs. This appears with them in the spiritual world; on which account also they are in the middle among Christians: for those are in the middle who are in interior light.

It was shown of what quality a book or writing appears to them, which has been approved by a man in whose erudition they have confidence; and of what quality a book or writing appears, which is not yet approved. In writings not approved, when they are read, they see nothing but the mere letter, or the sense of the letter; but in an approved writing they see the sense of the matter, and not of the letter; because they are then in enlightenment from the belief that it is so: so that approval gives enlightenment. On which account a writing, howsoever important, is not procured before it has been praised by a man worthy of belief.

Since the English are of such a genius, there are therefore set over them priests, and also magistrates, in whom they have confidence that they are intelligent and wise; and they then yield a favoring assent to them in everything which they say and teach. By this they are held in obedience, and likewise in doctrine. But they who are not compliant, and they who are wicked, are shut out of their society; for these loose the bond and unanimity.

I have had much discourse with English priests concerning faith, among whom also were bishops. Because it was according to their doctrine, they insisted that faith alone produces the endeavor to good. But to the question, whether by endeavor they meant man's manifest will, this they were unwilling to admit; because everything that proceeds from man's manifest will is in itself not good, and is meritorious; wherefore by endeavor they meant an internal operation, about which the understanding knows little: consequently that such endeavor is inwardly in faith, and that it is not manifested openly except by an inclination to doing. In this opinion they were so tenacious, and also in this, that faith produces the good which is called charity, that they were not willing to be led, although it was told them from heaven, that faith does not produce anything of charity, but that charity produces faith; and that faith before charity is not living faith, but only knowledge; and that a man ought to do good as of himself, and that otherwise nothing of good is inrooted and implanted: but to this they shut their ears. When they were told that one of the most talented of them 9-1 had thought out reasons and ways, even to a hundred, to confirm that faith produces charity, and that he had wandered through each way, as is done in the spiritual world by thinking that it is so; but still, when he came to the end of the way, he saw from enlightenment given him that he had been wandering, which he also as often confessed. Also when their solemn exhortation at the Holy Supper was read before them, wherein these things are said, 9-2... they thought, but were unwilling to say, that this is said for the laity, and that the doctrine is for the clergy: wherefore it was announced to them, that life according to the faith of the laity saves; but life according to the doctrine of the clergy condemns: since in the faith of the clergy there is no life, and in their life there is no faith; but there is in the faith and life of the laity.

In the spiritual world images and many other things can be formed from the ideas of thought, and be presented to the sight; which is peculiar to that world. Wherefore the same English priests undertook to form an image in the likeness of a man, from the ideas of their thoughts concerning faith alone, or faith separate from charity; which image, when it was made, appeared monstrous, as not unlike Dagon, the idol of the Philistines in Ekron; therefore it was cast into a certain lake.

It is said of the English in the spiritual world, that they love elegance in their discourses; and that such elegance has indeed a delightful sound in the ears, but still gives little instruction; especially when they treat of faith, and of justification by it: that they then so arrange their words, that scarcely anyone knows whether anything of good is to be done or not. They so weave together series of conclusions, that they sound as if good should be done; although these conclusions involve that faith produces them without their knowing it.

In the spiritual world the face of the earth is similar to what it is in the natural world. There are urban and country places there. They who dwelt in cities in our world, dwell also in cities there: in like manner those who lived in country places. Moreover, the cities in the spiritual world are similar to the cities in the natural world, but only as to the streets and public squares; but they are not similar as to the buildings. Neither do the good and the evil dwell promiscuously there; but in the middle of the city, where also are the public buildings, 12-1 dwell the best, who are the governors and magistrates. To the east there are those who are in the clear good of love, to the west those who are in the obscure good of love, to the south those who are in the clear light of truth, to the north those who are in the obscure light of truth. The good of love and the truth of faith decrease from the middle into the farthest circumferences. Since the cities there are similar to the cities in our world, there is also a London there similar to London as to the streets; but not as to the houses, neither as to the inhabitants, nor their habitations in the quarters. I was conducted into it in the spirit, and wandered through it, and recognized it. And I spoke with certain ones there, and said that men in the world would wonder, and would not believe that they who live in London see a London also after death; and if they are good, also dwell in their city: yet it is altogether so. They said that neither would they have believed it, when they were in the world; because such a thing does not fall into sensual ideas, but only into rational ideas enlightened by spiritual light; also that they did not then know that the spiritual appears before a spirit, as the material does before a man; and that all the things which exist in the spiritual world are from a spiritual origin, as all the things in the natural world are from a material origin: in like manner the houses of a city, which are not built as in the world, but rise up in a moment created by the Lord: so too all other things. They rejoiced that now as before they are in England, and in its great city; and they said that there is also another London below, not dissimilar as to the streets, but dissimilar as to the houses and as to the inhabitants: namely, that the evil dwell in the middle, and the upright in the last circumferences; and that those come into that London from the London in the world, who have not been in any spiritual love, and hence not in any spiritual faith, but have indulged the pleasures of the body and the lusts of the mind. Also that the city, in the middle where the evil dwell, sinks down by turns into the deep; and the evil are thus cast down into hell: and that the opening is renewed, and the evil are again collected into the middle of it, and again are swallowed up by hell. This is in the world of spirits, it is different in heaven, and different in hell.

THE DUTCH. They are quite clear-sighted, and remain constantly in their own religion; not receding unless altogether convinced; and if they are convinced, they still turn the back. They excel in judgment from natural rational light, from which they look into things in the world justly, especially in business. Their light appears more obscure, because their spiritual light is conjoined with natural light: the reason is, because they are continually thinking about business.

With the Dutch there is not that snowy appearance which is with the English, but in place of it something firm; which is an indication that they are constant in the things of their religion. But there is this difference, that on civil, moral, and likewise spiritual subjects, they judge from themselves, and not from others: and they reflect especially upon intellectual things, and upon the connection of reasons.

The Dutch appear in the angle towards the east and south; to the east because they love religion bare without images, that they may look at it in itself, but not from images; to the south, because they excel in understanding.

It is a general trait of the Dutch nation, that they are strong in judgment from natural light, from which they take a very just view of things, especially of those that are of the world: and because they are continually thinking about their business, the spiritual light hides itself in the natural; on which account also they are able to receive what is true in religion: but still, when they are convinced, they turn the back.

The Dutch are not so eager for money as for business itself. Business itself is their end and love, and is in the first place; and money is the mediate end, and is loved for the sake of business; thus it is in the second place. And they who are such, are loved in heaven; each one is esteemed according to his use. It is otherwise with the avaricious, as the Jews are, with whom money is in the first place as the very end and love, and business in the second place. Hence is avarice, which is sordid according to the love of money alone.

At the day of the Last Judgment, those of the Dutch who had done nothing of good from any religion or conscience, but only for the sake of reputation, that for the sake of gain they might appear sincere, were cast out of their cities, villages and lands: for with such, when the regard for reputation and gain is taken away, which is done in the spiritual world, then such rush into every wickedness, despoiling whomsoever they happen to meet in the fields or outside of the cities. I saw a great number of such cast into a dark chasm extending obliquely under the eastern tract, and likewise into a chasm extending under the southern tract. This expulsion was seen on the 9th day of January, 1757.

Those remained with whom there was religion and from religion conscience.

I was in the spirit, and it was then granted me to wander through a rather distinguished city, in which were Dutch. All the streets in it were seen to be roofed over, and in the streets were closed gates of wood; on which account, without leave from some overseer, it was not permitted to wander around. But afterwards it was granted me to speak with the magistrates, who dwelt in the middle of the city; by whom I was examined as to whence I came, and what I wanted: and when they understood that it was only for the sake of seeing, that I might make known to their brethren who were still in the world, what their lot was, and what kind of dwellings they had; they then related to me many things, especially that they who dwelt there were among the prudent and intelligent from that nation; and that there are many such cities, distinct according to the affections and perceptions of truth from good; and that they were in the world of spirits; and that after some time passed there, they were taken up thence into heaven, and introduced into societies there, and became angels: also that the city was double and triple, or city under city; and when one descends by ladders, he comes into a new city, where those reside who are different as to affections. They said that their streets are everywhere roofed over, because sometimes from the rocks round about, which are somewhat higher, they are looked at by the evil who are skilled in the perversion of souls by means of ideas, and in inducing lusts that are not congruous; and that they know how to bind the ideas, if by any means they penetrate; by which they were kept in anxiety, and as it were bound; and this even to despair: which was also shown me to the life. If anyone comes to them, who is of another genius, and therefore disagrees as to the affections and the thoughts thence, they order him to go away; and when he goes, he everywhere finds the gates closed: on which account he is led to other gates that he may go out, but he still finds them closed: and in the meantime they breathe into him a longing to go out; and this is done until he becomes so weary, that he can no longer endure it; and only then is he let out: and when let out he does not return, on account of the vexation into which he has been driven. The Dutch, more than the rest in the Christian world, know what fantasy is, and what reality; so that they cannot be deluded, like others.

It is not allowed to speak anything with them about religion; wherefore, when anyone comes to them from another religion, he is examined, not by the living voice, and by oral answer; but without his knowledge they explore his thoughts, and draw therefrom what is with them. It has likewise been given to speak with the priests; and I have spoken with them concerning the Lord from the Heavenly Doctrine; and they acknowledged the truths, and were affected. They were then in enlightenment from the Lord. From these things it was granted me to know, that they have a perception of truth above others, both spiritual and civil; and that they look out prudently for themselves, and that this is implanted in them.

In their cities, the men dwell at one side of the city, and the women at the other: and when the men desire, they send to them, and the women come; who are indignant at this, that they are thus to come at the command of the man. And they who in the world had ruled over their husbands, when the like is not given them, being kindled with indignation, wish to go out of the city. They are also sent out; but when they are outside of the city, there appears to them everywhere some obstruction and closure, now marshy, now watery, now something else. Thus they wander, and for a long time seek for places of getting away, and this even to fatigue: wherefore they are compelled to return into the city; and they enter their house, and so are amended. The reason is, that the desire of ruling in marriage takes away conjugial 22-1 love; which increases with a consort as the love of ruling decreases. In place of this then comes love, and with love enjoyment of life; and then neither the man nor the wife, but the Lord, rules: hence is happiness in marriages.

The Dutch appear clothed with coats and breeches altogether as in the world; and they are distinguished from others by the fact that their human derives more from the world than the human of others: for the spiritual does not shine through so clearly as with others. This they derive from their love for business in the world, and thence their continual thought and speculation about it. Even when they come into the spiritual world, they revolve similar things in the mind, and look around on all sides to see where there is trading, and what its quality is: for there is trading in the spiritual world equally as in the natural world; but still the difference is such that it can scarcely be described; and what I wondered at, when they meet with business men who wish to search into their thoughts and intentions secretly by close inspection, as is done there, they forthwith become invisible; which is from this, that they were unwilling in the world to divulge their business to others.

All, whosoever come among spirits after death, are prepared either for heaven or for hell, everyone according to the life formed from doctrine. The preparation is made with most by instructions from the angels. But the Dutch cannot be prepared for heaven and for receiving the spiritual of heaven, which is also the spiritual of the angels, by means of information, for they do not receive it; for they remain more constantly than all others in their faith. When they are informed, they still think from themselves against it. Therefore they are prepared in another manner. Heaven is described to them as to its quality, it is then granted them to ascend into heaven, and see it; and whatever agrees with their genius is insinuated into them, so that they return with the full desire of coming into heaven. But when they are sent back, they are reduced to misery, and business is taken away from them, until they see themselves reduced to extremities, and then they are led around to those who abound in all things, and who are rich; and then the thought is borne upon them what the quality of these is, and how they can be in such abundance, and in the delight of life. They thus reflect upon the life of these, that it is a life of mutual love; also upon their doctrine, that it is the doctrine of that love; and that all their good and pleasant things are from the Lord: and then they are not informed, but inquire themselves, and inform themselves, and thus think from themselves, that in order to get out of their misery they also must believe and do in like manner: and as they receive that faith, but of themselves through the life, abundance is then given them, and so on successively. They are thus prepared for heaven, not by others, but by themselves; not knowing then that they still are not prepared thus by themselves, but by the Lord; because they are such that they also afterwards acknowledge. They are afterwards more constant also than others, so that they may be called constancies; nor do they suffer themselves to be drawn away by any deceit, or by any art, or by reasoning, or by obscurity from insinuated doubts and from sophistries, or by any fallacy, appearance, or fantasy: especially they whose life's love was business, and not money; and whose end was not a sumptuous life.

CALVIN. It was said of Calvin, that he lived a Christian life, and did not place religion in faith alone, as Melancthon and Luther did; and that therefore he is in heaven.

Calvin was seen in a society of heaven, in front above the head, but not in the middle of it; and he said that he was in a like doctrine of the church, in which he was in the world. He told me, that he did not agree with Luther, nor with Melancthon, upon faith alone; since faith and works are so often named in the Word, and are commanded to be done; and that faith and works are therefore to be conjoined: but that Luther felt that if works were admitted, they would not recede far from the papists; but he believed that faith produces works, as a tree does fruit. Calvin is accepted in his society, because he is upright and does not make a disturbance; this I heard from one of the governors of the society.

MELANCTHON. I have spoken with Melancthon and with others concerning him. After he came into the spiritual world, Melancthon confirmed himself in faith alone more than before, so that he was scarcely willing to hear of charity, and of its good: and as he could not persuade any others but those who had led a life scarcely Christian, he therefore procured to himself a persuasive power; which is such that the speech flows into the thought of another, and thus binds it; so that the man is deprived of the power of thinking anything but what is said, though it be false. It fascinates the mind; on which account it is forbidden there; for it extinguishes all light of the understanding; and those whom he could not convince by reasonings, he looked into their eyes, and infused such a persuasion into their minds, that they could not see the falsities nor the sophistries, thus could not answer; on which account they complained about him. This he also tried with me, but with a fruitless effort. Leeks and the smell of them or garlic correspond to this persuasive power; which smell, by its pungency, hurts the left eye. I spoke with him concerning the power of persuasion, and concerning the Nephilim who were in it; who could almost kill a man by their persuasion; concerning which see in the Arcana Coelestia.

There came to me afterwards, from the northern quarter toward the west, certain spirits among the more cunning and malicious; and among them one, who was distinguished from the others by his heavy gait: it was a gait sounding like a bear's. He did many things maliciously; nor did I know who he was. It was afterwards disclosed that he was Melancthon. And that I might know that it was he, he asked where Luther was; and when it was told, he entered in to him, and spoke before him, and was recognized. It was said by Luther, that he spoke much with him about faith alone, or faith separate from good works. Luther inquired of him, what his lot now was: and he disclosed that he was by turns in a chamber paneled above, and by turns in hell under a judge: that when he was in the chamber, he was clothed in a skin like a bearskin, by which he protected himself from the cold; and that he wrote much about faith alone; that when he was in hell under the judge, he was held vile like the rest, and I heard the judge speak of him, that there he was evil, and was sometimes punished for his wicked deeds.

It was further said, that in that chamber the walls are of stone only, without decorations, as elsewhere; and thus it is rude and sad there. On which account, when any, because of his reputation in the world, wish to meet him and speak with him, he does not admit them, because he is ashamed of the rude things there. He sometimes acknowledges that he has been in falsities, and that thence he is such: on which account he sometimes prays that in his chamber he may write concerning charity, and its goods, which are called good works; and then some things are dictated to him from heaven by angels; and when he writes them, the chamber begins to be adorned with various decorations. But after he has written them, and left them upon the table, and read them over, he does not see them; and what he sees, he does not understand; and then the decorations of the chamber vanish: such is his lot.

I heard him speaking with Englishmen out of his paneled apartment. He spoke of faith alone. They said that they do not know what faith alone is. He said that God the Father sent His Son, who suffered for our sins. They said that this is historical: what besides? He said that by that faith they have eternal life. They said, "Did he have eternal life?" To this he could not answer. They said, moreover, that they hear preachers of faith alone, and of justification by it; and when they are hearing, the preaching sounds as if full of wisdom, because it is a well arranged and ingenious composition. But when they come home, they know nothing of what they have spoken, not comprehending their arcana.

I afterwards saw Melancthon among many who held to faith alone, in the place where they are separated, everyone at length goes to the place of his life; and I then heard a voice to them from heaven, that that faith saves no one, because there is nothing of the life in it, nor is there truth in it. On which account they asked, what truth is, and what life is. It was answered that truth and life is to live according to the commandments of the Decalogue: as not to steal, that is, not to act insincerely and unjustly; not to commit adultery; not to kill, or thus, not to burn with deadly hatred and revenge against anyone; not to testify falsely, thus not to lie and defame: and that he who does not do these things because they are sins, has life; and many more truths are afterwards given to him, what evil is, and what good is: and that no other one can be led by the Lord, and be saved; and that it may thence be known, that life and truth are one, as love and faith are; for life is of love, and truth is of faith.

LUTHER. There are places where they contend about religious affairs. Outside of these places their contentions are heard as the gnashing of teeth: and when they are viewed within, it appears as if they were tearing off each other's garments; and their sphere causes pain to the flesh of the teeth and the gums. There came one to me therefrom, with a religious garb, like a monk; and it was said that it was Luther. And he spoke with me, saying that he wished to be among such as contend about things to be believed; because he has brought with him from the world a persuasiveness of speech, and an authority from the consent of many of his time. I observed that he had communication with those who believe that they know all things, and that nothing at all is hidden from them, and who do not wish to learn, but to teach; often saying that is the truth, and that it cannot be contradicted. Such take away from others all freedom of speaking, by inducing their opinions as if they were from God, and by infesting all who contradict, unless for the sake of information. He said that he loves to reason about faith, and likewise about the good of charity; but that he rarely finds those with whom he could be in that delight, for the reason that he had hatched that doctrine from his thought, and that he is thence in the connection of things. It is otherwise with those who only learn it, and afterwards confirm it; they cannot be in such delight, because they are not in such connection of things. He said that they did not long endure his ardor of speaking, but withdraw.

It was given to speak with him concerning faith and love, concerning truth and good, and concerning their marriage, that no more is given from the one than from the other, consequently no more from faith than from life. I spoke with him for two hours with ideas from spiritual light, which are very many; and angelic spirits were then associated with him, for the sake of interior perception: and being at length convinced, he said that he wished to receive that doctrine; but that he doubted whether he could, before the principles respecting faith alone were cast out; which is a matter of labor; on which account also, when he went away, he returned to them, with whom he reasoned as before.

But the angels said that there was some hope of him; because as often as he had thought from his spirit in the world, that is, when left to himself in tranquillity, he had thought about good works, and made them a matter of religion; and it was thence that he spoke so much and wrote so much concerning the good of life, though he did not make it a part of his doctrine, nor to be done for the sake of eternal life; since man cannot do good from himself; and if he does, it is for the sake of heaven, and is a matter of merit. But yet, when he came out of the thought of his spirit into discourse with others, he then, as if turned round, spoke concerning faith alone. He does in like manner at this day. This was the reason that he rejected from the Word the Epistle of James, and also Revelation.

Some have two states, the one when in discourse from doctrine, the other when he thinks with himself. In the former state he is in the body and in its wakefulness, because he is in the lower thought of the speech, and is then in the pleasure of speaking, and for the most part in the pride of learning: but in the latter state he is in his spirit, and then in obscurity, because he thinks within the body, and above the thought next to the natural sensual. This was the case with Luther. He was in the pleasantness of his life, because in the pleasantness of glory, when he was speaking; and this was about faith alone, from his doctrine: but when he was deliberating with himself, he was in favor of good works. Such thought by himself in obscurity remained to him from boyhood, because he was born in that religion, and was a monk. But as he hatched out a new 1 he undertook to withdraw from that religion, by the separation of faith from good works.

Luther related that when he was in the world, it was told him by an angel from the Lord, that he should beware of faith alone, because there was nothing in it; and that for some time he guarded against it, and recommended works: but that he still continued afterwards to separate faith from works, and to make it alone essential and saving.

After Luther was informed by the angels, that no one has any faith unless he has the good of life; and that he has just so much of faith as he has of the good of life, and has no more of the one than of the other; and as he was many times convinced of it: he repented and labored with all his might to get out of the falsities, because he could not come into heaven until he did. I perceived several times that he had repented of it, and that he was laboring against his principles, but still in vain. He also prayed to the Lord that he might be able to recede from his falsities; and he received the answer, that it would be given, if he could receive it. On which account he was sent from one society to another, where those were with whom life was conjoined to faith; but still he could not tarry long, because it was contrary to the delight of his life. It was said to him, that truths of doctrine cannot be received by the life before falsities are rejected, because truths cannot enter where falsities fill the thoughts of the understanding; and that these cannot be easily removed. The reason is, because a man, while he lives in the world, conjoins himself to societies according to the principles of his religion, which had been matters of his affection. In these he likewise remains after death; and in those societies is everyone's life; on which account it is not granted to remove and extricate himself from them, and then betake himself into new ones. It is granted, indeed, as to the thoughts, but it is not granted as to the affections; and yet they act as one. Wherefore the man enters into the new ones; but still withdraws, when he feels undelightful things in the new societies. In a word, Luther sometimes execrates faith alone, and sometimes defends it: he execrates it when he is in fear, and defends it when he is in his love.

ZINZENDORF AND THE MORAVIANS. Zinzendorf. I spoke with Zinzendorf after his death, and then his life, his life's affection, and his principles of religion were disclosed; for a spirit can be let into such a state, that he keeps silence upon absolutely nothing, but lays all things open. It was then laid open, That he had been the greatest persuader; and that he persuaded by asseverations that he knew the arcana of heaven; and that no one comes into heaven but he who is of his doctrine. That at first he spoke with others according to their religion, thus simulating and thus alluring; and that he afterwards implanted his own secrets by first examining well whether they would be received and concealed. It was said that the mystery of his faith had been, that the Lord was born that He might be the adopted Son of God; and that he had at first believed that the Lord was simply the adopted Son of God, [because He had taken on Himself the passion of the cross]; thus that he was an Arian. That he had believed that His Divine was like the divine as with others; but now that it was something more. He hardly wished to hear about the Lord's conception from the Divine, as related in Matthew and Luke; but turned himself away, and was unwilling to say what he felt; and that this is the mystery which they are afraid to manifest. That he attributed sins to the Lord, and said that in the Evangelists He did not speak better than another man, calling them obscure things: that he cared nothing for the Old Testament, and was not willing to hear that the things written there are concerning the Lord. That he rejects all the life of charity, and says it is execrable to think of God and of salvation and the rest as to the life; and that faith separate from charity saves. He believed that he alone with his followers would come into heaven; and that these alone were living, and the rest dead. They speak of themselves what the Lord did of Himself, namely, that they are sons of God; that they are without sins; that they are life and truth; because there is not any evil regarded with those who are in faith: and that for that reason they are life and truth, and call their life blameless because they live by faith.

Still they love the Lord, since to love Him is commanded, because He suffered the cross to propitiate the Father; which is the faith that saves them.

Because he believed that he alone with his followers were to come into heaven, abundant opportunity was given him to ascend into the heavens; and wherever he was, he was ordered to go away, because they perceived from him falsities together with the delight of glory, from the fact that he had established a church. It was perceived that there was merit in the delight of glory. He also spoke with his brethren about heaven; they said that it is not heaven to them.

A spirit appeared to me in vision, bearing a stag in bonds; but which burst the bonds, and rushed with fury against those he met, wishing to lacerate and destroy them. But there then appeared an enormous dog, which, rushing upon the stag, lacerated him, and tore him to pieces. The stag was afterwards seen in the human form, —it was Dippel who [appeared thus,] because he was not allowed to go about refuting all from the delight of his life, and at the same time to excite disturbance. And Zinzendorf said that he had loved him, but that he had observed that he afterwards receded; and that he was such that he wished to lacerate all by his malignant writings; and that he could refute ingeniously, as if full of science and wisdom; and that this gift was natural to him; but that of himself he thought foolishly concerning things.

Zinzendorf, when he first came into the spiritual world, began to wander around to societies and preach, as he had done in the world. But it was said that he was nowhere received, and was conducted away to his Moravian adherents, and perceived that they were not in heaven, but were in misery, because they contemptuously rejected all uses of life, which are good works; when they wish to receive truths, falsities oppose which cannot be dispersed, because they have loved them exceedingly. They know how to falsify the Word and to twist it from its genuine sense in a dexterous and skillful manner; which is done when gathered in an assembly. Some of their attempts against their companions were disclosed, who wished to disprove those mysteries, or also to reveal them; and Zinzendorf said that he therefore removed himself from them. They say that the Lord is to be loved on account of the passion of the cross, but that He is not to be worshipped. They call the Holy Supper a reminder of the passion.

Zinzendorf was in an abstract idea, thinking within himself concerning the Lord. It was observed that he thought of the Lord as of another man, and not that He is God; and that the Divine in Him was as the Divine in another man; and that the Lord spoke in a very simple manner, and not wisely; and that Paul spoke more wisely: but it was shown him that all the Lord's words were words of life, because in each one of them there is a spiritual sense; thus that each one of His words filled heaven, because He spoke by correspondences.

He believed that all things were of mercy, and that if a brother commits a grievous sin, this is remitted to him, because to God that is the means of mercy: that they are altogether condemned; and that it is better for Sodom and Gomorrah than for those who do good works for the sake of salvation; and that this is the sin of sins, because they claim to themselves the merit which is God's alone.

When Zinzendorf was rejected wherever he came, as he saw his Moravian adherents in an unhappy state, he suffered himself to be convinced that he was in falsities, and for that reason labored with all his might and still labors to disperse his falsities, and to receive truths in their stead: but he confessed that he could not tear himself away from the societies in which he inserted himself while in the world; because every man is one with them, nor can he afterwards dissociate himself: for this is meant by the Lord's words respecting the five foolish virgins, that they afterwards wished to buy oil, and likewise bought it; but still could not enter into the wedding.

THE MORAVIANS. That the Arians induce pain in the right arm, near the shoulder blade; but the Socinians induce pain in the breast bone.

The Moravians conceal their mysteries of mysteries, and close up the ways, lest they should be known by others; insinuating themselves through such things from the Lutheran doctrine as agree, proclaiming that they are the remains of the Apostolic Church, who call themselves brethren; and that they have mothers, and certain statutes from the early Christians; but as to the interiors of religion they differ from them altogether. They do not acknowledge the Divine of the Lord as anything else than what is with any other man who is in that faith. They speak lightly of the Word of the Old Testament, and reject it as of no use. The Gospels they do not care for, only Paul's Epistles. They condemn the goods of charity or good works, as to salvation, professing faith separate from charity more than others. Because they are Arians, I spoke with them concerning the Lord. They said that He was sent by God the Father, that by the passion of the cross He might save the human race, and on account of it was acknowledged as a Son, and called the Son of God; that their faith is confidence, that they love the Lord as the best man, because He took upon Himself to propitiate the Father by the passion of the cross. They say that the Lord has power in heaven, and not over heaven. They call Him the Lamb, nor do they ever adore Him as God. When it is said to them, that He was conceived of God, that He says He was from eternity, and that the Father and He are one, they hear these things, but they think against them. They dare not say that it was so written, but was not said: and such things concerning the Lord they miserably distort, and as it were lacerate. They therefore take refuge in these words, that they themselves know how it is, but it is among their mysteries of mysteries.

They call only themselves who are of that faith alive, and all others who are not in that faith, dead; and they believe that they themselves are saved above all others, and that they are to come into the third heaven: but when they come into the first or lowest heaven among the angels, they do not endure the heavenly sphere there, which is derived especially from the goods of charity, and so far from faith; and they therefore flee away thence. Their aversion for that sphere has been perceived and felt by me. And moreover, in no heavenly society are they tolerated, because they think within themselves that all others but they are dead; thus also they have a dead idea concerning the angels themselves. If they come into the second heaven, and especially into the third, where love and charity, and thence the works of charity make the all of heaven, they are seized with pain as those who lie in the death struggle; and lividness comes over their eyes, and they make convulsive motions, and are tortured inwardly.

They have preached much that they have a certain interior sensation and perception, which they say is from an influx from God the Father through heaven, by means of angels or spirits. But it was told them, that they have that sensation or perception from spirits who were Moravians in the world, and that they are in the midst of them, and that these flow in from similar principles, and confirm; which is done strongly, because they love their religious persuasion and think much about it. This was shown them to the life; also that the Quakers are in society with Quaker spirits, Enthusiasts with enthusiastic spirits, and every man with spirits who make one with the affections, and the thoughts or principles taken therefrom; and that it is never otherwise. On account of the living experience they could not but affirm this, though they were unwilling.

The good which they do to the brethren of their assembly they call the good of friendship; and they have something of hatred against those who preach good works.

Footnotes

9-1 The author of The Whole Duty of Man. See SE 5058; CLJ 46.

9-2 The Exhortation is not quoted here. See T 722:3.

12-1 Tafel has, "aedificium;" in the MS. the words, "ubi etiam aedificium est," are written above the line. Possibly it should read, "ubi etiam editius est," "where, also, it is more elevated."

22-1 Tafel has conjugalem; but the MS. has conjugialem.

Because they observe that no one can come into heaven except those who acknowledge the Divine of the Lord, and they cannot do this, they recede from love towards the Lord on account of the passion of the cross, and act as one with the infernals. From that hatred they have it with themselves as it were implanted, that they persecute the angelic spirits in ways sometimes nefarious; but they are severely punished.

They rarely hold companionship with others: they appeared at first to the right in the plane of the knees; but by turns they were diminished, cast off, and scattered. Among themselves they speak of their mysteries with closed doors, and severely prohibit the revelation of these mysteries unless by general consent; yea, they threaten: whether from those threats something has broken forth in the world; they were not willing to be explored, what they had done against some.

They call all things with them, when in their faith and confidence, holy.

There flows out from their sphere a perception of heinous adultery, because they adulterate the Word throughout, and likewise mock at many things therein.

They appeared to the left in the plane of the foot, where it was disclosed that they made one with the evil, against those who have been in the goods of charity, and acknowledged the Divine of the Lord; all of whom are angelic spirits; and become angels: wherefore they were driven away towards the north. But because they were there not willing to become quiet, but that they would plot evil, calling to their aid the Babylonians, on this account they were driven still more remotely into the north, and sent into a cavern, which tended obliquely under the west, that they might no longer injure others. They form a brotherhood everywhere.

They were compelled to an interior confession of the Lord; and I then heard profane things, such as I should scarcely dare to publish; denying, yea, profaning the things which are said there concerning the conception of the Son by the Father; that He was carried away from the sepulcher by the disciples; that the transfiguration was a vision induced by fantastic spirits; that He was a man so low that He was lower than others; besides more heinous things from which it was evident that they are the worst of all in Christendom, and that they have hatched a theology out of their skull, and have afterwards consulted the Word, profaning it, because it does not make one with their vain delusions. The evils with themselves they call goods, because [they say] nothing of evil is imputed to them.

They were afterwards called together, and were explored whether they were all unanimous in professing those heinous things; and it was found that some of them had not such a heinous dogma; who were they that were ignorant of those mysteries. They constituted one-third part of them: these were separated; and the rest when separated were given to certain ones as servants: and it was forbidden them to thus gather together anymore. The rest also were separated, and sent into societies, with the prohibition that they should not be together. The Holy Supper they did not make holy. Concerning Baptism, they have it in use on account of the Reformed.

The rest were gathered together into congregations, and after visitation were cast down towards the lower parts, and were compelled to enter a cavern.

But because they had no food there, but vile chambers, they complained loudly; and were sent forth, and cast out into the deserts. Zinzendorf saw this.

THE QUAKERS. When other spirits wish to explore what they think, they conceal their thoughts in a certain way, saying that it is enough that they do no evil to anyone, nor openly speak evil of anyone. But it was said to them, that not to speak evil of anyone is a good in an earthly society; but that to think ill of others injures society in the other life, because there the ideas of thought are communicated. They do not wish to be instructed in doctrinals. They answer, "I do not understand this: What is this?" They have often affirmed that they have been taught by the Holy Spirit, and that they are taught. They most stubbornly resist, to prevent anything of their arcana from being published. The spirits who are with Quakers, whom they think to be the Holy Spirit, are they who were of the same sect in the world. To these after death they first pass; who inspire into them not to promulgate anything; wherefore they live separated; they are spurious spirits. 59-1 A communion of certain detestable wives was disclosed: they then expect an influx from the holy spirit, with a perception of leave that it is permitted. Their secret holy worship consists of such things, and by such things also the communication of their holy is effected. They do not at this day have the trembling and the total shaking, as formerly; but an uncertain shaking on the left side of the body and face. When they assert that it is commanded by the holy spirit, no one objects to adulteries and whoredoms. I spoke with their founder, who said that he never did such things, nor thought them. It was seen that Quaker spirits live in dense forests, like wild hogs: they become fantastic spirits. Those were also seen who believe that they are born holy, although he be one born from their adultery; respecting whom the rest say, that he alone drinks red wine in heaven; which wine they call celestial. But he appeared like a heinous man, and became black, and appeared to the angels like mucus of the nose. Such, dissociated, sit in their own places, like barks and the lees of oil, for ages. After those ages they retain very little of life, and serve societies for a vile connection. I spoke with Penn, who asserted that he was not such, and that he took no part in such things. It was said that the first of them were enthusiastic spirits, who are such that they wish to possess man. Those who from the dullness of the understanding wish to be called a holy spirit, are more corporeal as it were than the others. They say that they not only speak from the holy spirit, but also eat with the holy spirit; and that with some the spirit is infused into their feasts.

THE SAINTS OF THE PAPISTS. The papists, especially the monks, when they come into the other life, inquire for the saints, each one for those in his order; and the Jesuits do the same: and they likewise find them; but when they speak with them, they do not find more of holiness with them than with others. On being questioned, they say that they have no more power than others; and that they who have not worshipped the Lord, but only the Father, have no power; and that they are among the vile, whom their associates despised. Some of them know that they have been canonized; and when they are proud of it, they are derided by their associates; some do not know it. The most of those who affected sanctity in the world, are in the lower earth and in the hells, because they did this from the insane love, that they wished to be invoked and worshipped as gods; and that love profanes all the sanctity of heaven. But still the monks, and especially the Jesuits, conceal the lot of those, and lie to the common people, that they are saints on account of a restraint 60-1 and obedience; although they laugh at them in their hearts. 60-2

I heard the Pope who lived in the year 1738, -because he receded from the Babylonish error, and renounced all power over souls and over heaven, and became a Christian, calling upon the Lord alone, 61-1 he related to me that he had spoken with almost all who had been made saints, of both sexes; and, except two, he had seen no one in heaven; and that these two abhorred being invoked: and that many of them were not aware of it; and that some spoke foolishly.

St. Genevieve. She appears sometimes to the Parisians, in a middle altitude, in a splendid dress, and then as it were with a saintly face, and grants herself to be seen by many. But when some begin to invoke her, then immediately her face changed, and also her garments; and she becomes like another woman, and chides them, and rebukes them severely, for wishing to worship a woman, whose lot is no other than the lot of ordinary women, and who is not more highly esteemed among her associates than others: and she chides them even to shame, that men in the world are taken with such trifles. I will add, that the reason why she appears to them such at the beginning, was to the end that it might be known what kind of delusions these were. I heard the angels say that she sometimes appears so, for the sake of separating the worshippers of men from the worshippers of God. She also teaches them that she knows nothing at all more than others, and nothing whatever about invocation.

She says also that she is not among the best; and that he who wishes to become greater than others, becomes lower than others; and that it is an injury to the most of them that they have been canonized; because, when they hear of it, they become puffed up in heart from hereditary evil, and are removed away, that they may not know at all who they were in the world.

Agnes dwells in a chamber with virgins for her companions; and as often as she is called forth by any worshipper, she goes out, and asks what they want with a shepherd girl, who in herself is low, and is one with others in their work. And then her companions go out, and chide them even to shame. And as soon as they are ashamed, and desist from such things, she is also guarded, lest pride should enter into her. But she is now conducted away to another place; nor is she found anymore to the right among the upright women; in whose society she is not tolerated, unless she answers that she is filthy.

The saints adored in the world are of three kinds. Some are averse to the worship; these are guarded by angels. Some orally repudiate it, but still cherish in heart that they wish to be worshipped. Some receive it; but these are profane, miserable, and foolish.

Anthony of Padua appeared to me in front a little below, at the plane of the foot. He appeared in a dark garment; and I spoke to him as to whether he supposed he was a saint. He at first answered that he was not at all a saint: but still it was perceived that he retained the pride, that he wished to be one; on which account I spoke with him more severely. When anyone comes to him, he is led to say, that he can introduce no one into heaven, and that he knows nothing at all about being invoked; that this is a falsity. When they inquire of him what heaven is, whether it is the Lord, and whether it is love from Him and to Him and mutual love, this he does not know: on which account other spirits, from whom he wishes to get away, and cannot, mock at him. An interior craftiness has been observed in him. He endeavors to be worshipped in secret ways; but he fears: for he would be thrust down to lower places, where he suffers hard things. He can by art bind the ideas of the thought of others. He has conjunction with the Jesuits who appear in white.

Francis Xavier dwells deep beneath the back parts. He was a subtle magician, operating through conjugial love and through innocence; thus clandestinely.

Ignatius was in front above. He was a good spirit. He said that he was averse to being canonized, making himself filthy. He detested their making saints. He knew about the Jesuits, and called them atheists, and said that he shunned them.

The Virgin Mary, the mother of the Lord, was seen. Mary appeared to one side, in a snow-white garment, only as she passed by: and then she stopped a little, and said, that she had been the mother of the Lord; that He was indeed born of her; but that He became God, and put off all the maternal human; and that she therefore now adores Him as her God; and that she is unwilling that anyone should acknowledge Him as her son, because in Him all is Divine.

MOHAMMED AND THE MOHAMMEDANS. See some things concerning the judgment upon the Mohammedans, and that there are two Mohammeds under the Christian heaven, in the small work on the Last Judgment .

That a choir is when many speak and act together and unanimously, and that by choirs inauguration to unanimity is made and that in their speech there is singing, see in the Arcana Coelestia.

Mohammed. I have spoken with the Mohammed, who is in his stead, who had his seat under the Christian heaven: it seemed as if the glory of the Lord was shown to the Mohammedans, and that they then fell down upon their faces; and their Mohammed did the same.

I have heard the Mohammedans speak so skillfully and prudently as to affect certain Christian spirits with shame, acknowledging Mohammed but adoring the one only Lord of the universe: and Mohammed then testified that he has no power, and he also then adored the Lord.

I have sometimes seen that Mohammed drive away from himself the crowd that adores him, saying that they should go to the Lord, who rules the universe.

Spirits were sent to me from Mohammed, who could induce the appearance of a laver, pleasant through the form of its flow.

Both Mohammeds confess that the Lord is the fountain of all goodnesses and truths.

The spirits who are around Mohammed are inaugurated into unanimity and into agreement by angelic choirs, to the end that they may suffer themselves to be acted upon, and to think, will and speak from the Lord through angels; (respecting choirs see above;) and I have seen and heard them present by them beautiful representations concerning the Lord, the Savior of the world. The work of choirs is performed by Mohammedans with great merit. The Mohammedan choirs there became more familiar to me than others. I was with Mohammed on a remarkable occasion: it was also when I was in

Amsterdam, and in the courthouse there, which he saw through my eyes, and praised. He was delighted with the marbles there, which marbles correspond to the affections of the Mohammedans, who are in some degree spiritual; for all things are correspondences. Golden things correspond to the affections of the angels of the third heaven; things of silver to those of the second; things of copper to those of the first; and India porcelain to those of the last: to those of the Mohammedan heaven things of marble.

The two Mohammeds were once taken up into heaven, because they desired it; and they then spoke with me therefrom. They said that they saw thence, in one idea of thought, innumerable things, which, when below heaven, they believed to be one single thing: this was done, that they might know how the Lord leads man by innumerable things, which in the natural state appear to the man as one; when yet there are ineffable things in every one of them. This may be compared with the least things of an animalcule, which appears to the naked eye as one obscure point, but seen under a powerful microscope, is yet an animal endowed with members, and likewise with organs, and within with muscles, fibers, heart, brain, and many other things. So it is with one idea of a man's thought; therefore no one but the Lord alone knows what kind of thought the man has, and how much of what is living, that is, of heaven, there is in him: for as much of heaven as there is in him, so much of the human there is in him from the Lord. These things the two Mohammeds learned by being elevated into heaven.

There were Mohammedans in the western quarter dwelling upon rocks, who were rejected by the Mohammed in the Christian region, because they worshipped Mohammed as God, and adored him; which was forbidden them: and it was found that then they thought nothing respecting the Lord, not even respecting Him as the greatest Prophet, and the Son of God. And when it was inquired what kind of idea they had concerning God the Father, and it was found that they not only had not the idea of Him as a man, but none at all, and without an idea of God there is not given conjunction with any heaven; it was said to them that they could rather have the idea of God respecting the Lord, because He was the greater Prophet, and the Son of God: but they said that they could not, for He was of a wandering nation. Since they worshipped Mohammed, therefore Mohammed himself, who wrote the Koran, and was buried at Mecca, was taken from his place, which was to the right deeply behind the right foot, and he was elevated a little above the earth, and was shown to them. He appeared gross and black, altogether similar to corporeal spirits, who have little of life. He spoke with them, confessed that it was he, and that he was such: and after he had been shown, he was carried down into his place; but those worshippers of Mohammed were dispersed.

It was afterwards disclosed whence were the two Mohammeds, who had obtained a seat in the Christian heaven: because one of them was born in Saxony, and taken by the Algerians; and he there adopted the Mohammedan religion, and became a ship captain. He was then taken by the Genoese, where he received the Christian religion: thus he became imbued with both religions, because he acknowledged the Lord: and being led by the love of ruling, he was therefore taken there instead of Mohammed, and infused into the Mohammedans the belief that he was Mohammed himself: he was clever.

[Marginal Note:] I have heard that Mohammed say that he acknowledges the Lord as the only God, in whom is the Father, who is one God with Him: and that the Holy proceeding from Him is the Divine filling the heavens, and making the heavens.

But the other Mohammed was disclosed as being a Christian from Greece. He was also acknowledged by those who in the world had thought of many Mohammeds.

With the first Mohammed there appears something luminous, as if from a little torch; and the Mohammedans look thither, and there is influx thence into then through the medium of spirits: for in the spiritual world distances are only appearances; and when anyone is thought of, the distance perishes, and there becomes presence; Mohammed is skillful in instructing those who inquire of him. It has been granted me to perceive the sphere of his life: it was exteriorly pleasant, but interiorly concealing lasciviousness, which they have from matrimony with many wives and concubines. It was an unclean heat, but which is a pleasant heat, to the Mohammedans.

The reason that Mohammeds are continually substituted in place of another, is because everyone after death is led into his religious persuasion which he had in the world: it is a continuation of life. But he is afterwards gradually led away either to goods or to evils, according to his life; according to which also he receives truths or falsities.

THE MOHAMMEDANS I was conducted to a region where the Mohammedans were, which region was towards the right in the plane of the sole of the right foot: and when I was there, I was held in the thought concerning the Lord, that the Father is in Him, and He in the Father; and that the Holy Spirit proceeds; thus in the thought that there is one God, in whom is a trine. All those who were there were then in the same idea, and altogether acknowledged it; and this through all that tract. It was thence granted me to know, that there are many from the Mohammedans who receive the belief concerning the Lord, that He is one with the Father.

When I was conducted by the Lord through all the places, that I might know the quality of those there from their various nations, I came also to two mountains, upon which were Mohammedans. On one were those who lived well morally; they said that they have good, because they obey their governors. On the other were those who were very perceptive of spiritual things. They stated at first that no others can come to them but they who are of a like genius; and that Christians cannot; and that if they come, they appear to them as if they were being swallowed up by wolves; and that those who still come, they send to prison, and treat badly, and afterwards dismiss: these are monks who are able to introduce themselves by their arts, but are detected. I spoke with them respecting many wives; and they heard the reasons why it is according to the Christian doctrine, that only one wife is to be received. They perceived the justice in the reasons, but answered that they cannot as yet recede from matrimony with many, because it was conceded to them by their religion in the world, for the reason that they are orientals, who, without many wives, would have burned forth into adulteries, and so would have perished.

I spoke also with the firstborn of the Christians, who are the military guards of their Sultan, called Janizaries, and became Mohammedans: they said that they were still Christians in heart; and that some were intermediate, but some Mohammedans.

When I spoke something from the Word with those who were upon the other mountain, I apperceived something holy from them: as when I said that the Lord was conceived from Jehovah; and for that reason He called Him Father; and it is thence that He is the Son of God; and thence the Divine is in Him; and therefore He could glorify His whole body; so that as to that part of the body, which from those who are born of human parents is rejected and putrefies, was with Him glorified and made Divine from the Divine in Himself; and He rose with this leaving nothing in the sepulcher, altogether otherwise than takes place with every man. They heard attentively and said that they wondered they had not heard of such things.

I saw an infestation of Mohammedans by Christians in a certain city; from which infestation they could with difficulty be rescued. It was done by arts, of which there are many in the spiritual world. It was then seen that the city sank down in the middle part, and there was a wall made round about. But the sinking down was little, so that they could ascend and descend. Thus those who withdrew were transferred, and exempted from the infestations.

I was conducted to the Mohammedans who are in the eastern quarter, and it was granted me to speak with them. They said that some Christians of the Roman Catholic religion come to them; and they observed that it was done by them only for the sake of gain and dominion: and further, that they wish to possess all the things of the world, and also to have dominion over all who are there. There was a conversation with them concerning God: they said that they cannot comprehend how they can perceive one God, when they name three, and call them persons; when yet there is but one God; and that they still heard from the Christians, that they also say one God; because this is a contradiction. They asked what I knew concerning God. I said, that in the Christian heaven that is not believed, nor is it so said: but that the trine is in one Person; and that the trine which is named in it is the Father, the Son, and the Holy Spirit, that this is in the Lord, in whom the inmost, which is the esse of life, is called the Father; the second, which is the existere of life thence, is the Son; and the third is the proceeding, and is called the Holy Spirit: and that such a union was effected by God the Father, by His coming in the world; and that Christians might also be enlightened in it, since the Lord teaches openly, that the Father is in Him, and that the Father and He are one, and that the Holy Spirit does not speak out of itself, but from Him: but they who are of the Roman Catholic religion do not admit this, for the reason that they are lords on the earth; neither the Reformed, who are in the religion of faith alone; for so far the Mohammedans comprehended this. They said that they thought, desiring illustration, which was afterward given them; since this thing cannot be comprehended, without instruction from the Word.

I spoke with the Mohammedans concerning the resurrection; that the Christians believe that the resurrection is first to take place with the destruction of the world; and that the bodies are then to be united to their souls, and to be gathered together from every quarter where they have been scattered; and that in the meantime they are spirits, of whom they have an idea as of wind, especially of the breath; and that thus they flit about either in the ether or in the starry heaven, without hearing, sight, or any other sense; and that they are in expectation of the judgment; and that those also are in this expectation who have died from the very beginning of this earth; who have thus flitted about in the universe now for six thousand years; and that some think that they are together in a certain place, which is not a place, but a somewhere or other; as also that the angels are such. Also that the Christians scarcely comprehend that man lives a man after death as in the world, for they cannot have an idea of the spiritual body; but that still, when they do not think from doctrine, they think of themselves after death, that they live as men, as when they are near to death: and that for that reason those who treat of the deceased write openly that they are among the angels, are speaking with them, are in white garments, in paradises; yet as soon as they come to any ideas from doctrine, they think, as was said, of man after death, and of an angel, as of wind. When these things were said, the Mohammedans then answered, that they wondered that such a fallacy can reign with Christians, who call themselves more enlightened than others; saying that they know that they are to live after death, are to live in happy marriage, and are to drink wine; and this after they have rejected the castoffs, which had served them for their ultimate clothing in that gross sphere, as a body there.

There are many Mohammedans who become Christians, acknowledging the Lord as the only God, because the Father is in Him. These, when they are led into heaven, are led first to the east, and thence to the north, and thence ascend higher and higher to the west, and are there in a higher place; but still by a circuit, or going round, according to situation below; some appeared to ascend towards the south, who were they that confirmed themselves in the Divinity of the Lord.

Many Mohammedans, from natural light, comprehend better concerning spiritual things than the Christians do; because they think much, and desire truths. They understood well that all the things in heaven and in the world refer themselves to good and truth; and that truth, when it is believed, is the truth of faith; and that good, when a man is affected by it, is the good of love: and therefore two faculties, understanding and will, were given to man; the understanding by the reception of truth, thus of faith, and the will by the reception of good, thus of love: and that good and truth, thus the understanding and the will, must be one, that the man may be truly a man; thus also a man of faith and of truth. They clearly perceived thence that they who are in the good of life, are in the perception of truth; for the reason that good desires truth, and wishes to be conjoined, and as it were nourished; and that truth is as spiritual food to good; also on the other hand that truth desires good, that it may be anything; because without good there is no life in truth; thus that there is the reciprocal desire of the one for the other, and that from this man is man.

In the Judgment I saw that the Mohammedans were led from the west and round about in their circuit around the Papists, by a way towards the north to the east, in a circular way to appearance: and that on the way the evil were cast outside of that sphere where there is a space of great extent; some into a wilderness there, some into swamps and pools, some into dark forests. These things were on the backside of their mountain: on the side of that space in the north there was an immense and extended whirlpool, into which also many, who had led an evil life, were cast. The rest proceeded by a circuit towards the east, and spread themselves into an ample space that extended itself more to the back. Thither those were led, who acknowledged God the Father, and the Son as the greatest Prophet, who is with the Father. That space was broad, divided into mountains, hills, and valleys, upon which they were arranged; and there it is well with them. They who were still better, enjoying more intellectual light than others, were likewise led to that place, where there was communication with the Christian heaven, a space which separated intervening. These were they, who, being instructed, received the Lord; and they who received well, were led into the south, where they obtained their heaven behind the Christians there.

There were those who feigned themselves Christians as to the belief in the Lord's Divinity. These insinuated themselves among them by craftiness, but were forthwith detected and separated, and cast into the desert and the adjoining chasm; and some were led back and dispersed.

There were some from the Mohammedans who acknowledged only the Father as others do, and the Lord as the greatest Prophet. They said that they could not understand that the Divine is divided into three Persons, thus into three gods. They said that the Holy Spirit was God speaking by a spirit, and an angel; a certain one from the Christians now drew near to them, asking why they do not acknowledge the Son of God as God. They said that there is one God, and thus there would be two; on which account they asked him how many Gods he worshipped; he replied One, because God is one. But they explored the idea of his thought, that he did not think of one God, but of three. This is easily done in the other life. They said that they saw that he said one God with the mouth, and in heart and in faith believed in three: and yet it behooves a Christian to speak as he thinks, and not to divide the mind from the speech, as do flatterers and those who lie; and as he could not deny this, they said that the Christians ought to be ashamed to think of three gods, when no Gentile who has any intelligence thinks so; who have not three in their idea, when they name one. He wished to say that the three were one by unanimity; neither could this be given without the idea of three conversing and consenting among themselves; and besides, three essences which make one could not be given, unless they were also one person: one and the same essence of three is not given; still less in God, who is not divisible: and who, moreover, can give it from an essence, such as this is among the metaphysicians, and have it be thought by the common people, when it cannot be by the learned? On which account he was affected with shame, saying that he would in no wise return to them, and that he would inquire of someone concerning the triune God. The angels afterwards spoke with the Mohammedans, instructing them that God is one both in Person and in essence, in whom is a trine; and that the Son of God, who to them is the greatest Prophet, being sent by the Father, cannot but be God, because He was conceived of God the Father Himself: thus the Divine itself was in Him from conception; and the Divine is indivisible.

The mansions of the Mohammedans, after death are palaces. They are for the greatest part in the western quarter. After the Last Judgment there came many anew into that quarter, who thought little respecting the God of the universe, and nothing respecting the Lord, but worshipped Mohammed as God.

And because they did not find him, they elected another, on a mountain elevated above the Christian region, with whom they consulted, and whom they obeyed: and then, by the command of their new Mohammed, they poured themselves into the Christian region, and infested them in various modes. But after visitation, and the disclosure that they were a wandering nation, and one that delighted in idleness, and wished to do nothing useful, they were cast into their hells. As long as they consociated themselves with the Babylonians, they were also able to render themselves inconspicuous. At length the earth upon which they were was rolled over above them, and they were cast into hell: their hell appeared fiery.

. The judgment upon them proceeded still further into the west, in a long tract; and likewise towards the north, where they mingled themselves with the evil Papists; and I saw them cast into the hells and whirlpools there.

Many of the Mohammedans, when they had heard many things concerning the Lord, wished to go and join the heavenly Christian Church. But it was told them that they should remain still in their religion, or in their doctrine from the Koran, that the Lord was the greatest Prophet, the Son of God, the wisest of all, sent to inform the human race; for the reason that they cannot in heart acknowledge His Divine, but only with the month; since they imbibed those things from infancy: and their spiritual good was formed in part from such things as had been of their faith; which cannot be extinguished so suddenly by a new tenet of faith, let them only live in sincerity and justice, and so in their good: because all sincerity and justice is in itself the Divine proceeding from the Lord; and because they can in their manner still live faithfully, and be gradually led on to the Lord. It was said to them, that many Christians do not think of the Lord's Divine, but only of His Human, which they do not make Divine; for instance, the Roman Catholics, as also the Reformed; who for that reason go to the Father, that He will have mercy for the Son's sake and rarely to the Lord Himself: on account of which belief and prayer, they continually retain the idea concerning the Lord, that He is a man like any other.

It was told me that there is a book among the Mohammedans which is common in their hands, in which some pages were written by correspondences, like the Word with us; from which pages there is some light in the heavens.

There were with me many from Greece, who had dwelt in the world with the Mohammedans; complaining that then as well as now they inveighed against them because they worship three Gods; to whom they also replied, that they worship one God, and that the three are one: but they still persist that they are three which they worship, since they name three; and they ask which God of the three they worship the most: and when they reply that they worship all together, they then say that thus there is one God, and the rest are little gods; and that it is only said thus. But when they hear it said that they are equal, they withdraw, and set themselves against the Christians, as having little or no judgment in spiritual things. They complained that they do not give up the infestation, until they say that they are three names of the one God: then they acquiesce. They afterwards inquired respecting the three names of the one God. It was told them from heaven, that the Christians derived those names from the sense of the letter of the Word, where three names of the one God are mentioned: and by the Father is there meant the Creator of the universe; by the

Son, the Savior of the human race; and by the Holy Spirit, enlightenment; and that these three are in the Lord alone; and that in Him the three are one; and that He teaches this in the Word. But on account of the class, who are not willing to regard the Lord's Human as Divine, because they have claimed all His power to themselves, they were not willing to have it said that it is Divine power, and thus that they were gods on the earth; and when it was read to them out of Matthew and Luke, that He was conceived from God the Father, and thus the Divine was in Him, and He was from it; they said that they supposed He was the son of Joseph. And when it was said to them that He did not come into the world to reconcile the human race to the Father, but to conquer the devil, that is, to subjugate the hells, that He might reduce all things [on earth] and in the heavens to order, and might at the same time glorify His Human, or might reunite it to the Divine, which was the soul itself in Him from conception; and that thus and no otherwise could the human race be saved. On hearing these things they were silent, and many acquiesced.

Footnotes

59-1 [MARGINAL NOTE.] There are Quaker spirits who, from their worship by Quakers in the world, believe themselves to be the holy spirit, and to have been from eternity but in process of time they come among the profane who are called stercoracenus and cadaverous spirits, abominable excrement.

60-1 The M.S. has, mucus narium; Tafel, mercurius vivus. See SE 3811, 3812, where mucus narium occurs.

60-2 The M.S. has a marginal note which Tafel omits, namely, Sunt spiritus quaqueriani qui ex cultu a quaqueriis in mundo se credunt spiritum sanctum et ab aeterno fuisse, sed successu temporis veniunt inter prophanos, qui vocantur spiritu stercorei et cadaverosi, excrementum abominabile.

61-1 Clement XII, Pope A.D. 1730-1740.

It was said to them that there are Mohammedans who receive the belief that the Lord is one with the Father, and that they have a heaven in which all things are happy; and that they live there from the Lord in spiritual marriage of good and truth.

SOME THINGS CONCERNING THE PAPISTS. When the Last Judgment was going on, he who was Pope in the year 1738, and was then blind in his old age, dwelt on high near a city in the northern quarter; and I saw him then brought away, and carried sitting upon a litter, and sent into a secure place; and as everyone after death is first led to his own religion, and afterwards is led away from it, as far as he can be, they also, for that reason, seek for the Pope: on which account someone is always appointed, who takes on the name and the function of Pope. He was for a long time in that function after that time; but when he observed that he had no power at all of remitting sins, nor of opening heaven, and that this power was Divine, and thence the Lord's alone, he therefore began to be averse to that doctrine, and afterwards to abhor it, and he abdicated that office, and betook himself among the Christians who worship the one Lord, and is with them in heaven. I have often spoken with him; and he called himself happy, that he had embraced those truths, and had removed himself away from that idolatrous religious persuasion. He said that he revolved in his mind similar things in the world, and acknowledged in heart that the Word was holy, and that the Lord was to be worshipped; but that he could not then recede, on account of causes which he also mentioned.

But it happened otherwise with his successor, Benedict XIV. He declared openly that he had confirmed in his own mind, that since the Lord had transferred all power over the heavens to Peter, He had no power at all left, and no longer any holiness. I saw him speaking with Sextus V, who was called up from below, and after the conversation sank down again. I heard him speaking many things in regard to the Word with someone concerning the Bull Unigenitus, but this is not the place to make them public. He was cunning, and at first civil, and then very sharp-sighted: he loved the Jesuits more than others, and went down to them into their hell; nor have I as yet seen him come up therefrom: and scarcely is he to come up thence, because he said that he had confirmed and established the Bull Unigenitus, and because he said that the Sacred Scripture was not equal in his mind to the papal decree, but inferior to it. When it was shown him that the Word was holy in every word, and that they were perpetual correspondences, and that thence it was for the whole heaven, he made this of no account, saying that the papal decrees were of the same holiness. But then it was said, that there is in each thing which the Pope pronounces in the Consistory, something derived from the infernal love of ruling over heaven and earth, and of ascribing to himself the Divine power, and so of being worshipped as God; and that hell, and not heaven, is in such a decree. And it was shown from what spirits it is said, and who it is that then breathe into and move the breast; that they are infernal spirits, who are not willing to believe in salvation by the Holy Spirit, 103-1 but he reasoned against those things.

Louis XIV, king of France, is at this day among the happy. He was made by the Lord the governor over the best society of the French nation, over those who are arriving in the spiritual world from the world. He acts uprightly and justly, and is diligent in looking out for things useful to his subjects there. He acknowledges the Lord, and that He has power over the heavens and the earth. He reads the Word, and shuns cunning and craftiness. He said that he was such in the world. Once when I was speaking with him, he suddenly descended seemingly as if by steps, to a place below me a little in front; and it was perceived that then in vision he was as if he was at Versailles. And it was then perceived that he had come as if into a kind of sleep; and it immediately became silent around him, and also with me; which lasted two hours. Afterwards he ascended, and spoke to those who stood around him, saying that he had spoken with the king of France, his grandson, who reigns at this day; and that he exhorted him to desist from confirming the Bull Unigenitus; and he said that otherwise misfortune would come upon him. He said that he did not know whether he perceived that in clear vision, or obscure vision, which are in the thought with some emotion of the mind. This took place Dec. 13, 1759, about seven or eight o'clock.

After the Last Judgment, the Babylonians were for a long time gathered together upon mountains in the west as before. The reason is, that a spirit after death can go nowhere else than the place where his life is. They were thus there upon mountains, where a part made to themselves as it were new heavens. But as soon as it was calculated that there were about two hundred there, they were cast down into the hells, as before; and this was done until all things were reduced into such order; and no one after death can go anywhere but into his own hell; nor can a part remain upon the earth there; and this is done when those places are taken possession of by societies, where they are in the acknowledgment and adoration of the Lord. The southern quarter, where the richest were, and where the great city of the Jesuits is, which quarter was altogether overturned, as may be seen from the description of the Last Judgment, is still a desert land; and I saw the monks there sometimes, who, as they had heard that treasures were hidden away there, still flocked thither for the purpose of exploring; but in vain.

Nor do they still desist from sending out their emissaries into the Reformed Christian world, for the purpose of seducing as in the world. They are monks, who thirst solely for gain and who aspire to supreme, yea Divine, power and who are so barren that they know nothing at all of Divine truth; but yet they prevail over others by cunning; nevertheless they are investigated, and those who have been investigated are miserably punished.

It was shown me to the life, why Babel or Babylon was called Lucifer, son of the dawn, Isa. 14 and Gen.. That by Lucifer there Babel is meant, is manifest from what precedes and follows there, concerning which the things there may be quoted. And that Babel in the beginning adored the Lord, and observed the commandments more than others, bearing domination in the mind; but that in process of time domination becomes the head, and at length endeavors to drag the Lord Himself from His throne, and to place itself thereon.

The women and virgins who have lived in convents, and have thought lascivious things, and still more those who have done lascivious things, are cast into hells where there are direful things. But they who have cultivated piety alone, and have not done any work, are divided among the adherents of their own religion, to act as servants, learning that bare piety in idleness does not conduce to salvation. But they who were diligent and loved to work, are allotted places among those women in the churches, with whom it is well. They who have been diligent in the convents, by serving others there in various ways, as to food, clothing, and other functions there, and who did these things from charity and affection, are conducted away beyond that mountain into the confines between the south and west, and form a society, which is protected from infestations from the men, and they are sent to those who teach the truths of faith; for they are more teachable than others.

There was a vast multitude of Papists dwelling to the east, occupying all those mountains, 109-1 even from the eastern quarter to the southern, who introduced themselves to the Gentiles upon the mountains and plains there. All that multitude was transferred by a direct way to the west, where a settlement was given them upon hills and plains for a great extent. They were those who had lived in goods, although not in truths, who had performed good works according to their religion, and were of that genius that they would not injure others, nor plot evils. That they desired truths is manifest from the fact that while they were on the way they appeared as if they were borrowing silver and garments, as the sons of Israel did from the Egyptians; by which was signified that they desired truths, and were receiving them from them; from those who do not do anything good.

The vast multitude was explored as to the quality of its affection of truth from good, and at the same time whether they had lived in the good of charity. That exploration was seen as a sudden and instantaneous transference to various quarters. They who were in the middle remained there; because they were in the affection of truth, and wished to be imbued with the truths of faith. The rest were sent back, that they might first be instructed below by their own people, who had been upright monks, and at the same time had been in some doctrine of truth from the Word; and they were afterwards transferred to those of the Reformed, who, on account of a life according to the truths of the Word, were angelic spirits.

I also saw a vast multitude of the Catholic nation, who had been hidden away and reserved by the Lord for a long time, and were reserved from the idolatrous contagion of the others; because they had lived well, and had acknowledged the Lord: and some were transferred to the south, some to the east, some to the west, and some to the north, that they might form some heavenly society, and be further instructed. For this end angels were sent to them, not only to instruct them, but also to guard them from the cunning and deceitful of their own nation, and from the influx out of their hells. In a word, many and great societies were instituted out of Catholics, and partly inserted into societies where the Word is read freely and the Lord is adored. If, after being instructed, they have received the truths of faith in the good of love, they are elevated thence into heaven. It is not their fault that they were born there. All their infants are in heaven: but these are ignorant of the falsities of their parents, not knowing that they are such; and they are educated under the Lord's auspices by the angels.

The most malicious of the Roman Catholics become the most stupid, for the reason that when malice penetrates all the interiors of the mind, and destroys all spiritual truth, they then first become insane, and afterwards stupid, and are sent under the earth between the west and the north. When anyone passes to that place, great stupor occupies his thought, and torpor his body. Many of them were worshippers of the devil, and had books where the doctrine of the worship of them was contained. One or two of their books were taken from them and read before others. The doctrinal teaching was this: that they petition God the Father to excuse them for betaking themselves to the devil; because they petitioned for help from God the Father, and had not obtained it, knowing that they get help from the devil; on which account they betake themselves to him, calling him their patron. Another book was opened, written with various characters and flexures, and being deciphered, taught that they had nothing from the Divine, but all from the devil. Being asked the reason they said, that they had not obtained from God by prayers their request that they might rule as in the world, over the souls of men and over the goods of that earth. It was told them that no one obtains this by prayers. Being detected, at first they became insane, and were cast down from the mountain on which they were, from the southern side of the mountain, into a direful hell where the worshippers of the devil are; and their houses collapsed together into heaps. One of them ran to me, and he was dusky like a devil.

Those of them who are upright by nature, cannot dwell together with those who have attained spiritual uprightness from the affection of truth; for those who are upright from any natural uprightness are easily seduced. They believe all things, even things of cunning, and adore idols; on which account also they are among those who serve others as handmaids and servants; by whom they are guarded, lest they should be approached by the monks.

THE AFRICANS. There are, among the blackest of the Africans, those who love to be punished and treated harshly; and who come into heaven, saying afterwards that they detest blackness, because they know that their souls are white and their bodies black.

I have heard it announced that at this day a church is being established with many in Africa, and that revelations are made at this day; and that they are receptive of the Heavenly Doctrine, especially concerning the Lord.

I was conducted through several regions in front towards the left. Afterwards I saw a great palace, and a spacious court there. A certain one spoke with me there, saying that a revelation had been promised, and that he was expecting it. And then something luminous appeared in obscurity, which was an indication that now there will be a revelation. And as I was attending, I heard that they were expecting a revelation concerning Christ, whom they call the Only Man, from whom every man is a man. And one of the angels then spoke with them, and instructed them concerning the Lord, that He is the only God. They replied that they perceived this, but not as yet that He was born a man. But when they were instructed by the angels, they understood this also, saying, that this was done for the sake of the salvation of the human race. Moreover, they knew many things respecting heaven and hell, of which Christians are ignorant. It was said that they were Africans. I was afterwards conducted thence towards the right, where I heard them saying that they had expected a revelation, and that angels were now speaking with them from the Lord, and were instructing them concerning the Lord, with the promise that they were about to receive the Heavenly Doctrine. These said that it could not be otherwise than that God, the Creator of the universe, should appear in the world, because He created men, and loves them; and that His appearing must be made even to the ocular sight in the human form.

It was afterwards shown in obscure vision how the Heavenly Doctrine would proceed in Africa; namely, towards the interior parts, even to the middle of it; and that it would then proceed towards those who were at, the sides on the Mediterranean Sea, but not to the coast; and then, after a time, would turn itself back towards Egypt. Thereupon the angels were glad, that there was now the Lord's coming anew, and that a New Church was being established, with whom they could be conjoined. That doctrine does not extend as far as to the Africans that dwell near the coasts, since the Christians come thither, who insinuate scandals, and who have a human and not a Divine idea concerning the Lord. The Africans are more receptive of the Heavenly Doctrine than others on the earth, because they freely receive the doctrine concerning the Lord, and have it as if implanted in themselves that God will altogether appear as a man. They are in the faculty of receiving the truths of faith, and especially its goods, because they are of a celestial disposition. It was told them that a prediction was made by the Lord concerning His coming, and concerning the New Church after the old one; and that His appearing is made through angels who teach.

I was conducted again to the Africans by a way running first to the north and afterwards to the west; and I saw there as it were a palace, where someone walked; and afterwards higher up, where I stopped, and heard a vast number sent forth out of the Christian heaven to those who were Africans; and those were there who in the world had lived according to their religion and had acknowledged one God under the human form. It was told them that he who has lived in good according to religion is also in the affection of truth, because the good of life desires nothing more than truth; for it desires to know how one is to live well. Thence they rejoice when they are informed; and that all such receive truths from the Lord, and are enlightened according to the quality and quantity of their good of life: this they acknowledged, and were glad. The African race can be in greater enlightenment than others on this earth, since they are such that they think more interiorly, and so receive truths and acknowledge them. Others, as the Europeans, think only exteriorly, and receive truths in the memory; nor do they see them interiorly from any intellectual light, which they do not acknowledge in matters of faith. I said there, that few Christians live according to religion, but only according to the civil laws, and live well morally for the sake of fame, honor, and gains; and that they rarely think of living according to their doctrinals; believing also that they are saved by the faith of doctrine, and not by the life: on which account they have no doctrinals of life. At this the Africans wondered exceedingly, not being willing to believe that it is so; believing that there is no man who does not live according to his religion; and if not, that he cannot but become stupid and evil, because he then does not receive anything from heaven.

All are explored after death as to what idea they have concerning God. That idea is the chief of all, because conjunction with the Lord and conjunction with heaven is according to it, and all of the love and faith of the church is hence according to it, because the Divine is the all of the church, yea, is God: hence the all of the church with a man is from his idea of God: such as that idea is, such is heaven to everyone. The Africans also differ from each other according to their idea of God. Some worship an invisible God, and some a visible one: some make of them two, and some make of them one and the same. Some have been instructed by Christians that God was born a man, and they receive this; and when they hear that they distinguish the Divine into three Persons, they go away, believing, however, that the Christians, although they say three, still think of one: for they do not comprehend what a Son born from eternity is. Some, who are the best of them, believe that God is altogether a Man. They say that those who believed that God was born a Man, formerly saw a bright star in the air. The wiser of them believe that God was born a Man in the world, and so manifested Himself.

It was said that in a certain region of Africa there is from ancient times a book which they regard as holy. It is written by correspondences in a similar manner as the Word is with us.

A certain priest, who had supposed that the idea of the Divine Human is not given with anyone, was transferred into societies of Africans, and he found that they had no other idea than that of the Divine Human.

In Abyssinia, in Africa, they have some psalms written in a style similar to that of our Word, and they sing them in their temples, and spirits are sensible of communication therefrom. In the spiritual sense they treat of one God, the Redeemer of the human race; but these things have been treated of before, where the Word is spoken of, Spiritual Experiences.

It has been granted me to speak with African spirits on various subjects, and they perceived all the truths of the church with a clear perception; and when the Word was presented to them, they understood it as to the internal spiritual sense, and carried it to their elders, who said that they have a Word with them, and that it is most holy.

They afterwards showed me the quality of those who are in Africa, which they know from the societies of that race in the spiritual world; namely, that interiorly in Africa are the best and the wise: that those that are not good are near the Mediterranean Sea, also near Egypt, and at the Cape of Good Hope. The tract where the good are, lies from Ethiopia towards the middle, into which part strangers from Europe are not admitted; and if they enter, and are not willing to perform service, they sell them to the Asiatics; and they said that at this day some speak with Africans in the world, and instruct them orally; and that their speech with them falls especially into their interior perception; and that they perceive the influx, and so receive the revelation with enlightenment; and that such speech is with their instructors, in whom they have confidence.

THE GENTILES. Concerning the lot of nations and peoples outside the church, see what has been written in Arcana Coelestia, and in the work on Heaven and Hell ; also something in the little work on The Last Judgment. That a new heaven has been formed both from Christians and from Gentiles, and also the Lord's Church on earth, see The Doctrine of the New Jerusalem.

About the time of the Last Judgment, Christians appeared there in the middle, where they were arranged at a distance from the center 2 to the circumference, and also at the various quarters according to the light of truth from the love of good. Around this middle were seen the Mohammedans arranged in like manner at the various quarters, near to the Christians according to the light of truth from good. Outside this compass were seen the Gentiles arranged according to their religion and according to life therefrom. All have similar lands divided into mountains, hills, rocks and valleys, and above them are expanses where dwell the best of them who have received from angels truths of doctrine concerning the Lord and concerning life. Beyond them appeared as it were a sea, which was the boundary. All these circuits taken together are extended not in a plane but in a globe like the earth, so that when I was conducted to the Gentiles, after passing through the Mohammedans, I descended by a declivity.

When the Last Judgment was going on, those who were in the western quarter beyond the Mohammedans, were led away towards the east. They were led, not by a circuit, but above the northern plane of the Christians, and, what I wondered at, on high, so that they were transferred by a way above the Christians, and yet did not communicate with them. And they were then allotted places around the Mohammedans at the east and also at the south. On both sides of where the Mohammedan heavens are, there appeared openings descending into the depths. Thither were cast those of them who were evil, who had worshipped idols, and had thought nothing about God, and at the same time had lived an evil life.. There is also a similar chasm on the northern side of the Mohammedan desert. Into this were cast the worst, and also many of the Roman Catholic religion who had worshipped the images of saints, and had thought nothing at all about the Lord. These latter were gathered from the northern quarter under the mountains there and were mingled with the Gentiles because they are similar. I then saw the whole northern valley even to the mountains there torn up to its foundations, and all who were there, scattered, and then there appeared in that place as it were a smokiness.

I was afterwards led beyond the Mohammedans to certain Gentiles who were in the eastern quarter, with whom it was granted to speak. They said that they were sad because the Divine does not appear to them, when yet they think of the Divine and speak about it; and, therefore, if there is a God [they had hoped] that He would send to them those who would teach them; but that they had long waited for this in vain, lamenting that perchance He had deserted them, and that thus there seemed nothing else for them but to perish. And then I heard angels speaking with them out of heaven, saying that God could not have been manifested to them because they had not been willing to believe that God was born a man in the world, or that He had taken on a Human, and that until they believe this, God cannot be manifested to them, nor can they be taught, because this is the primary thing of all revelation. They said that they did indeed believe that God is Man but that they could not comprehend that He was born Man in the world. But answer was made them, that He was not born Man like any other man, since He was not born from a human father, but from the Father Jehovah, and by a Virgin, and that thus He was unlike any other man; for a man's soul from a human father is a recipient of life, but the Lord's soul from the Father Jehovah is life itself, which gives life to all; and that the difference is as between the human and the Divine, and the finite and the infinite, or the create and the uncreate; and because He was such as to His soul, it could not be otherwise than that His body should become like His soul, after He had rejected that of the body which He had taken from the mother; and that therefore He rose as to His whole body, nor did He leave anything of it in the sepulcher, as is the case with every other man, who rises only as to his spirit, and never as to his material body. And further, it was said that the Divine itself, as it is in itself, which is infinite, could not have done otherwise than reject the finite which was from the mother, and put on the infinite from the Father, thus the Divine. They said that they had known no other than that He was like any other man born from a human father, and also that He so died, and was afterwards received by men as God, and that they now know that the Lord is not such a man as others are. After they received these things they were divided, and those who had received the faith were instructed by angels in other matters of faith and love.

I was conducted to those who in the world had known nothing about God, but who nevertheless had led a moral life amongst each other; they were said to live on a certain island. They appeared to me not like men but like apes and yet with a human face. 129-1 They so appeared because they knew nothing about God, and the Divine is in the likeness of a man. One of the Christians is set over them by the Lord. I have spoken with him, and he said that they obey him and love him; that they are modest and are engaged in employments, but that at first they could hardly comprehend the things of religion. But after some time, there was given them a nearer communication with the Christians, and they are beginning to receive something of religion, and he cherished the hope that they could be reformed, for the reason that they had lived a moral life, and are in obedience and are industrious. As to similar people elsewhere, see below. 129-2

There were likewise seen others, who had lived in an island in the West Indian seas, who had no thought at all about God, thus no religion, and who yet had lived together in a sincere and friendly way. It was told me, that at first they appear destitute of rationality, but that nevertheless, because they had contracted no false principles against religion, some of them suffer themselves to be instructed like infants, and they are perfected. It was shown that the delight of their life was to will to serve others under others. Some wealth was once given them, but they offered it to the angel who was instructing them, in order that he might receive them as his servants, that thus they might be instructed as to how they should live. It is an angelic delight to inform such spirits and to lead them to heaven.

I was once in a sweet sleep, and when I awoke I saw around me some Chinese, 131-1 and I noticed that they sat with their legs crosswise, and were talking with each other. And it was ascertained that they had been sent to me by the Lord in order that I might know of what quality many of them are. The angels said that the delightfulness of my sleep had inflowed from the fact that angels had been speaking with them about God and about the wonderful things of wisdom, and that they had been so delighted at this that they had been in the tranquillity of some celestial peace; and that evil spirits could not approach, because they were of a spiritual celestial genius.

There were with me some spirits from Tartary, 132-1 who dwelt outside the Chinese wall, saying that their country is populous; nor do they know anything about war, saying that they are without the love of reigning and that they give the government to those who say they can rule and govern, but if he cannot, he is rejected with a fine; those who do what is right and just are loved. They said that all are engaged in work, and that the lazy are cast out. They say that sometimes Christians come to them, and they marvel at their sayings that God is a Man, for they believe that all men know this. They also say that they have the commandments of the Decalogue, and that they live according to them because God so wills. They said that they have a holy book of which others do not know, and which they understand. Inquiry was made, and it was the Psalms of David. They call the Chinese their friends because they are of their nation; nor do they think of war, saying that if any strangers should come, then, unknown to them, they would all depart, taking their provisions with them. I also saw a Christian preacher with the spirits of that region. They are of a tranquil disposition.

THE LAST JUDGMENT ON THE PROTESTANTS OR REFORMED. Before the Last Judgment which was a general one, less general judgments preceded which might be called preparatory, by which those who were more exteriorly evil were cast into hells. It should be known that between the judgment effected by the Lord when He was in the world, and that of the judgment which is now effected, spirits who had outwardly lived a moral life, and had confessed God with the lips but not interiorly or in heart, had ascended upon mountains and hills and had there made for themselves, as it were, heavens, where by various arts, which are very numerous in the spiritual world, all of them unknown in our world, they had ascended on mountains; so that the world of spirits which is mediate between heaven and hell had been filled up with such heavens, and thereby the communication of the Lord and heaven with the human race had been intercepted. This also was the reason why the spiritual things of the Word and of doctrine therefrom were not disclosed until after the Last Judgment, for by the latter the world of spirits was purified and communication with man opened. If the spiritual things of the Word and of doctrine therefrom had been disclosed before, they would not have been received nor understood; and if they had been received and understood, still hell, which then prevailed, would have secretly snatched them away from men's hearts and have profaned them. Those fictitious heavens are meant in Revelation by the heaven and earth which passed away. These could pass away, but our visible heaven, which is the firmament of all things, was so created that it cannot pass away, for if this should pass away, the angelic heavens would also pass away. It would be as when the foundation is taken away from a palace, or the base from a column, whereby the house and the column would fall. For there is a connection of all things from the first to the last, from the Lord Himself to His last work which is the visible heaven and the habitable earth. The case would be similar if the human race were to perish, for thus, for a like reason, the angelic heavens would also fall to ruin.

Before the Last Judgment I often saw societies, which had made for themselves semblances of heavens, purged and also destroyed. There was one rock on which was quite a large city, where those were who were in faith separate from charity, believing as in the world, that faith alone saves, and this from mere mercy whatsoever the life may have been. They were in the lust of commanding; and therefore they stood at the sides of the rock, and in various ways infested those who were beneath. When visitation was made, and all there were found to be of such a character, I saw that the rock sank down into the depths together with the hill and the inhabitants. The like was done elsewhere. But prior to this being done, the good are separated from the evil, and the evil are in the middle; and then the middle sinks down while the borders remain; in the borders are those who are in the good of faith, that is, who are in charity.

All who have not denied God with the lips, although they have in the heart, and have led a moral life on account of the civil laws and also on account of reputation and consequent honors and gains, when they come into the other life betake themselves into societies where there are cities; and there as in the world they live well morally, from fear of punishment and of the loss of honor and gain. But when their externals are taken away from them, and they are let into their internals, they rush into infamous crimes. But when the wicked increase in number the society is then perverted; wherefore angels are then sent thither who search out the state and separate the good from the evil; and the good are either sent to the sides of the society or are taken away. Then the city with the evil sinks down into hell, to a depth according to their wickedness. Once I saw that four angels were sent to such a city, who when they came thither entered into a house; 135-1 but the criminal spirits who were there, being excited by their presence into interior malice, as takes place, rushed to the house where the angels were, shouting out to them, Did they wish to come out and commit whoredom? They wished to urge them to it, and even attempted to offer violence, but in vain; in a word, they did like what was done in Sodom. And that city was completely destroyed and its inhabitants cast into hells. The reason why they wished to lead them forth to commit whoredom, was because in that city were gathered those who in the world had accounted adulteries as allowable; also because they had been in falsities of doctrine, by reason of having regarded life as of no account; moreover, to confirm these things they had falsified the Word, and all those who falsify the Word in order to confirm evils of life and falsities of doctrine, account adulteries as allowable and are led into them.

I also saw a rock on which there had been such a city; torn up from its place and carried away to another place at a remarkable distance; it appeared carried away like a cloud. And when it came to that place I saw that it also sank down, because there was their hell. The inhabitants had been first reduced into a state of stupor.

A great number of those who are in faith separate from charity betake themselves to rocks; while those who are in the love of self betake themselves to mountains which are higher than the rocks. Hence it is that in the Word, a rock signifies faith, and a mountain love. And when, before the Last Judgment, the evil had been thus gathered together upon rocks and upon mountains, first there were suddenly felt concussions and earthquakes, by which are meant perversions of state in respect to the church, and afterwards follows the overturning, which is effected either by sinking, or by carrying away, or by casting out and thus thrusting down into hell. On the mountains and hills upon which are angels, the wisest are in the middle and the less wise at the circumferences; but on those upon which are the evil, the worst are in the middle and the better at the circumferences. The sinking in the middle appears like a vortical gyration, but in a spiral.

There was a plain somewhat more elevated than the valley. In this plain was congregated a multitude of spirits who had learned to practice evils by means of cunning, and to station themselves invisible behind others, and thus force them to think and speak what they wish them to, yea evils and falsities. They have contracted these arts by reason of their having been in the insane love of ruling over others. As it was then disclosed that their wickedness was consummated, their destruction followed. The whole of that plain was overturned; and the earth was then opened elsewhere and there rose up good spirits who had been kept concealed by the Lord in the lower earth and guarded lest they should be infested by the evil; and they succeeded in place of the former, and came in full number into possession of their land. Such things are represented by the sons of Israel to whom the land of Canaan was given after the wickedness of its nations had been consummated.

After many destructions and partial judgments had been executed, which were premonitory of the general destruction and judgment, and hordes of spirits who were impure had been cast into pools, 139-1 lakes, and chasms, that is into hells, then some came who were skilled in the art of breathing into others and exciting them to evils of interior thought. They incited some souls against the Lord and against Divine truth from Him, and from these the multitude, like one mass, began to be fermented. The tumult spread thence in every direction, as when a rebellion is started by a few persons, and yet at length stirs up a crowd. I there saw the disturbance widely spread to many rocks and mountains, even to their peaks, and thence to the sides down to the bases. Their intent was to destroy those who acknowledged and worshipped the Lord and were in Divine truths from Him. When it was noticed that the contagion had grown so wide, then was the Lord's coming for the general judgment. This coming was the Lord's influx into them through the heavens, an influx which appeared like a misty sphere spread around over those mountains and rocks; and it carried off the dwellers there, not by casting them down but by bearing them away. The Divine sphere entered into their interiors and laid them bare; and what lay concealed in their will and heart was thus made manifest. And it snatched them away and carried them down to hells according to the evils of their life. That Divine sphere was seen carried around in gyres, sometimes returning; and it also drew them out of the places where they had concealed themselves. This was done with some myriads within the space of an hour. When these things had been accomplished, the tops of the mountains receded, and the mountains themselves sank down even to the plain, and there was seen a solitude. Such things are meant in Revelation by the former heaven and the former earth which John saw pass away; for the mountains there, with the rocks and valleys, appear like the earth in our world; and the habitations upon the mountains are there called heavens. Those who were thus carried off and cast away, are they who are meant in Revelation by the dragon and his two beasts (Rev. 12-13), and by the false prophet who was cast into the lake of brimstone and fire (Rev. 19:20; 20:10).

The judgment upon the Protestants or Reformed was effected as follows: They who had led a life of charity, which may also be called a life of faith, had all been carried up into heaven long before the universal judgment; and all who in heart had denied heaven and had led an evil life had been cast by turns into hell as they came from the world. On those only was the judgment effected, who had professed religion and had acted as if from religion but only hypocritically; to these it was conceded to gather themselves together in many places in the spiritual world, and, as in the world, to simulate religion, but still they had no religion. These are they who made heavens for themselves and who are meant by the former heaven and the former earth; and by means of arts unknown in the world they are able to produce splendid things, and to persuade those who are similar that they are in heaven. Their exteriors communicated with the ultimate heaven but their interiors with the hells; and it was on account of the communication with the ultimate heaven that they were tolerated, according to the Lord's words concerning the pulling up of the tares. The angels of the ultimate heaven were first separated from them and the communication was broken; as takes place comparatively with seeds in fruits when they ripen, in that when the time comes for them to produce a new tree they separate themselves, as it were, spontaneously from the body of the fruit.

All the Protestants or Reformed of whom there was still some hope, were collected in the middle, where they were arranged according to their kingdoms in the world; for according to these were also the diversities of their dispositions or affections. But above them 141-1 and also around them were those who had read the Word and had frequented temples, but yet had made nothing of evils of life, loving themselves and the world above all things; there was an immense multitude there. Surrounding the middle region, in which were Christians who had been in the good of faith and charity, were dark caverns stretching obliquely into hells which occupied a wide space below the heaven of spirits, where were hells beneath hells. Such gulfs and chasms lay around that middle region on every side, east, west, south and north; thus the hells extended even under the circuit made by the Papists round about the Reformed. All who were interiorly evil had been disposed around the Christian middle, and from every quarter they were led down into those gulfs and cast into them. Thus, into the eastern gulf were cast those who had been collected from the east; they were such as had been in the love of self and especially in the love of ruling, nor had known anything whatever except that faith alone is saving. Into the southern gulf were cast those who had been versed in the doctrinals of faith; into the western gulf those who had been in the love of the world; and into the northern, those who had been in no understanding, but had merely heard preachings and had received no instruction afterwards.

Those at the south were led down first, then those at the west, and, lastly, those at the east. This happened at the same time that the eastern Papists were being led down beyond the northern tract.

When this had been done their dwellings were laid waste and destroyed.

Afterwards I saw an immense number of those who had lauded faith alone, and yet had possessed no faith because they had paid no attention to the evils of their life, both the learned and the unlearned, saying that they have the Word and the true doctrine, that they know the Lord, and many other things, and that, therefore, they, above others, would be saved. They were led away in a multitude, first to the west, afterwards to the south, on the other side of the waste Babylonish tract there, and even towards the east and still farther. 144-1 And they were divided; were scattered towards the north, nor were they seen anymore. And many were led back, but hither and thither; this transfer was effected in order that they might be explored as to whether they had any faith such as they had boasted of; namely, whether their faith was only a science, which is not faith; or, whether there was anything of life in it, which is faith. And it was given them to perceive that they had had no faith, but only something scientific without life.

When they were in the southern quarter near a gulf there, there came forth a multitude which had been concealed there from early times, who likewise said that they had had faith, and that they would be saved by reason of faith alone, and they had thought nothing about life. This multitude then approached them and was mingled with them.

From a certain mountain region a multitude was brought forth, who had led a moral life, not from any religion, but merely from fear of the law and of the loss of fame, honor and gain; thus without any Christian life; wherefore, so far as they could do it unknown, they perpetrated evils. Because they had not acquired to themselves any communication with heaven by means of a life from religion, they were led around to the southern and western quarters, that they might be explored as to whether they had any religion of life; and because they had none, they were rejected.

Finally came those who had been versed in the doctrinals of the church, and, in like manner, had led a moral but not a Christian life, because they had lived, not from doctrine, or the Word, but for the sake of fame, thus before men and not before God. And, being explored [it was seen] that they had nothing of conscience, because nothing of the religion of life. These were cast out of that mountain region.

All these, who were divided into the three classes, were driven so far away that they could not be seen except as a dark cloud; and they were dissipated. It was told me from heaven that they were cast down into uninhabited and desert places, and thus were separated lest they should consociate together.

The dispersion of these three classes was made to all the quarters, east, south, west, and north, whence they can never return; and this all the more, since every knowledge of religion is taken away from them. Concerning life in deserts, see elsewhere.

The angels wondered that there is so great a multitude in the Christian world who are entirely ignorant of the truth that religion is a matter of life, imagining that religion consists in thinking something or other, and that by thus thinking they absolve themselves from every obligation of life, which they have made up from this: that, by the Lord's merit, they are exempt from the yoke of the law, and that no one can do good from himself, and that if he does, it is meritorious: and yet this is so far from religion of life that it is no religion at all.

Footnotes

103-1 Tafel has, qui non volunt credere salutem per spiritum sanctum. The reading is doubtful. Acton translates it, "Who at heart wish to be saluted as the Holy Spirit."

109-1 See SE 5341-5343.

129-1 See SE 5822.

129-2 See SS 116; SE 393, 5822.

131-1 See AC 2596; SE 6067.

132-1 See SE 607; R 11; T 279; Coro 39.

135-1 See SE 4932

139-1 In the M.S. stagna is written twice; in SE 5202, lacus, "lakes," is given in place of the second stagna.

141-1 See SE 5347.

144-1 See SE 5355, 5535, 5538.

But all who have thought with themselves that evil must not be done because it is sin, and is against Divine laws, and who thus, so far as they could, have abstained from evils, all these have received something of conscience, and, in the things which were of their faith, although they were spurious, there was much life; and they were saved.

The cleansing of the middle where the Reformed were, lasted a long time; and those who were in the church without the church in themselves, or without doctrine and religion in themselves, were, by turns, cast into the gulfs surrounding the middle, and many of them into deserts. These cleansings lasted for a long time after the judgment.

I once saw many spirits, sitting around a table in a certain house, who looked like rich merchants; and still more spirits were approaching so that there were quite a number of them. In face they appeared as though upright, and they were clothed as though they were angelic spirits. But I saw that they were all cast into desert places, and into woods, thus outside the societies of the upright. The reason was stated, namely, because, in the world, they had lived, in external form like Christians and had acted well, but this solely for the purpose of acquiring a reputation for sincerity and honesty in order to make gain therefrom; and that they had not done the least thing for the sake of God or the neighbor, but all for the sake of themselves; and that, therefore, they had no communication with heaven. Hence it is that they were cast out thither, where they roam about amongst robbers, and themselves commit robbery. For when external bonds are taken away from such spirits they become robbers. They were robbers even in the world, were it not that externals, which are fears for the loss of fame and hence of gain, held them in bonds.

In the western quarter was seen a multitude whose speech sounded sincere, so that from their speech they might be thought to be, as it were, sincerities. By their speech and reasonings concerning sincerity they could induce the simple to believe that they were of such a character. But still it was found out that, within, they were like wolves, because without religion and hence without conscience. I have heard them consulting together as to how the simple might be deceived and their goods stolen away from them; some were consulting to do this, in order that they might thus obtain dominion. And then they assailed them from behind and inspired evils into them, for in this way they are able to subjugate. But their doings were seen in heaven and they were cast into a hell about the western tract of the middle region; 154-1 for they were insincerities and also wickednesses - devisers of arts with the end of gain and dominion.

Afterwards those of the Reformed were explored, as to what idea of God they had. Who had led merely a life of piety. Who had frequented temples and made themselves guilty of all sins, but had not explored themselves. Who believed that they had led a Christian life, in that they had lived well morally because of the civil laws. Who had been hypocrites.

They were explored as to what idea they had concerning God. It was found that they had thought only of God the Father, and of the Lord as like themselves; this is their belief, that the Father has compassion for the Son's sake. And they had then thought nothing concerning the Divine of the Lord. Thus, when they thought of one God they had not at the same time thought of the Lord; when yet the Father cannot be approached, since no one seeth Him but the Son alone; and that the Lord is the Way, thus that the Father is to be approached by Him; and that faith must be a faith in Him, and not in the Father. Hence they could have no determinate idea of God except as of wind, or ether, or as of nature in its leasts; and there is no Divine idea of the Lord when He is thought of as a common man. The angels complained that they were disturbed by their idea, which was communicated to them; and very many of these spirits were brought down into the quarters round about. And the places to which they came then appeared gloomy; for the true idea of God makes clearness itself. Some of them were brought into places underneath according to their life; some in order that they might be further informed. And then only those who have lived well receive a Divine idea concerning the Lord. I saw that those succeeded to their place who had been kept concealed by the Lord lest they be hurt by the contagion; these are meant in Revelation 20 by those who were slain and were delivered out of the sepulchers.

Afterwards I saw those who had led a life merely of piety, and in idleness, led away from the others. They had been continually in prayers, and not at all in truths, merely knowing that salvation is from mercy, and that sins are remitted, but knowing nothing as to what sin is. They had despised others in comparison with themselves, and had also condemned them on account of cares of the world. Most of them had placed merit in prayers. Of these also the angels made complaint, especially because they induce sadness upon them. They dwelt at the side, 157-1 wherefore they were driven away to their own places; there they retain their worship, but they are driven to work. They were brought down into the northern plain because they were in ignorance of such things as lead to heaven.

Hypocrites who have spoken well concerning God, the neighbor and the country, but in themselves have thought the contrary, were explored and cast into hell. They wished to speak well concerning the Lord's kingdom and concerning heaven, for this is then the country, but their interior thought was explored, which was for themselves alone, and against the rule of the country; wherefore, when they were let into their interiors they perpetrated criminal things. They were cast into hells, being first deprived of all that they had drawn from the Word and from doctrines by which they had deluded others.

Preachers who know something of the doctrine of their church, and, after they have been instructed in the schools, and have come into their functions, no longer care for it, nor for the Word, except that they may preach and be elevated to higher offices or may gain wealth; and thus who live in ease and are merely worldly and not Christians, these are sent into a hell in the northern quarter towards the west, far from the middle, where a dense fog is seen; and they then become stupid. 159-1

All are separated according to their life, thus according to their affections, not according to their external life, but according to their internal, for this is the life of the thought from will or affection, and no one has internal life except from religion; external life is from morality and the state, and according to its laws; wherefore moral life, unless it draw its quality from spiritual life, and thereby change its appearance, is not spiritual life with any man; consequently there is no conjunction with heaven, and they who are not conjoined with heaven are conjoined with hell; and in such case, although, in the world, they have not done evil, yet, after their departure from the world, they do evil from delight; thus their state is changed.

Concerning the Dragonists. Who are meant by the dragon, may be deduced from what has been said in the of the Apocalypse; also that by the tail of the dragon is meant faith separate from charity, which drew down the stars from heaven, that is, the knowledges of truth and good.

The dragonists were separated; many of them, when in the world, had been priests, who had confirmed themselves in faith separate from charity. They were explored in various ways, as, by the inspection, in light, of the back of the head. With those who were merely natural and hence infernal, the back of the head is filthy, hollowed out, and altogether bony. They are led down to places where they are deprived of the exteriors which have been induced on their faces by art, and the face is regarded according to the affections and the interior thoughts thence. What was human in their face is then taken away and something diabolical succeeds in its place. They are also explored by being turned to the east, and thus to the Lord; and then from the east there flows in a spiritual affection concerning the Lord. And then they instantly turn themselves back again to the west, like a spring, which recoils when it has been twisted backwards. In this way, also, angels explore newcomers to their heavenly societies.

There are also some who desire to hear truths; they believe they are saved if only they know them. But when they hear that truths are for the sake of life, and that so far as truths of life become actual, so far truths of faith also live, they then depart, feeling the utmost disgust for life, but not so for the truths which are of faith, because these they can talk about. 163-1 The truths of faith which do not live unless truths of life become actually such, may be enumerated; and it may be mentioned which are truths of faith, and which truths of life. 163-2

Everyone can see that charity consists in not stealing from anyone, either by artifice or openly; that charity consists in being wholly unwilling to commit adultery with the wife of another; that charity consists in not doing injury to the neighbor in hatred and revenge; that charity consists in not reviling another, and so forth. He who abhors these things as sins, has charity, for he loves the neighbor.

Afterwards I saw an immense number, both sent forth from the heavens and rising up from below, and also of those who had been left, who were allotted their places, mansions and habitations; in the east, those in the clear good of love and of charity; at the west, those in the obscure good of love and of charity; at the south, those in truths from good in clearness; and at the north, those in truths from obscure good; all acknowledging the Lord as the God of heaven and earth.

Many in the Christian world were also cast down who had an understanding of truth but not a will of good. In the beginning such spirits are accepted among the upright because they can speak about many things, even truths; moreover in the beginning, the understanding with them is enlightened but the will is laid to sleep. Such spirits were collected together on the mountains in the western quarter. They league themselves with the upright who are in the ultimate heaven, who do not inquire as to things of the will, but believe that those who speak intelligently are also good. But I saw such spirits, that they were altogether devoid of charity; and they secretly consociate with the evil and, first by reasonings and afterwards by arts, they infest the upright, until they are conjoined and devoted to themselves; for in this way they prevail against others. Many such were in heavens which they had made for themselves; and they interposed themselves between the Lord and man in the world, and so obstructed the way that the Divine operation could not have its force. Very many of this character are in the pride of self-intelligence from the love of self, and in the delight of domineering. I once saw such spirits in a somewhat high mountain in the western quarter toward the north, and everywhere round about on the sides of the mountain; and they persuaded themselves and others that one is in heaven from mere intellectual light and not at the same time from heavenly heat; they are most dangerous. I saw them cast down from the mountain and from the sides of the mountain, and a gulf underneath opened itself and swallowed them up, 166-1 and they sank deep down and were let into darkness. For they then received falsities in place of truths, and turned themselves to things contrary. Such is the understanding which is led by an evil will. The evil who had conjoined themselves with them, because they no longer had the power of resistance, were cast down into their various hells, some into hells under the mountains, others into hells under the plains. 166-2

Those who were in faith separate rose up in insurrection, exciting a rebellion well-nigh universal. Their dogma and their learned leaders rose up against those who acknowledged the Lord and a life of love from Him. They stirred up all, except those who were in the eastern quarter, these were guarded by the Lord, even to certain Mohammedans who were in the northern quarter. They sent forth companies of fifty to many places, in order that they might stir up those who were there; 167-1 and those who remained and directed were divided into companies of ten. Their purpose was to destroy all those who acknowledged the Lord alone, and works together with faith as being saving. Almost all of them were without religion, and hence without conscience. But when they set out to do this, and were in the endeavor to destroy others that were evil, a force flowed down from on high, or from heaven, by which they were cast down to the hells, to a number exceeding many thousands. They also conjoined themselves with Papists and with monks who in the world had proclaimed themselves Christs and had thought nothing of the Lord's Divinity. When the whole crew had been cast down, the leaders were taken; and they became black as devils, both within and without; and they became so monstrous that they would be scarcely recognized as men. For man is such as he is as to life; he who is black as to life, afterwards becomes black even from head to heel. It was found that they had not rebelled from zeal on account of the doctrine of faith alone, but from the delight of ruling and of doing evil for the sake thereof. This was the combat of Michael with the Dragon; for all such who have insinuated themselves into heaven are drawn forth thence and cast down. They are Michael who worship the Lord and [who make] works conjoined with faith saving; for since the one is not given without the other, therefore they save conjointly.

The combat of the Dragon with Michael was afterwards as follows, for it lasted some days: A hand was seen stretched out over the heavens by the Lord. In the western quarter towards the west 168-1 there appeared as it were a great back raised above the middle towards heaven; angels in immense number were seen there. In that entrance were the dragonists; and they spoke with them concerning the Lord and concerning the goods of charity and thence of faith. All then turned towards them to hear what they would say. And the dragonists were forced into the thoughts concerning the Lord and concerning faith alone which they had in the world; and then most of them had no Divine idea of the Lord, nor any idea of charity and works. The angels answered them wisely on this matter, but in vain. They said, moreover, that all the angels in the heavens do not perceive the matter thus; but it was in vain. 168-2 And at last, after the combat, when the dragonists were only willing to give further response outside of the matter or the truth, but could not, they were adjudged to be cast down from every place where such spirits were. But when they said they would resist, the Lord was seen descending from the sun in a bright cloud, and He gave judgment that all who were found to be such should be separated and alienated. And then they were cast down successively and by turns according to the connection of the societies of heaven; towards the western quarter an immense number, and a thousand then appeared as one. The grievous collision of truth and falsity which pertained to temptation was felt within me. The whole western quarter was full of such spirits who had been cast down from the heavens; and then the earth was seen to open, and they were cast down and were covered over with a dense cloud. They were all such as would never have abstained from thinking and willing evils but only from doing them by reason of fear. This happened in 1757 on the 11th day of April. 168-3 From the southern quarter to the western the dragonists were seen in a curved line under the figure of a tail; at the south, there, were those who had been skilled in the degrees of justification and had confirmed these with themselves.

The Lord's heaven was first inherited by such as had acknowledged Him and had lived well, who had had heaven in themselves; afterwards, succeeded those who wished merely to have heaven outside themselves. To these latter it was also granted to make heavens for themselves, which they called heaven when they saw the magnificent things, such as palaces, porticos, paradises, and many serviceable things. But, since their internals were not in correspondence, such things disappeared; and then by phantasies and the abuses of correspondences and by many arts, they provided for themselves things similar. This did not last long, however, for they placed everything in delicacies and in bodily pleasures, and thus they became wholly external such as they had been in the world; and then came the judgment, after which followed continual purifications of the societies from such spirits.

Many of those who are in faith alone, because they have no conjunction with heaven but all conjunction with hell, are in the love of ruling. They are explored in the following way: From the societies of heaven they look down to the places beneath; and where they see spirits, whether many or few, walking about there, they rule their thoughts, infest them in various ways, and by phantasies cause many things to appear to them to which they are led; their joy is to precipitate them into hells. They are of such a character that they do not want to be led but to lead; this is their delight; wherefore they cannot be led by the Lord, for the Lord leads through the affection of use, and this is not their affection. With them use is to domineer, and, therefore, they successively deny the Lord, and rely upon arts, which are many, by which they have dominion. They put their trust in their own prudence, and ascribe nothing to the Divine Providence and when the reins are loosened, they rush finally into such a state that they think there is no God. And yet inseated in them is the purpose of domineering over heaven and to be there in place of God. This is inseated in the love of ruling for the sake of self. I once saw that a certain spirit in a small society was permitted to set in order those who were there. He set them in order as a spider sets its webs, placing himself in the middle and making paths in every direction, with the command that all should look to him; but that society was swallowed up by the hells which were below. All who are of such a character wish to be in the heavens; and they climb up into high places, where they believe that the exercising of dominion is the delight of life, but use is this; but when they have been explored they are cast down. They are wanderers; they direct their course from one society to another, often seeking to obtain office.

They are distinguished according to their ideas of the Divine, as They who have an idea concerning the union with the Father. They who have an idea solely of the Lord's Human and nothing of the Divine, although they had known of it. They who have acknowledged three Persons and have not made them one God by essence; these are specially distinguished. They who have an idea solely of the Father; these are without a God. They who have not believed in the Lord from eternity. 171-1

All those are preserved who in the world had acknowledged the Divine of the Lord and had shunned evils as sins, especially those who had acknowledged the Divine Human, and had approached Him. But the rest who had thought of the Lord as of a common man, are cast back among the Socinians and Arians who, at first, are under the heavens nearest above the hells, and afterwards are in the hells.

They who were in faith alone persecuted me. They brought persecution upon me 173-1 by bringing me into a state like that in which they themselves were by means of a like respiration and a like pulse; thus also into like thought and affection. And, in respect to God and salvation, I was in an obscure cloudiness as though immersed in water; and it was perceived that I had no communication 173-2 with heaven; and it was said that they have a similar communication.

Many of those who are in faith alone and had committed nothing of truth and good to life, for the reason that they had rejected all moral life from a spiritual origin, saying that it effects nothing, and that evils do not condemn, and that the Lord had fulfilled the Law for them, and had taken away damnation, and that of themselves they cannot do good still less fulfill the Law, many of these become rebels and put forth various scandals against the Lord, as is the case with all who have not lived their religion, even if in the world they had not thought wickedly concerning the Lord. They were explored and it was found that they had committed nothing of truth and good to life, and that they merely knew something from the Word which was like any other scientific matter in which there is nothing vital. And they then appeared without clothing, for clothing signifies the truths of life; and then they understand nothing at all, even as to what was right and just. It was said to them that they had lived without religion, and they were cast into the southern gulf, and were thus carried away.

Some of this character were let out of hells in order that they might be transferred to another hell. And it was then permitted them to act according to their will. Then they at once desired to force their way up to higher places by means of phantasies, and they were in the endeavor to do evil. It was recalled to their memory that, in hell, they had said to each other, that if it were allowed them to go out, they would be just as wise as others. Certain ones then spoke with them, saying something of intelligence in which was the light of truth; and when they heard them they were seized with such anguish that they fled away. This was done several times in order that it might be confirmed that such spirits, even when the state is changed, do not sustain the light of truth, thus of intelligence. They said that they were doing them harm, but answer was made that with each other they said otherwise. Hence it was made clear that they who are in hell can never live in the light of heaven, thus in heaven; and least of all in the heat of heaven, which is love.

After the judgment, all societies were disposed according to nations, in an admirable order. The order was according to affections in the heavens, and according to cupidities in the hells. They are then straightway purified by means of communications with the evil, and thence as it were by a fermentation; and then the alien are cast down like things heterogeneous. Sometimes the purification is effected by the society becoming like one man; they who are in the man remain, they who are outside the man are rejected. After the judgment, it is not permitted to thus ascend into heaven and be cast down thence, but each one is determined in such direction that he may go the way that leads to his society.

Afterwards societies were formed most distinctly according to all the genera and species of the affections of good and of truth; and also corresponding infernal societies. All spirits, after they have been vastated, are now led along by designated ways tending to the interior societies which correspond and are analogous to their life; nor are they allowed as before to turn aside in any other direction, or to stay in other places, still less to form for themselves societies and as it were heavens, according to life in externals. It is perhaps believed in the world, that man is saved and comes into heavenly societies according to his thoughts which are of the understanding of truth; but no one is saved according to these, but according to affections and thoughts thence, thus according to the good of the will and thence the truth of the understanding. For man is man from his will and his understanding thence, and not from the truth of the understanding separate from the good of the will; the understanding merely teaches how man must will and act. Many are led along the designated ways with difficulty, for they wish to go to the sides where they are sensible of the presence of the good both below and above, to whom they are eager to do evil; for all ways are such as are the societies above and below them.

The arranging of the Reformed after the judgment lasted a long time, for the reason that the Word is with them and the Lord is known, and they are therefore in the middle; and the greatest light is there, which passes from that middle to the peripheries where are also the Gentiles. On this account the arranging of the Reformed lasted a long time.

All those are retained in the heavens who have had the delight of some use, or of some function for the sake of use, whether it be the delight of business from sincerity, or of some study, provided only there be the delight of use and the acknowledgment of God. These can be held in order by the Lord, because the Lord inflows into uses. But they who have led a life of idleness, merely in social companies, or in offices solely for their own glory, cannot be ruled by the Lord; and because they are not members of the society, considered as a man, they are rejected. There is an application to the function of the blood.

HE-GOATS; THEY ARE THOSE WHO ARE IN FAITH SEPARATE FROM CHARITY. Speech was held with some in regard to the he-goat mentioned in Daniel and to its combat with the ram; and also in regard to the judgment on the goats and sheep mentioned in Matthew. And beneath me there then appeared a he-goat with great horns which was seen to infest the sheep and to treat them badly with its horns, and also to toss them hither and thither. And inquiry was made as to what this was, and it was said that this was the appearance of those who are in faith separate from charity, and of their combat with those who have been in the life of charity. And it was said that before their own eyes they do not look like this but like men sharply disputing with each other; and that he who seemed like a he-goats, was one who was in faith separate, while they who seemed like sheep were those who were in the life of charity. For sometimes, and especially at a distance, spirits appear according to their affections, inclinations, and their principles therefrom. For example, when anyone is thinking from the understanding, he appears as though sitting on a horse, and some appear in other ways. Hence it was made evident that by the horned he-goat in Daniel, and by the he-goats in Matthew, none others are meant. It is supposed that all the evil are meant by the he-goats, but no others of them are meant than those who have lived wickedly and have nevertheless confessed faith alone. [Marginal Note:]   After the Last Judgment was accomplished many were seen who had been scattered among others at the back in the west; at a distance they appeared like he-goats, and some like dragons; who because they wished to seduce the upright were removed thence and driven into deserts where there was scarcely a shrub.

In like manner afterwards, those who were in faith separate, appeared as he-goats, and those who were in the life of charity as sheep, and their argumentations and wranglings, as combats.

. THE DRAGON. By "the dragon" (Revelation 12), and by his "two beasts" (Chap. 13), no others are meant than those who are in faith separated from charity both in doctrine and in life, by "the dragon," all those who have confirmed themselves in that faith, and by the beast from the sea, they who have confirmed those principles by means of reasonings from the natural man, and by "the beast from the earth," who is afterwards meant by "the false prophet," are meant confirmations from the Word in favor of that faith. That such are meant by "the dragon and his two beasts," may be clearly seen from each particular there written about them, understood in the spiritual sense;

which can be seen to the life if the things written on Revelation should be given to the public, for they are all confirmed from heaven; also that by "the tail of the dragon," is meant the confirmation of that faith by means of the degrees of justification which are treated of in [Spiritual Experiences.

The Apocalypse treats of the two religious systems in the Christian world, that with the Reformed and that with the Papists, for the whole of Christianity is from these two, since they are the ruling systems. The religious system with the Reformed is a system of faith alone, which has devastated the church; and that with the Papists deals with the Lord's vicarious authority over the church, thus over the souls of men, and also over heaven, that resides with the popes and the primates and subordinate officials of the church. It is these two ruling systems of religion which [have been rejected] by the Last Judgment, concerning which we will treat later.

That they who are in faith separate are meant by "the dragon and his beasts." That by "the dragon" are meant those who are in faith separate was made evident from the following circumstances: It is related that "the dragon stood by the woman about to bring forth, that he might devour her ;" and that, by "the son, which the woman was about to bring forth," is meant the doctrine concerning the Lord and concerning the life of charity, was made evident from this, that when that doctrine was being written many of those who are in faith alone were present, and in such fury, that I could scarcely have written had I not been guarded by the Lord by means of angels; and it appeared as though they wished to rend it and tear it to pieces. By "the woman" there, is meant the New Church which is the New Jerusalem, and by her son, the doctrine concerning the Lord and concerning the life of charity; and by "the dragon," are meant those who are in faith separate, because such then was their nature, and because they were about to do what is described afterwards, by persecuting the woman, and casting forth water like a flood, that he might swallow her up; by "water like a flood," falsities are signified.

There was a certain preacher who was in faith alone; he appeared to others altogether like a dragon, and he also seemed to hover around a woman about to bring forth, eager to devour her child; and yet, seen near at hand, he was standing near those who defended the life of charity and the Lord. He was a preacher at The Hague.

Of those who are in faith separate there are some who correspond to the head of the dragon, some who correspond to his body, and some who correspond to his tail. The latter are they who are in the conceit of those principles, for the tail is the continuation of the spinal cord, and this again of the brain. There are some who correspond to the poison.

Concerning the back and hinder part seen like the tail of a dragon, see above 134-179]. [On the Reformed], towards the end of the chapter.

Moreover at the left was seen a hillside upon which ascended many of those who were in faith alone; and on the summit there, they have some bearded old man who had been bearded in the world, and sometimes of lowly condition. This man persuades them that he is God the Father. It is a rock and rocky places are around about it. And when they do not wish to be seen they betake themselves behind the mountain. These are they who have laid snares for all who do not believe like themselves, believing that this is allowable. The life of charity they make of no account. By their interiors they make one with the hells. They who appeared round about the bottom of the mountain were seen like an immense dragon stretching itself towards the places below; and its tail was seen elevated and extended from the mountain to the lowest parts thereof.

FAITH ALONE. The interior sphere of spirits was perceived to be completely filled with affections, which are ends, of becoming great, of growing rich and of being wise for the sake of glory, and little, if at all, on account of the common good.

When, from the Lord, I was in the faith of the knowledges of truth it was found that evil spirits were powerless to refute them or even to reason about them as when I was in the knowledges that the Lord rules the universe, that the Lord alone is life, and that the proprium of man is nothing but evil, and others of a like kind. Evil spirits hearing these, although they did not believe them yet could not contradict, for truth is averse to it, because the intellectual does not admit any thinking against it. From this it was made clear that those who are in the simple faith of truth resist evils. I also saw some, who were in truths, who passed through many hells and all the infernals retreated, nor could they approach, still less do any evil. But he who believes in the faith set forth in the church at this day, cannot do this; the infernals are in no way troubled at their approach, because truth from the Lord is not in that faith.

Concerning certain spirits who have no spiritual life because they are in ignorance of truth; and that life is inspired into them by the Lord through angels. I once felt a somewhat intense cold from the soles of the feet up to the knee; it became evident that there were cold spirits. It was told me that they were those who in the world had lived in absolute ignorance of God. After they had been elevated I heard them talking, and I could perceive scarcely anything vital in their speech. They spoke as though they were making inanimate statues speak, and I despaired of any life long remaining in them. They were like automatons or sounding sculptures. But presently I heard that they had been let into a species of activity appearing like a species of gyration. Angels were caring for them by infusing life into them, which they did with such solicitude and devotion, that it can scarcely be described, nor did they suffer themselves to be wearied. In the meantime they waved them, as is said in the Word of the things sacrificed, that they were waved by the Levites, the reason being, that they might receive spiritual life. When this had been done for some little time, they began to be vivified, and to be no longer of such a nature as before; thus they began to speak something in consociation, saying that they were in heaven. The work was continued by the Lord through angels during the whole night, and after this they became such as to be capable of being insinuated or inserted into some companies in which they were afterwards perfected. For they were receptive of life because they had nothing repugnant thereto, as have those who confirm themselves in falsities against truths. The manner in which life was successively insinuated into them was represented by colors, the first of life by a marble color increasing in whiteness, the second by a growing azure color in which was the white, and the third by patches of bright clouds rising up. Their quality was afterwards shown me by a blowing from them on my face, and also into the anterior region of the breast. It was somewhat cold but verging to heat. This was from the Lord alone by means of angels. They may be said to be resuscitated from no life into some life.

There was one who held it as a principle that faith alone saves; it was said to him that faith is like science and knowledge which should be for the sake of use and good, and that otherwise it is nothing but a science; also that he is insane who believes that science alone saves, when yet all science and knowledge has good as an end.

He who has fought against evils, and, from the Lord, has come into the love of good and truth, is in the knowledges of truth and good as it were from himself; he sees them in himself, and they are inscribed on his heart, as is said in Isaiah and Joel. The rational is then enlightened. But prior to this he does not know them, except from the memory alone, in which case he does not see them except externally, and if they are not seen internally they are dry and transitory. This is the life in truths; for all the things of truth are inscribed on the love, just as, with every animal, all things which are for use are inscribed on the affection, as in the case of bees, birds, and other animals; so also are they inscribed on man if he is in the genuine love of truth and good. It is from this that the angels have their wisdom.

I was led through societies or mansions of heaven, and I spoke with many. And when I came to mansions of the third heaven, where are the celestial, I wished to speak with them about the knowledges which are called knowledges of faith and which in themselves are truths. I marveled that they did not wish to make any response to these things. They said that they see all things in themselves from the love in which they are, which was love to the Lord and mutual love, saying that the truths of their faith were inscribed on their life, and that therefore they see them from the light of truth which is from the Lord, and this because in good is contained all truth. They also said, What are knowledges except for the sake of uses? and uses are goods, and goods are of love. It was told me that they are of this nature because, in the world, they had applied all the truths they had heard to their life. All their love and all their faith consists in deeds.

Those who are in faith alone believe in instantaneous salvation and pure mercy; and therefore they implore mercy alone and believe that they are instantly saved the moment they receive faith, even though it be in the last hour of death. They also believe that the remission of all sins consists in the wiping away of all evils. They have no comprehension of remission by means of repentance of life, but only of remission by means of faith arising from thinking such things as they call of their faith; thus they are ignorant of all the means of salvation. It was shown them that such things are a phantasy; and this phantasy was represented as being interiorly full of poisonous serpents. The nature of the phantasy was shown in a ludicrous manner, namely, that they think and also wish to void those serpents through their posteriors.

When they think from their doctrine about faith alone, and are opposed by the statement, in The Epistle of James, that men should show their faith by works, there appears as it were a knife flying forth to slay those who perceive this to be the case. And from one side comes forth an idea of Luther, and from the other, whither the knife flies, an idea of James, although Luther and James themselves are not there. The reason is, because, Luther excluded the Epistle of James.

Below, at the left, are those who from doctrine have confirmed themselves in regard to faith alone, but yet have lived a life of charity from the principle that faith produces the works of charity. These, because they have lived well, are accepted and have conjunction with heaven. Still it is not a direct conjunction, and this for the reason that they hold it as a principle that it is faith that produces the works of charity, when yet faith is of the thought, and thought produces nothing; it only teaches what should be done, and if a man does what it teaches, then it is not from any faith; for knowledges of truth do not become knowledges of faith until man has done them. It is like one who believes that the sight operates into the hands to enable a man to work, or into the feet to enable him to walk and not stumble, when yet the sight does not operate in this way, but it teaches and brings things to view. That this is an inversion was shown by it being given to a certain spirit to walk on a road and to then believe that it was the understanding that was leading him. He then went from the east to the west or from the south to the north, thus from truths to falsities, and into obscurity. But his state was changed [so that he believed] that the will or love was leading him; he then walked from the west to the east and from the north to the south, thus into good and into truth in light. It was told them that with those who have had this belief the state is successively inverted, and that then they begin to be regenerated and come into the angelic life.

They who, from doctrine, are in the principle that faith alone saves, and yet have led a good life, constitute certain societies in which they are in the middle, while at the circumferences are those who are not of such a quality, and lastly those who are evil, so that they are surrounded by the evil. It was told them that they still dwell among the evil.

It was made known by living experience that those who have been in faith alone and have led a moral life, had made heavens for themselves, where they seemed to themselves to have been in light; but it was shown that it is a wintry light, for when angels looked thither, in place of light there appeared a thick darkness. Those who go there, and are at the same time in charity, feel a pain in the breast, the stomach and the knees.

Concerning those who are continually wrangling about truths. There are hells where they do nothing else but wrangle about truths. One of them was under the groins. In that hell were those who believe that they know everything and that nothing is hidden from them, when yet they do not know anything, except that their faith is the all of the church with men. There are those there who, by reason of their belief that they know all things, think that they alone are entitled to talk; they despise the laity. They are continually saying that this is the truth itself, and that it cannot be contradicted. I have there heard perpetual contradictions and quarrels which went so far that they wished to attack their opponents with their fists, but they are held back by others. They appear in that place as if they were tearing garments; and from the place is heard as it were the gnashing of teeth. Thus do they go forward and back and thus do they wrangle, not at all for the sake of truth but for the sake of themselves from the pride of their own intelligence and from the itch of domineering. They are removed from others, because they disturb all tranquillity of mind and take away the freedom of thinking from the Word, inducing their own opinions as though they were from the Divine and infesting all who do not receive. At this day there are many such consociations drawn from the Christian world, because there they have divided the church on questions of opinion concerning what is to be believed, and the good of life they not only reject, but they also say that they know not what it is unless it be to give to the poor and to hear preachings.

Footnotes

154-1 See SE 5398.

157-1 See SE 5392.

159-1 See SE 5514.

163-1 See SE 5540, 5541.

163-2 Tafel has, delati, possibly it is detecti. See SE 5696, 5698.

166-1 See SE 5698.

166-2 See SE 5699.

167-1 See SE 5731 1/2, 5758.

168-1 The M.S. has, ocvcidentem, "west." In SE 5742 it is septentrionalem, "north."

168-2 See SE 5722.

168-3 See SE 5746.

171-1 See SE 5821.

173-1 Tafel has, eamque mihi intulerunt; the MS., me persecuti mihi intulerunt. In SE 5827 it is, Se congregarunt, et violentiam inferebant, "They gathered themselves together, and inflicted violence."

173-2 See SE 5827.

Those who have said that they had faith have been seen many times; and when they are explored it is found that they had no other faith than that which was spoken of above. This they call the only saving faith, and also spiritual faith, and yet they have not lived any Christian life by shunning evil because it is sin. They were sent into places where faith was constituted of truths which had their essence from the good of life, and their communication was granted them to discover whether they had faith. And, from the perception then given them, they themselves openly confessed that they had nothing of faith, it was mere knowledge like any other mere knowledge of the world, and that they had not known what faith was; also that faith was truth, and that, unless truths are from good; they are not truths, but are only articulated expressions of sound.

Very many of those who are in faith alone and in no life of charity are sensual. For evils of life, which they neither see in themselves nor have endeavored to see, occupy their voluntary and make it; and, as a man is in respect to his voluntary such he is as to his interiors. Therefore these interiors are shut up, and all things which are of the church and heaven are below or without, thus merely in the memory where they reside as historical faith or as science. This is the reason why, when men hear something of the truths concerning the Lord, the Word, eternal life, heaven, the state of the angels and the state of men after death, the things they hear are received as matters of the memory; but as soon as they think about them, as to whether they are so, then the sensual corporeal judges and makes its own conclusion. The conclusion reached is that what has been heard cannot be true, and this because what is previously in the memory from doctrine must be believed; as, that there are three Persons of the Divinity, that the Human of the Lord is not Divine, that angels, because they are spirits, are like winds, and so likewise man after death. The reason is because it is the sensual that makes the conclusion, and [in that] light from heaven which enlightens cannot be received, the interiors being closed to the transflux of that light. Investigate for yourself as to whether this is not the case, whenever any such truth is laid under direct examination, and inquiry is made as to whether it is so. The sensual man is such that he comprehends fallacies and believes in appearances and speaks truths, but the truths themselves, which are of the light of heaven, he rejects. This is the effect of faith alone, and therefore they cannot be led on into any understanding of truth.

It was said by angels that there can be no such thing as faith alone. Spirits who, in the world, had been in faith alone, being indignant at this, came running up from every direction to where the angelic spirits were, and inquired, "Is there no such a thing as faith alone?" In this manner they ran to ten or fifteen places, and everywhere received the answer, that there is no such thing, because faith without love is mere knowledge, and their faith the mere knowledge of falsity; and if they wish to call mere knowledge faith, because they have persuaded themselves in it, although they do not understand whether it is so, [their belief] is nothing but persuasion because it is so said, and is scarcely different from the belief that corpses and bones and men's graves are holy, when yet they are stercoraceous and signify damnation and hell. When they heard this they ran on and inquired what love was, whether it was not faith alone. Angelic spirits thought them insane, and still more when they said that works were faith, which is as if they had said that thinking was doing. They ran on still further and said, "Is not faith thus a nonentity?" They received the answer that faith separate from charity is a nonentity, because faith is called faith from charity which is its soul; and faith separate from charity is just such an entity as is the body without the soul.

I have heard many of the learned reasoning about various matters of their faith, things which they had held from birth, thence as truths of their religion. Their reasoning was sharp and vehement and each one was refuting the other. There were angels who were listening and they said that with not a single one of them did they perceive any affection of truth, nor therefore any sight of truth, and thus no delight of mind arising from any truth. They wondered that these spirits were able to confirm falsities; and they said that it was merely the delight of reasoning springing from pride, and that thus they cannot progress into any wisdom, for they are at a standstill. But those who are in the affection of truth are ever progressing from truth to truths, and this continually until at last they come to wisdom and thus to angelic happiness. They said that as soon as they hear such reasoners, they turn themselves away and have no wish to join company with them because they see nothing. Of such quality are very many of those who have confirmed themselves in faith separate, not only in doctrine but also in life; for they think to themselves, "What need have I to know what evil is since this does not condemn? or what good is since this does not save? Only let me think, from that faith, that the Lord has fulfilled for me all things of the law and that His merit will be imputed to me."

It was disclosed by angels of heaven that those who are in faith alone have no conscience, yea, that they do not know what conscience is; and he who has no conscience has no religion. The reason is, because they make goods of life of no account, and they who make these of no account can by no means have conscience, and hence cannot know what it is; for conscience is a grief of the mind that one has done contrary to the Divine precepts and that one has thought against them. Grief of conscience arises from this, that they see themselves as it were in damnation.

They who believe that man is saved by charity and not by faith alone, if they do not live the life of charity, differ little from the others. For to say charity or to say faith, and not to do them, are both equally of the thought, in which there is nothing of life because nothing of the will. Such spirits inflict pain in the breast and in the right shoulder blade.

How greatly the principles of falsity injure the mind and turn it away from deeds, may appear from many examples. Thus he who believes that works contribute nothing to salvation turns his mind away from doing goods. He who believes adulteries are allowable turns his mind away from chaste conjugial love, thus from chastity, yea from purity of faith; for purity of faith is wholly discordant with adulteries. He who believes that nature operates all things, and that God operates only in a universal way, trusts in his own prudence, and does nothing of good except from himself. Wherefore principles of falsity inflow into the life; for the will does not act contrary to the principles that have been received, but with them.

I have spoken with Melancthon about faith alone, to the effect that he could see from reason alone, that faith alone is not saving because every man is his own good and his own evil; and that every spirit is a form and image of his own good and his own evil; and this not only as to his face but also as to his whole body. For according to the quality of a spirit's affection such he is in respect to his mind, and at the same time in respect to his body. This may be manifestly known from the fact that when anyone speaks contrary to the affection of any spirit or angel, he immediately changes his countenance, yea, becomes invisible and disappears. And, therefore, because faith alone is merely of the thought and not of the will, and thus only of the memory and not of the life, it follows that it is as yet outside the man and not within him. Wherefore, since a spirit is a complete spirit in the degree that he is his own good or his own evil, and since faith separate from good is not within the man, it follows that it is merely like a skin, and that men of faith separate are not men except as to the skin; and thus that they are to be called cutaneous.

The truth is, that he who confirms faith alone with himself both in doctrine and in life cannot be reformed, and thus cannot be saved; that is, he who, while in the world, has thought, "Since I am justified by faith nothing of evil will condemn me, because it is not imputed, and nothing of good will save me;" and has thus cast out of his thought all reflection upon the evil and the good of life with himself; and if he apperceives any evil or good he is not concerned about it as being a matter of no importance in respect to salvation. Such are spirits who cannot be reformed, for they think like things after death.

That the Lord is love; that hence the whole heaven is arranged according to the genera and species of love, and thus according to its varieties; that in like manner every society of heaven, and every spirit and angel; that it is similar in a spirit and angel in whom heaven is, in that all things in them are disposed from love and, according to it in their understanding, yea, their whole body. How then can there be such a thing as faith alone, since faith is according to love?

There was a certain Englishman, who had written learnedly and skillfully about faith and charity, and this from considerable ingenuity. But he had come to the conclusion that faith produces charity, and that when man is justified by faith he is in the endeavor to do good, and that this is the effect of faith; thus that faith first leads to charity and afterwards in charity. It was told him by angels that it so appears to man, and yet that it is not so; and, because it so appears, that this is the way of reformation, for thus man learns many things which are of faith, believing that in this way he is saved; but when man is not regenerated the order is inverted. And, moreover, that if he should make inquiry he would never find that faith produced charity, but that faith was produced by charity. And, therefore, because he was gifted with much ingenuity, he thought out many reasons for confirming the idea that it is faith that produces; and it was permitted him to produce these reasons, and to show whether the case was so. Wherefore in his meditation he was left to follow out each reason; but when he came to the end of his production there always appeared, as it were, an obstruction to the way which he was unable to penetrate so as to arrive at charity. Therefore, abandoning this reason, he acted in a similar manner with another reason, and so on with a hundred. In this way he went on in his ingenious meditation every day for an entire year, and not once did he see a conjunction on the part of faith. Wherefore he afterwards confessed that the thing was impossible, and that the fact that some said they had felt it with themselves was due either to their having thought of charity outside of faith, or to other causes, etc., etc., which arose from the fact that the things which are of faith have taught them, for the truths of faith teach and man acts according to them, and that from a principle either adopted or heard, they have attributed it to faith. Moreover, after a man has done charity, faith is then living, and then, in the single things, charity and faith work together, and it can hardly be seen which is prior and which posterior. The truths of faith which are of the thought and understanding are prior-but still truths do not live and become truths of faith or saving until man lives according to them.

I read before Englishmen their exhortation used before the Holy Supper , how they should act that their sins may be forgiven, and in which there is no mention of faith; and I said this is true religion itself. Certain preachers who were in favor of faith alone, hearing this, said that when reading that exhortation in their churches they had fully believed it to be the way of salvation, but when thinking from their doctrine of faith alone they had thought differently. The English were praised for that exhortation, and many of them believed that it belonged to their doctrine; but more of them said that this was for the common people, faith alone being for the learned. They were asked whether they wished to thus invite the curse expressed in the words, that unless they do this Satan would enter into them as he entered into Judas. They then went away and spoke about the matter among themselves.

I once saw some leaders of the English, among whom were also one or two bishops, who fought for faith alone as for their altars and hearths. And from the ideas of their thought concerning faith alone and justification thereby they formed an image, that it might represent that faith. In the spiritual world this can be done skillfully and easily. They there made their images by means of ideas, and these images also became visible, for appearances are merely from their ideas. Into their image they fitted all things of their faith. But when it was finished it appeared in the sight of the angels as an enormous monster, and as though it would frighten them away. This was in the light of heaven; but before their own eyes it assumed a different appearance, as monstrous things are wont to do, when seen in darkness and from phantasy. They gloried in it at first, but afterwards they became ashamed.

The English said that faith produces charity as a tree produces fruit. But it was shown them that by a tree there is not meant faith but man, and by the branches and leaves are meant the truths of faith, and by the fruits the goods of love; also that natural affection or natural good, which is of the love of self and the world, cannot be conjoined to a faith which is spiritual; if it is conjoined, the result is an adultery; and that spiritual good is not possible except by means of the good of life, which is the good treated of.

An argument on which they lay stress is, that man cannot do good which is good of himself. This is true, but still unless man be in good as from himself it is not appropriated to him, and so he is not conjoined to the Lord. In order for conjunction there must be something reciprocal, and thus a covenant, which is, If you do that I will do this. And, therefore, that man may do it as if of himself freedom is given him, and this freedom is freedom to think, to will, and to do; reason is given him that he may see what salvation is; will is given, and choice and election; and he is commanded to act. All these are given in order that he may act as if of himself, and yet it is not from him but from the Lord. If he did not act of himself he would be an automaton, and all influx would pass through him. The Lord is continually with man pressing and urging him that he may act, and that, for the sake of appropriation and conjunction, it may appear no otherwise than that he acts of himself. A thousand passages can be adduced showing that man is condemned if he does evil and rewarded if he does good; those where doing and works are mentioned might be brought forward.

Many were explored who at the last hour when they had received the Sacrament believed they would be saved by that faith. They said they had believed with trust and confidence; yet it was the life of evil that remained and not the faith. They were told to hold their breath and, at the same time, retain that faith, but still, as soon as they breathed, the delight of evil, from which was their life, returned; and they were cast into hell.

After the judgment those who had been scattered amongst others round about were collected together. And when they had been collected, there came into their mind a cunning of seducing the upright [by teaching them] that faith alone is saving. Wherefore the latter complained about them to the Lord. And then I saw them receding more and more, even till they came to the bounds of the Christian world; there, at the back, were deserts, and I saw a great part of them driven thither. Afterwards it was granted me to see the nature of this desert. There were vile huts and hovels wherein they dwelt almost solitary, with some harlot, and round about them it was stony, with great heaps of rocks between which were a few ways. Nor does one dare to approach another. They all fear each other lest they do evil, nor do they believe even when they stand outside and invite them in. A piece of bread with water is given them daily; some send them something eatable. I saw no shrub, still less any tree; but sandy and rocky places.

Many of them said they were desirous of being instructed and thus of rejecting that faith, but in vain; 218-1 the inrooted faith clung to them because it had been the principle of their life. What is marvelous, the learned of that religion regard justification by faith alone as such a Divine mystery, that touching it is like touching the pupil of the eye; saying that they have bound themselves to it by oath. But it was shown them that in the Revelation it is described by the beast from the sea [Rev. 13:1-10], and in Daniel by the little horn which waxed great towards all the quarters, and cast down from heaven the host thereof [Dan. 8:9-10]. But when they hear this confirmed from heaven, where correspondences are perceived, they still worship justification as their idol. The justification that is meant is justification by faith separate from charity. I also spoke much about the endeavor to do good which follows justification, asking them whether this endeavor is anything of the will on man's part. They said that it was: others said that it was not, but was to be carefully separated.

Some say that we have no free will, but that it was destroyed by Adam; that we have some freedom of belief or faith, but none of doing or acting. But it was shown them that no man, not even Adam, had freedom from himself, but only as if from himself; and that everyone has freedom to act from the Lord, thus to be led by the Lord: and that each one is in this freedom so far as he is led. 219-1

All those preachers who in the life of the body have confirmed themselves in faith alone, and who cannot recede therefrom on account of their life, are not admitted to preach. Their priestly garment is taken away from them, and afterwards they do not know that they have been preachers. Very many are admitted to preach, but as soon as they preach faith separate from charity, and justification by it alone, all who are present go out, and the temple becomes empty. Thus those preachers who can recede from that faith are amended, and receive the doctrine of heaven. The case is similar with those who separate the Lord from the Father and do not make them one, and what is new, all of them, after they have been in the spiritual world a month, reject the third Person, acknowledging that the Holy Spirit is the Lord speaking through angels and spirits. The reason why they reject is because enthusiastic spirits, Quakers and many others, who are infernal, call themselves the holy spirit from eternity. I have had much speech with them in respect to this matter, to the effect that they have rejected the third Person of the Divinity, and that now they think of two, in order that they may see, whether from the two they make one.

One whom I knew in the world, had confirmed himself in faith alone by many arguments. I said to him that he should go and see those habitations in the desert, and when he went he saw nothing but a sandy waste, with rough stones and rocks all around, but not a single shrub nor a blade of grass; and, therefore, returning, he grieved over their miserable lot. There also he met and spoke with some who in the world had been acknowledged by him as learned men. And when he still wished to defend faith alone there appeared serpents which darted at his feet and coiled themselves around them. He was afterwards led to plains where those dwelt who were in a similar faith, where there was grass, shrubs, trees and buildings, and the inhabitants were of a cheerful disposition, and industrious in their work and business. They confessed that they had merely known of that faith from having heard it preached, but had thought nothing about it beyond the literal sense, and had not confirmed it any further; and that still they had lived a life according to the Word; thus that the faith was only a faith of science in their memory, but not a faith in the life. They are afterwards instructed and receive truths which they had not known in the world.

A learned man, who, in the world, had thought solely about faith alone, was examined as to whether he knew any truth of the church, whether he knew what faith is, or what the life of faith, what charity is, what love, what truth and the affection and perception of truth, what free will, what regeneration, what spiritual temptation, what Baptism, what the Holy Supper, what is heaven with man, and what and whence is hell, wherein is the holiness of the Word, what Providence is, what God and whether He is one or three, what conscience is, also what is the church in man and what heaven in him. And the angels heard; [and they saw] that he knew nothing of these things. The responses which he made were falsities derived from reasonings, and were also things from the Word which had been falsified. It was said to him, How could he be in the light of heaven, and hence in angelic wisdom, and from this in the felicity of heaven? Being convicted, he wished to learn, but because he had confirmed faith alone he could not.

I spoke with angels concerning the progression of truth to good, saying that the angels have joy when an infant or boy learns truths and acquires them from affection, thus when truths become truths of knowledge; they have greater joy when they become truths of the understanding, still greater when they become of the will, and the greatest joy when they become of the act. Then they love him because truths have taught him and led him to good. And they are gladdened when he knows that it is not truths which lead to good, but that it is good which leads him into truth and thus into wisdom. Man does not know this, but the angels perceive it and rejoice.

How Englishmen who wish to acquire a reputation for erudition compose their discourses with great elegance and as it were profound wisdom, especially concerning the influx of faith, and the endeavor to the doing of good, and of man's state then as to affection, reception and enlightenment by the Holy Spirit. Some of the English complained, saying that these elegancies delight their ears and are pleasing to them while they listen; but when they wish to apply anything therefrom to themselves they know not what the preachers have said, and whether it is allowable to adjoin the will, and thus to openly will, and act, or not. When they ask them, they say such sounding words as, that they may, and may not, and finally that it is a transcendent mystery. They speak in this manner so that their hearers, being able to gather either meaning from them, may praise them. And yet, by reason of these words with their double meaning in which something lies hidden like a snake in the grass, those hearers do not love them. They tell them that they should remain in the doctrine that is taught in the exhortation used at the Holy Supper, and that if they do not so from the will, the devil will, perchance, enter into them as he entered into Judas. Their discourses are also filled with the perception of trust and confidence in themselves.

I have sometimes heard it said from heaven that that faith saves no one because there is no life in it; and that true faith is truth; and that man has truth only so far as he shuns evils as sins. Particulars concerning the Decalogue and its Holiness, —See Spiritual Experiences.

The truths of faith are compared with the ornaments and utensils in palaces; unless man lives according to them they are, as it were, in a dark room with the windows shut, but as soon as a man lives according to them he is then elevated into heavenly light, the windows are opened, and he then sees those things and is delighted with them.

CONCLUSION. Lastly, it shall be told what the state of man is after death, whatsoever his religion may have been. They who have led a good life, who are such as have shunned evils because they are sins, and have conducted their business with rectitude and sincerity, are not let into the evils of their will, but are held by the Lord in good, and in intelligence and wisdom therefrom. But they who have lived in evil, are let into the evils of their will, and then they can think in no other way than in agreement with those evils; and when in that state, they appear as if insane, more like beasts than men. The love of doing evil then rules them, and they now rush into all things which they have coveted. They who have been in the love of ruling for the sake of self are more insane than others. I have seen many such spirits, and they appear as if utterly deprived of all rationality; and yet they then believe that they are wise, yea, the wisest of all. But it is allowed them at times to return into the rationality which they had in the world, when, from shrewdness, they had feigned themselves gifted with every virtue. Still, even then, the pleasure of returning into the delight of their will draws them on so that they cannot be led away except unwillingly; they wish to be insane. And because they are of such a character they are sent into hells, and then it is not permitted them to go out. And they there remain under the supervision of a judge who imposes tasks on them which they must do daily. If they do not perform them, they receive neither food, clothing, nor bed; and if they do evil they are severely punished. Thus by means of adequate tasks they are led away from the delights of their will. In such a prison all are held, both men and women, who have lived in evil, that is, who have given reins to their sins. But before they go, they are deprived of everything which they had formerly learned from the Word, and of everything which they had known concerning faith, and also of the knowledge of who they had been in the world, whether kings or magistrates, bishops or elders, rich or poor, or of the common people. And they are then all alike among themselves, nor is one greater than another. A low countryman may be together with an eminent man, nor does either know who had been the more eminent in the world; for elation of the mind exists equally with those who are of the common people as with those who are in the highest places. And, what is wonderful, they cannot go out to all eternity; for if, perchance, they put forth a foot, they are punished; and if they are taken out by others they become more insane than before. I have sometimes seen this done. They are like robbers who, from fear of punishment, live honestly in a house in a city, but as soon as they come into the woods they constantly think about robberies.

All the states of man can be recalled after death, the states of age, as the state of childhood, of adolescence and of youth; they who come into heaven come into the state of their adolescence, return into all the states of innocence, charity and affection with all their delights, and this with ineffable increase. With those who have lived well good states are recalled, with those who have lived in evil, evil states, concerning which various things have been said above.

That at this day they crucify the Lord, see Lord; and that they are like the Jews in their time: experience.

LOVE. From the ideas of spirits passing into the world of spirits after death, may be known all the ideas which they have had concerning God, heaven, love, and faith. Concerning God most of them have an idea as of a cloud or mist, because they have thought that God is a spirit, and of a spirit they have no other idea. Concerning heaven they have the idea that it is in the air, some that it is in the stars, others that it is in the universe, and scarcely any that it is with man; for they cannot remove the idea of space. Concerning heavenly joy they have ideas of delight, each one of the delight of his own love, especially of the delight of ruling and of living happily and continually in external luxuries. Few have an idea of living in internal delights; not knowing what they are. Concerning love they have so gross an idea that you may call it filthy. They think from the delight of the love of adultery. Some have no idea of love, because they have not known what love is. And so concerning mutual love; some have an idea of external friendship. In a word, all their ideas of love partake of the idea of lasciviousness. Concerning faith they have no other idea than as of the received faith, the quality of which has been spoken of above.

This is no idea of genuine faith since it is an idea of faith separated from charity, and what this is, is unknown. When the angelic idea concerning God, heaven, love, and faith flows in, if it is not perceived, it becomes in their minds like an obscure darkness; for the light of heaven does not enter in. Such, from faith alone, is the world at this day. For when that faith enters in and is received, then nothing of truth is loved. They say, "In this faith I know the truths of our church in one complex."

After death man comes into the world of spirits which is intermediate between heaven and hell; and there he changes his societies, and is thus prepared either for heaven or for hell. This change appears like a transference from one place to another, and also like a journey. He goes to various quarters, now ascending to higher regions, now descending to lower; and yet it is perceived that these journeys are only changes of state. This has been the case with me when I have been in the spirit. And at last when the man has been prepared, then that love leads him which is the head of his other loves. And he then turns his face to the society where his ruling love is, and thither he betakes himself as to his own home.

The knowledges of truth are inscribed on the affection or love, so that it is the affection that produces them as though they had been known to it. Affection sees those things which are consonant and concordant with itself, for some have the faculty of confirming. Wherefore if the affection is good, and it becomes good by means of life, it straightway has inscribed on it the knowledges which serve it; and when it hears and sees them, then, from things in itself which are similar and analogous, it discerns them; this therefore is of the love. But he who is in faith alone and in the love of self and the world, cannot be affected by other things than those which agree with his love; these are inscribed on his love. They are contrary to the truths of faith, which are: That God should be loved above oneself, heaven above the world, the good of the neighbor, and every use for the neighbor, and the like [above self]. The truths of faith are then cast out, which is also actually the case after death, and those things remain which are of the love, or, which are of the will.

All who are in the love of ruling for the sake of self and not for the sake of uses, retain that love after death; and wheresoever they come they wish to rule. This love rushes on as its bonds are relaxed. It spurns everything Divine, unless this afford it the means of ruling; in which case, so long as it serves as a means, it loves it; but when it does not serve as a means it not only rejects it but also holds it in hatred. The reason is, because this love is opposite to heavenly love. They are not admitted into heaven, and if, like hypocrites, they insinuate themselves into heaven they fill the whole neighborhood with an idea and image of themselves, and this even when they speak of God. This love turns aside the ideas of the angels, which are directed away from themselves and towards God; therefore they are driven away. This has been shown. For the most part they are corporeal because immersed in the proprium, and not elevated above it. Such spirits are taken to the boundaries of the world of spirits of our earth where there appears a lake smoking with fire; and first the spirit is rolled in the dust and let into his life in the world, and thus he is cast into the lake.

Let all who are in the world and read these lines know that the love of ruling for the sake of self and not for the sake of uses is diabolical love itself and in it are all evils. Let them know this and be on their guard. All evil loves are in that love and with it, even those of which the man had been wholly ignorant while in the world. I have examples in all abundance, showing that those who, in external form, appear to be moral and Christian men but interiorly in themselves have thought of nothing else but themselves and the world, after death are consociated with devils. There was one whom I saw during a long period of time, who was so haughty in his disposition that hardly anyone could be more haughty; and yet in the world he could talk with theologians and speak morally with other men; and he feigned justice and equity more than anyone else. But after death he became such a fiery devil that he not only denied God, but he also wished to be the devil himself, in order that he might continually fight against God and destroy heaven; and he was enflamed with hostility against all who were in the acknowledgment of the Lord. He was punished frequently, but in vain. If I should mention his deeds of malice, cunning, and crimes I would fill pages. In him I saw what the devil is, both in his own hell and with men (C. XII.). 234-1 Such men do not acknowledge God, but believe all are gods who are powerful; and they wish to become gods themselves, and be worshipped.

There was once some conversation respecting the love of ruling, to the effect that many believe that those who worship the Lord in the world, although they are His enemies, [will be saved and will rule over all in heaven]. 235-1 And it was said that a devil can be driven to worship the Lord, if only he be promised that he will be great, and still more if he would thereby become the greatest. It was then permitted that they should take from hell one of the devils there, who was most bitterly hostile to the Lord; and it was told him that he would be made the greatest by the Lord. He then put his whole mind to this object, and this to such a degree that he wished to lead all men to the Lord and to drive them by threats; saying, that the Lord alone should be honored and worshipped, and repeating it with earnestness and persuasion; but in his mind he cherished the thought that he would become the Lord's vicar. When, however, he saw that he had been deluded, he began to detest the Lord, and became as before, His most bitter enemy; but he was cast into hell. In a word, the delight of commanding exceeds every delight of the body.

Concerning the two rules or dominions, one from the love of self, the other from love towards the neighbor, see in the work on Heaven and Hell, in The Doctrine of the New Jerusalem, and in the little work on The Earths in the Universe, all of which works may be adduced.

With those who are in the love of commanding, the interiors appear black, and this because they are closed against the influx of heaven; but their inferiors appear as it were misty because they are opened to the hells. 237-1 It is said that with those who are in the love of ruling, the superiors, thus the interiors, can never be opened towards heaven.

There were seen men who belonged to the nobility of various nations. They had cordons lying over their breasts suspended from the shoulders, and also diadems. A number of them were seen. And being inspected by angels it was observed that they were continually directing their looks to themselves, and were thinking about their own superior eminence and excellence, and desiring that all men should turn their eyes to them. And because they believed that they were more worthy of being set over others than other men, therefore offices were given them. But when they were making conclusions with respect to subjects that concerned the common welfare, it was then perceived that they had no affection for the community, nor for uses; thus they were unable from judgment to discern good from evil, or truth thence from falsity, but could only speak in a high-sounding manner from the memory. And because they were of such a character they were cast out of their offices; and it was allowed them to wander about and get offices for themselves. But wherever they came they were told by the spirits there that they were thinking only of themselves and not of them, thus that they had no thought except what was from the sensual corporeal; therefore they were nowhere received. They did this for some time, afterwards I saw some of them reduced to extremities and seeking alms. Thus is the love of ruling brought low. One spirit who also wore the insignia of a nobleman confessed that as long as he wore that insignia he could not think as before, because he was interrupted by thought concerning himself; but whenever he was at home and put it off, he returned to his own judgment as before. 238-1 Diabolical spirits are skilled in the art of seducing the upright. They do this by turning their thoughts to themselves and their own proprium; by praising them in various ways; by placing themselves at their back and breathing into them the love of self; and where they observe anything black, which is the proprium, they inquire what is there; they then infuse it with their own thought and pervert, yea lead him. Some look into the forehead and act in like manner; others proceed in a different way. 238-2 Wherever blackness appears, there is the love of ruling, because this blackness is the proprium.

Love, which is of man's will, corresponds to flame, and faith, which is of the thought from the understanding, corresponds to light, this is derived from the Lord's influx from love and wisdom, or from the sun of heaven. From this sun proceed Divine love and Divine wisdom, love into the will and wisdom into the understanding. But only so much of intelligence [is received] as there is of love; just as is the case with light from flame.

They who worship the Lord from love, worship Him from all the truths of faith; therefore the more the truths the fuller and more acceptable is the worship. The reason is, because love excites all the things which have entered from love into the understanding. When the man is in worship only those things appear before him which he then speaks or prays, but all the rest are in vain and not in their series. When love produces truths, then these latter are disposed by the Lord into the form of heaven, and the man then adores the Lord as it were from heaven. This has been made known to me from experience in the spiritual world. When I see anyone, all those things come up which I know and have heard about him. The angels see these in their series, and so forth. Hence it is evident of what quality is the worship of the Lord by those who, from love to Him, are in genuine truths.

For the sake of instruction it sometimes happens that one spirit is allowed to change the affections in another, even into contrary affections; and according to the changes of his affections his face is changed so that it becomes wholly unrecognizable; there is also induced a monstrous form of face and also blackness according to the affections. Moreover, the body also is changed, becoming taller or shorter, taller from haughtiness and pride, and shorter from humility and the disparagement of self. It thence became evident that affection or love makes the man from head to foot. A like change takes place when a spirit is carried transversely through various societies, which was also seen, so that at length he is not recognized. Hence it is evident that he is altogether such as his love is. It was also shown that faith, which is of the thought, conjoined to corporeal love, and which also is various, makes man to be deformed according to the kind of love, and therefore in order that faith may be faith, it must be conjoined to spiritual affection.

The quality of the delight of the love of commanding was perceived, namely, that the sweetness within it is ineffable. From this sweetness man believes that it is heaven and heavenly joy, when yet it is hell. This delight is also turned into what is direful. It is similar with the love of doing evil, the love of hatred and revenge, the love of theft, and also the love of adultery, and their delights. Man does not know that when, by means of reformation by the Lord, these delights recede, then for the first time the delights of heaven enter in; which delights infinitely surpass the former. Nor does he know that the delights of those evils are then undelightful and stinging. Before reformation he does not know that such is their quality.

I saw many who had lived in this and former centuries, some of them military officers, of higher and lower rank, and others civil functionaries, all of whom, under the favoring influence of fortune, had contracted such a delight of commanding that they aspired to dominion over all things. Their delight was perceived as being to them like heaven. Moreover, they were gifted, above others, with talent and natural light in regard to civil affairs. After their decease, they had at first spoken about God; but after a short time they not only denied God and acknowledged nature; but at last they became like fools, sitting in dark shade; and in this way they led a miserable life. The reason is because the love of commanding is opposite to heavenly love.

After death every man is bound to many societies according to the number of his loves; but after vastation he comes into that society where his ruling love is, for this is the center of his other loves.

There was a certain man (Fr. G.) 245-1 who in his boyhood had cultivated piety, and who remained therefrom in the acknowledgment of God even to the end of his life. And yet under the favoring influence of fortune he came into the love of commanding and hence into evils of every kind. He did not indeed perpetrate them, but still he excused them and accounted them lawful. In the other life he prayed to God as he had done in the world, and with such fervor that scarcely anyone could pray more ardently; but it was to God the Father, for he believed that by doing this all things were forgiven him. But he began to burn with such hatred against the Lord that he denied Him; and afterwards he persecuted those who adored the Lord. At last he denied God and became like a fool; and he was sent among those who have little life.

They who are in the delight of the love of commanding cannot become spiritual. They become corporeal for the reason that they immerse everything of affection and hence of thought in their proprium, which in itself is corporeal and evil, so that they cannot be withdrawn from the proprium. Everyone who acknowledges God in heart, is elevated above his proprium; for man cannot look to God, acknowledging Him in heart, from himself; and he who cannot be elevated above his proprium has heaven closed to him. And since through heaven there flows in from the Lord intelligence, because it is spiritual light, therefore when heaven is closed they become stupid and like fools.

I once saw what kind of love to the Lord exists among Christians at this day. A number of them were let into their loves; and in phantasy it was granted them to see as it were the Lord. 247-1 And they then came into such fury that they wished to drag down and slay Him. They were all in faith alone, and, at the time, in the love of self. Thence it became evident that in the Christian world at this day they are against the Lord as were the Jews of old. In a word, all who are in faith alone and in the love of self and the world, and hence in evils, come into fury if they merely feel the Lord's Divine sphere.

THE JEWS. Before the Last Judgment, the Jews, for the most part, were at the left in the plane of the heel. I have often spoken with them there. They were then under the middle region where is the Christian world. 248-1 But after the Last Judgment they were driven away, and now being removed to the left, they dwell there in certain cities where the streets appear filled with filth and impurities, and where the houses are undergoing continual variation. This arises from the fact that newcomers are ever arriving and departing. They are there explored in order to find out who among them are able to acknowledge the Lord as the Messiah, whom they still look for in the world, and who are not. The former are taken to synagogues where they are instructed.

In that city an angel with a rod sometimes appears on high; and he gives them to believe that he is Moses. He exhorts them to desist from their madness in expecting the Messiah, when yet the Messiah is Christ, who, being now one with the Father, rules the whole heaven; adding that He knows this Himself, because He had known it in the world. They hear what he says; and when they depart those who cannot acknowledge, because of their life, forget it, but they retain it in their memory who can.

Of Abraham they have a Divine idea; of Jacob, and also of their fathers they have some Divine idea, but a lesser one. There is always set over them by the Lord, some converted Jew in whom Judaism lies hidden within or in the heart, and Christianity, without or in the mouth; and he is taught by certain angels from the Lord, in order that he may rule them according to their genius and disposition.

Footnotes
218-1 See SE 6023.
219-1 See SE 6024
234-1 See SE 4748, 4884.
235-1 The words in brackets are supplied from a corresponding passage in SE 4817.
237-1 See AC 1507.
238-1 See SE 5461 1/2.
238-2 See SE 5463.
245-1 See Se 5976, 5977.
247-1 See SE 4725.
248-1 See T 841.

They still retain from the world the carrying on of trade, especially in precious stones. These by certain methods they procure from heaven; for thence come precious stones, of which much more might be said. For in heaven are all things which are in the world. There is gold and silver there, also gold and silver in the form of coins, and also stones of every kind. Like all other things which appear before their eyes; they are from a spiritual origin, and hence are correspondences. They appear just as in the world. Divine truths are their origin; and therefore, with those angels who are in truths, the decorations in the houses are resplendent with silver and gold, and diamonds. Precious things of this kind are given from heaven to those below who are studious of truths; and because of their origin they also remain forever. The Jews get them from these and sell them. The reason why Jews have this business in the world, and also after their departure from the world, is because they love the Word of the Old Testament in the letter, and the literal sense of the Word corresponds to precious stones of various kinds. It is this sense that is meant by the twelve stones in Aaron's ephod, which were the Urim and Thummim; by the precious stones in Tyre, concerning which in Ezekiel; and by the precious stones with which the foundations of the wall of the New Jerusalem were adorned. Now because it was foreseen by the Lord that Christians would not hold the Old Testament so holy as do the Jews, therefore, the Jews have been preserved up to this day, and have been scattered throughout the whole Christian world, in order that the Word might still be in its holiness by means of correspondences. This also is the reason why it is still allowed the Jews to trade with similar things as in the world. If there had not been this reason, that whole nation, by reason of its perversity, would have perished.

There are also those who make precious stones for themselves artificially, so that they can scarcely be distinguished from the genuine. But these, when they are found out, are severely punished; they are put into a prison where they suffer harsh things, and are cast into the hells.

The Jews have no other delights than to acquire gain. Of interior delights they have no knowledge. Most of them are external men.

I have often spoken with the Jews on various subjects, namely, Concerning their sacrifices, that they refer to things heavenly; and in what way their various sacrifices signify the Lord. Concerning Isaac, why he might have been sacrificed by Abraham; and that these things had not been disclosed to them in the world because they were so external that they would not have received, for they were not willing to receive; and that they would have profaned them. Concerning the things which are contained in the fifty-third chapter of Isaiah. At this they became altogether silent; for the chapter was explained, so that they could make no answer. They were afraid lest it should be read again, for they were not willing to be convinced. Concerning eternal life, that it consists in the unanimity of all and in joy therefrom; and that as for them, they are at enmity with each other and thus cannot have the felicity of heaven. They answered, that they look for the Messiah who will unite them. I spoke with them about the signification of Jacob's sinew which was put out of joint, about Esau's heel which Jacob caught hold of, and about the heel which the serpent bruised, that these signify themselves; about their origin from a Canaanitish woman, and from whoredom with a daughter-in-law. And it was explained what all these signify, and that the things there meant are such as are signified. Then that the Jews and their tribes mentioned in the Word are not they but are things celestial and spiritual. I spoke about the land of Canaan, to the effect that they believe they are to be introduced into that land by the Messiah when He comes; that He will walk before them with a rod, and will dry up the rivers; that a wall of fire will be round about them; that they will go through Christendom, and that Christians will take hold of their garments and beg to be allowed to follow them; and that they will admit these and hold them as slaves provided they give their money; and many similar things. They were asked whether the dead and those in the world of spirits are also to follow the Messiah, or whether it is only those who are in the world; whether the land of Canaan would be able to hold them; where the Messiah was to be born; whether they knew the line of David, or the situation of Bethlehem; and many similar questions; why they look for an earthly kingdom when the kingdom of the Messiah is a heavenly one, which those who have now departed from the world might know. All this was said and heard. Those of them who were evil could not be convinced, but some who were upright wished to be instructed. It was explained to them what the land of Canaan signifies, and what Jerusalem; why these are called holy; what Zion signifies; what the twelve tribes represent and hence signify; also the passages where it is said that they who had been in captivity would return, to the effect that it was by no means they who were meant, but that it was so written on account of the spiritual sense in each particular. I spoke with them about the spiritual sense; at which they first said that they knew there was a mystical sense in the Word, and that they knew that mystical sense, which was that they receive gold and that they are able to make gold. To which I answered that, mystically, that is, spiritually, this is also true, because gold signifies the good of love, and they who are in that mystical or spiritual sense of the Word, receive this love. But they wanted gold, not love, saying that the possession of gold is love. 254-1

Before the Last Judgment they called the two cities Jerusalem. But after the Judgment they changed the name by command; because the name Holy Jerusalem, mentioned in Revelation, then came everywhere into general use; by which is signified the New Church into which none shall enter who does not make the Messiah one with Jehovah, thus only he who worships the Lord alone. The Jews are treated of in the Arcana Coelestia.

The Jews strive much after heaven, believing that heaven is theirs, and that to inherit the land is to inherit heaven, that the land of Canaan is in heaven, and that the Messiah is with them. They marvel that He does not descend to them from heaven, but I answered that He does not will to do this because there is so much discord among them and such enmities and hatreds, and contempt for others; and because they pray to the God of Israel not for the sake of salvation but that they may become rich.

Those of them who are evil are cast down into the hells which are under their great tract; many into woods and deserts where they commit robbery, but still they are miserably punished. The Word is taken away from them.

They have been preserved also for the sake of the Hebrew language. They also have the Word written in the ancient Hebrew language where all the letters are curved, because in such a letter the Word has a more immediate communication with heaven.

THE TEN COMMANDMENTS. Ten articles, what is effected with man when he fights against evils as sins, as before.

Then the commandments of the Decalogue, where the evils are which are sins, against which one must fight. —Then of the spiritual which is then given to him, and in which he also comes; there is the spiritual there in every precept.

What charity is, is; it is to do uses, everyone in his own function.

What faith out of charity is, and what faith from charity is.

Something concerning faith separated from charity, what its quality is when man is in it both as to life and doctrine.

OBSERVATIONS CONCERNING FAITH. In a particular small work faith will be treated of, thus concerning faith separated from charity, after the work on the Last Judgment, in which all things will be described by articles, which are:

What charity and faith are.

One cannot be separated from the other. There is no charity where there is no faith, and there is no faith where there is no charity.

As far as there is one, so far there is the other, in equal degree and in equal quality.

Faith is truth.

Faith does not produce charity, but charity faith. —Before there is charity, those things which are supposed to be of faith, are only knowledges without life.

Faith without charity is not possible. —Faith without charity is no religion. —Faith without charity falsifies the Word. —Faith without charity blinds all the understanding of truth. —It is the end of the church when there is not the faith of charity. —Every church ends in Babylon, and in faith separate. —Faith separate from charity is predicted in the Apocalypse, and is meant by the dragon and his two beasts. —Faith without charity is meant by the he-goat in Daniel and in Matthew. —Faith without charity is meant by Philistea. —Faith without charity is meant by Cain. —Faith without charity is meant by Reuben. —Faith from charity, also faith without charity, is meant by Peter. —Charity is meant by James, and the works of charity by John.

The quality of the faith of the present day is to be presented, such as it is, and the degrees of justification such as they are, they are to be described briefly, and that it is the whole of theology at the present day, also that if it is confirmed there arise many falsities, but not if it is not confirmed.

The will is double, spiritual and natural. Knowledges are the storehouse of faith. All things of faith can be seen. Falsities of faith are not faith. Faith is truth.

. THE LAST JUDGMENT. What the Last Judgment is.

The Last Judgment has been effected three times.

The Last Judgment was effected and is effected by the Lord from firsts by ultimates.

The Last Judgment could not have been effected the second time, unless He Himself had come into the world, and by that as (in firsts) be also in ultimates.

Without the Last Judgment effected by Him, thus without His Coming into the world, no one of mortals could have been saved.

Unless the Lord had glorified His Human, even to its ultimates, no Last

Judgment could be effected at this day. —Thus hereafter no one could be saved.

After the Last Judgment a new church is always to be established and is established, and before [the Last Judgment] it could not be nor can it be.

Therefore it is predicted in the Apocalypse, that the New Jerusalem will descend from heaven after the Last Judgment, by which is meant the New Church.

No one is received in that church thus in heaven, after this except he who acknowledges God, one in Person and Essence, in whom is the Trinity, thus the Lord; and unless by some combats he has removed and shunned evils as sins against the Divine laws.

THE ENGLISH. The English have a double theology, one for the learned and one for the unlearned.

The preachers compose their discourses so that the learned understand their theology and the unlearned theirs, and this is done from a certain fear on account of reputation and favor on both sides.

To the question whether they believe that the theology for the unlearned is true, they reply that they do not know otherwise when they utter that prayer in their temples, but not so when they compose their discourses.

It is then said to them, that the reason they do not know otherwise at that time is from influx out of heaven; and that it is not so when they compose their discourses, is from influx from their proprium; because they then think concerning themselves, their own learning, and fame and favor there from.

VARIOUS THINGS CONCERNING THE SPIRITUAL WORLD. Various things concerning those things which are in the Spiritual World, from which some things have been quoted in the Continuation Concerning the Spiritual World. To Be Observed. LEIBNITZ AND WOLFF. I spoke with John Wolff and his preceptor Leibnitz concerning the simple substance and preestablished harmony.

Concerning the simple substance Leibnitz said, that his opinion concerning the monad was never like that of Wolff concerning the simple substance. He said that he indeed acknowledged monads as unities but that there were in them simpler and purer substances by which the monad was formed, from which changes of state existed therein; since if there were nothing therein, it would be nothing, in which there cannot be any change of state, for a vacuum admits of no change. Leibnitz therefore wondered that Wolff held that his monad, which he calls a simple substance, was created out of nothing, and that when divided it falls into nothing; and yet he had attributed changes of state to it; and also that he had called some existences simple substances, and which are in nature, which anyone can see are aggregations of substances, like the parts of the air and ether, the elements of metals, and also souls. Wolff said that he wished by his definitions of his simple substances to captivate the minds of theologians, who want it to be believed that all things have been created by God out of nothing, immediately; at that time not knowing that his followers, by confirming these principles in themselves, would close in themselves the ways to angelic wisdom, which nevertheless are founded on natural truths.

Concerning preestablished harmony, Leibnitz said, he had considered and deduced it from this, that thought acts as one with man's speech, countenance, and action; and at that time he had not thought of interior thought, from which many men do not speak nor act; and which with many combats with the exterior; and still less did he think of spiritual thought, into which man does not come until after death; then that he considered nothing else in the world but thought, which at that time he acknowledged in place of the soul; and he did not consider affection at the same time, from which and according to which he thinks. Therefore now, after he has been instructed by angels he confesses that he erred, and he knows that the case is altogether otherwise.

NEWTON. I spoke with Newton concerning a vacuum, and concerning colors.

Concerning a vacuum he said, that in the world he had believed in the existence of a vacuum; but when the angels perceived that he had an idea of a vacuum, as an idea of nothing, they turned themselves away, saying that they cannot bear the idea of nothing, since when there is an idea of nothing the idea of the essence of things perishes. And when the idea of the essence of things perishes, the idea of thought, understanding, affection, love, and of will with men and angels perishes, which things are not given in nothing. They asked him whether he believed that the Divine, whence is all angelic wisdom, and all intelligence to men in both worlds, the spiritual and the natural, is a vacuum, and thus that any Divine operation inflows through a vacuum into their vacuum and can present itself to perception. At that question he was disturbed. He replied that it cannot through an absolute vacuum, which is nothing, but through an apparent vacuum, because the Divine is the Esse itself of wisdom and love with the angels in heaven and with men in the world, and it fills all things. Also Esse itself and nothing are so contrary to each other, that if one be admitted the other cannot. Therefore the angels entreated that he and all those who cherished the idea of a vacuum as of nothing would desist from it, that they might be together, knowing that nothing of their life can ever be given in nothing, but in those things which are, and which are or exist from the Esse. They added that not anything can be said of a vacuum which is nothing, which has relation to acting, reacting, receiving, or attracting, thus to the life of their wisdom and love; in which there are so many infinite affections with their variations, perceptions, and sensations; for nothing is nothing, and of nothing we cannot predicate something. When he had heard these things, Newton said that before this he had desisted from that idea, and he would desist from it hereafter; knowing that he is now in the spiritual world, in which, nevertheless, according to his former idea, would have been his vacuum; and that even now he is a man, and therein he thinks, feels, acts, yea breathes, and this could not take place in a vacuum which is nothing, but in something which is, and from Esse exists and subsists, and that an interstitial nothing is impossible, because that would be destructive of something, that is of essences and substances which are something. For something and nothing are altogether opposites, even so that he was horrified at the idea of nothing, and would beware of it, lest his mind fall into a swoon.

Concerning colors he said that in the world he had believed that they originated from the substances, as it were, of different colored materials continually flowing forth from the solar ocean, and adding themselves continually to like things in objects in the world, likewise when they pass through pellucid objects following then the ways of light, according to its diffractions and refractions, and proceeding as like to like, thus red to red, blue to blue, yellow to yellow, and so on, as in prisms, crystalline globes, and vapors whence come rainbows. But the angels did not acknowledge this cause of colors, saying that there are colors in the spiritual world as well as in the natural world; and in the spiritual world they are vivid, splendid, and variegated more than in the natural world, and that they know that they are variegations of their light corresponding to their love or good, and to their wisdom or truth, and that the sun from which their light proceeds, is the Lord Himself, whose Divine love presents around Him the appearance of a sun, and the Divine wisdom therefrom the appearance of light, and that from that sun, which as was said, is pure love, no such substances or matters flow forth, but that pure light presents to view variegations of colors in objects according to the reception of wisdom by the angels; the color red according as their wisdom is derived from good, and the color bright white according as their wisdom is derived from truth, and the rest as they partake of the defect and absence of them, which there correspond to shade in the world. Moreover the angels, by their spiritual ideas, by which they are able to present and bring forth the causes of things to the life and to full consent, demonstrated that colors are nothing else than variegations of flamy light and bright white light, in objects according to their forms; and that colors are not materials, so neither is light, because they correspond to the love and wisdom of the angels, from whom they proceed by Divine operation; and their love and wisdom are not material but spiritual. Neither are heat and light in the world material, but natural, and they inflow into matters, and they modify themselves in them according to the forms of the parts. Therefore neither are colors material, as they would be if they existed from different colored atoms. At length from some indignation they said, "Who cannot see a paradox in the Newtonian cause, yea what is absurd?" And they departed, saying they would return if he would discern spiritually or even naturally concerning colors, and not so materially and sensually. Then some spirits approached, and said to him, "We entreat you to think of colors not as originating from some small prism or from some wall, but from the green color of all the woods and grassy fields of the whole world in which you were; can you conceive of a continuous efflux from the sun of a green color alone, and at the same time an influx, and a continual restoration, likewise of a continual influx of gray or stone color into the mountains of the whole earth, and so on? Can you then conceive of a continuous ocean of green alone, and of rock color alone? Tell us where they go, where they subsist, do they proceed into the universe? Or do they fall downwards somewhere, or ascend upwards? From these things perchance new earths exist, for they must be in great abundance because they are material." After he thought of this thing more deeply, he said, "Now I know that colors are modifications of light in objects, in the forms of which they make general planes, upon which the light is variegated according to the forms of the parts, whence are colors." These are the words of Newton himself, which he wishes me to communicate.

LONDON. London in the spiritual world appears like the London in the natural world as to its streets and quarters, but is dissimilar as to houses and habitations; this difference is not apparent, because everyone there dwells in a quarter and in a house corresponding with his affection and thought thence derived. In the middle of the city is situated the Royal Exchange. To the right of it dwells the moderator, and round about it his officers. The middle street of it answers to Holborn; the east is in front, toward the back even to Wapping is the west; the south is at the right of that street; and the north is on its left. In the eastern quarter, which is of considerable length, reaching far beyond the city, dwell the best of them, where they all worship the Lord. Those who are distinguished for intelligence dwell in the southern quarter which extends almost to Islington, where there is also an assembly. They who dwell there are also prudent in speaking and writing. Towards the north those dwell who are illiterate, and who are in the greatest degree of liberty of speech which they love. In the west are those who are in the obscure affection of good. Those who are there are fearful of manifesting their thoughts. In the southern region answering to Moorfield's and round about it, is a promiscuous multitude; thither from the city are sent away all those who incline to evils, wherefore the multitude there is cast out by turns, and thus continually, through this way the city is continually purified, and those who are led away therefrom appear no more. Sometimes they see about the middle of the city a certain malicious person sitting on a seat in a pulpit, and the inhabitants are called together and ordered to go thither to him. They who approach and hearken are led to the place of exit, where there are promiscuous crowds, and as was said, they are sent out through the ways there. Every society is purified, this is the manner of purifying them there. Their houses, clothing, and food are similar to those used in the world. I asked about wine, strong drink, beer, chocolate, tea and the like, and was told that they had similar things. I asked also about the liquor called punch, they said that they also have that liquor, but it is given only to those who are sincere and at the same time industrious. They do not tolerate in the city any ruler who directs or dictates to them what they must do, for they wish to be in full liberty.

The English live together, and do not travel about in other regions, for they are of a different genius and disposition from others, and their disposition is such, that they do not admit others into intimacy with them.

It was also shown to them that they speak, write and think spiritually, and that they themselves do not know otherwise than that they do all things naturally; from which they were instructed by me that there is no ratio between the spiritual and the natural, thus there is no conjunction through what is continuous, but through what is discrete, that is, by correspondences; which conjunction makes a likeness as if they are one. They were a little envious that they had not discovered this. Moreover in each degree there is an internal and an external, and the external corresponds to the internal, and the externals are appearances like material things, although they are not material. It was shown to them also by ascent to the third heaven, that there is a similar difference between the celestial and the spiritual, as there is between the spiritual and the natural so that there is no ratio between them, that is, the natural cannot become spiritual by any continuous purification, nor can the spiritual become celestial, thus not by any approximation, but it is like the difference between cause and effect or between the soul and the body.

I afterwards spoke with them concerning priests. And I saw that there is one kind of priests that supposes they are more erudite and learned than others. These all dwell in the west, and when they come to preach, they go forth from the west a little into the north, and so towards the middle of the city to the temples. This is a sign that they go in the way of taciturnity and ignorance, for in the west those dwell who are taciturn, and there near to the north those who are ignorant of truth. They appear to themselves to preach learnedly and with erudition, because they preach about the Divine operation into the actions of men, when they are justified; thus concerning the effort, which is the fourth degree of justification, which inflows into the act with men, they themselves being ignorant of it, and that the voluntary of man is not present, since that is evil. The hearers complained of them that they cannot understand them whether they wish them to act of themselves or not; because they can take both senses from their ambiguous teachings. It was perceived that they wish such discourses to sound learned before preachers and bishops, and that they do not dare to preach otherwise before them. But there are also preachers who dwell in the south, who altogether preach that they must shun evils as from themselves, and that they must do goods as from themselves; but that still they must know that they are not from themselves, thus the citizens love these; they speak in harmony with the prayer before the Holy Supper.

In the suburbs at the left dwell many of their learned and with them Newton, they go down thither by a sloping way.

In a word they who teach according to their prayer at the Holy Supper, dwell in the south towards the east, and they are loved because they think as they preach, the rest do not, but dispute continually with them, and reply that they cannot do otherwise. I saw them recede to their habitations in the west, which are at the right side there where there is a place of exit, and some also are led out.

It was said of those preachers in the west, that they do not care to know evils or sins, because God knows, and not they, nor do they wish to know from affection any other knowledges than what confirm their faith. They despise those who are in the south and east as simple, who as it were with their thought are low; and that their thought is not elevated but depressed, when yet it is altogether contrary.

I heard a conversation with presbyters in the west, which was effected by representatives. On one side the devil with hell was represented, on the other side the Lord with heaven, and then it was said, that the devil or hell dwells in the evils with man, and that the Lord with heaven is in the goods with him. Then that the Lord through heaven continually drives away the devil with hell. But the man who excuses his evils, and who lives in them, retains with himself the devil with hell, nor does he permit him to go away, although the Lord drives him away. Also the devil then speaking with him, says what need is there to know evils, so as to combat against them, when God does that? and so he confirms man, therefore he is retained and thus they live together as friends; besides many similar things. Also the devil by that faith confirms them, saying what need is there of other knowledges, than those which belong to that faith? they are of no help; what need is there to know evils, because man from himself cannot combat against them? What need is there of combats, because man of himself can do nothing? When nevertheless everything of life, everything of reason, and everything of freedom man has from the Lord, and He wills that man should act as of himself, and without man's cooperation as of himself, the evil remains, and the devil with evil, etc.

Those priests in the west complained that those who were in faith alone, or in faith separated, disappeared, saying that they do not know where they went, some said that they saw some in the hells.

Footnotes
254-1 See T 845; SE 2256, 2257, 4388.

THE MORAVIANS. I do not write of those who are in the world, but of those who are out of the world, I spoke with these and I heard. They are mere Arians, and deny the Divine of the Lord, saying that He has the Divine, such as man has. When it was said to them that He was conceived of Jehovah, they come together, nor do they wish easily to admit it, wishing to deny the Scripture lest they should be refuted; but still they say something that the Jews do. Others when they are convinced, say that He was born that He might be adopted. They confirm themselves by the Lord's word that in His freedom He was left to suffer the cross, not knowing why this was done. They say that they love Him, because He took it upon Himself to suffer the cross, and also because it is commanded by the Father, then especially because He is loved by the Father on account of the passion of the cross. They reject the Old Testament as no longer for them but for the Jews. They also despise the Gospels, saying that the Lord is spoken of as a simple man, and thus that there is nothing Divine in them. Concerning faith in Him spoken of in the Gospels, they say that He so wished it, and that it ought not speak thus. They acknowledge the Epistles of Paul only, and also the historicals of the Word, but they do not believe in the holiness of the Word. They say concerning good works and charity, that they ought not to be together with faith, and that they shudder at doing good works for the sake of heaven, and that in their heaven they would rather adopt the most malevolent than such; in a word they condemn them to hell. In speaking they utter the greatest fallacies; they speak with each one according to his heart in religion. They guard lest those mysteries should be disclosed; the rest which are concerning the Holy Supper and Baptism they think and teach violently. They are such things as do not agree with the faith of the Reformed, nor do they admit to the Holy Supper any others than those who receive those three mysteries, because they have confirmed them. From these things it is evident that they are among the worst who profess Christianity. They make much of their sensation, but it was shown to them, that their sensation is with their spirits, who were enthusiastic spirits from their assembly in the world, who come nearer to them, who think much of their religion and love it, saying that they are more loving and happy than others. These confirm them very greatly, thence is their sensation.

They are held in the lower earth to the left in a society separated from the rest; because they are among themselves, and they are a society of interior friendship, which if it should be in the neighborhood of others, they would destroy their delights. They recede by turns from that society towards the left, into a desert which is for them alone, where there is no grass, where there are crags and cliffs.

THE DUTCH. How formally and courteously they invite their wives and bring and lead them to their house, and show how well it is with those who act together in unity in their houses, and also how clean and well furnished their houses are; and on the contrary how unclean those are where there is the dominion of one over the other; savory food is also given those who act in unity, and they are taught by these things the quality of their delight when one is of the other mutually and reciprocally. Therefore when they see those things and apperceive them to be true they desist from dominion; and then they obtain a habitation nearer to the middle, and are led into a house better furnished. The reason is that there is then conjugial love, which regarded in itself is celestial love itself.

THE MORAVIANS IN LONDON, THE HERRENHUTERS AND THE JEWS. The Moravians dwell in the furthest corner of the place of exit mostly at the side there, but when they journey into the city as to their sanctuary, they appear to proceed towards the middle and thence a little to the south, and thus to their corner, which is done because they wish to appear to others as Christians, of a similar doctrine. Afterwards from their corner they go into the west where the presbyters are who are in faith alone, concerning whom we have before spoken, and they return thence. From their corner, which is as it were their inn there, they go out by turns, and descend into a vault which stretches deeply under the west, where the presbyters are of whom we have before spoken, and their hell is there, from which they are no longer let out, except some into deserts. It is not allowed them to dwell near others, nor elsewhere, because they form a society of interior friendship, which takes away the spiritual delight of others. They say to others that they should dwell here and there even to the middle, but still they dwell at that corner, of which they have an idea as of their inn. They appear in a way towards the middle, because they persuade that they are of the Anglican religion and speak with the English piously as if they were; and that they differ only as to ceremonials, which are like those of the Apostles. When they are asked why their preachers are clothed in blue, they say because that color is loved; nor do they dare to say that they should be clothed like the English preachers in a black gown, because they fear lest their mysteries should be disclosed. They very greatly fear to be sincere and just on account of religion. They are altogether averse to this, wherefore they are prone to all kinds of evils, taking care only lest they be discovered, because with others this would be hurtful to their religion.

Moreover the Jews do not dwell upon the earth in London, but under the earth there, on the northern side below, where Towerhill is. They enter there through a dark opening. And the citizens of the city do not know where they dwell.

THE LOVE OF KNOWING. The love of knowing is the external of the will, the use on account of which [it is done] is the internal of the will.

With infants and boys the external rules, in process of time the internal is formed. [Marginal Note:] Use of life makes the internal of the will originating from the sun of heaven. It [that is the exterior] is as in the time of winter, and like what is foul shining exteriorly.

Then there is formed the love of knowing for the sake of use, these are formed whether they are good or evil.

But the love of understanding whether a thing is true or not, and thence the love of being wise, is also the external of the will, originating from the light of heaven and its variegation.

This love, because it is the external of the will, can be separated from its internal, and then it is the love of one's own glory, on account of glory and not on account of any use then. Therefore it can be given also with the evil.

Or the external of the will in the understanding is the love of truth on account of glory, thus on account of the external.

THE JEWS. The Jews less than others know that they are in the spiritual world. They think there of the Messiah as they did in the world and expect Him. And they say that He will come. But when it is said to them that it will be in Bethlehem, and from the house of David, and they are asked where is Bethlehem now, and where is the house of David, they do not know how to answer other than that He knows where that city is, and where that family is. Some of them in the other life say that the Messiah is in heaven, and that He will not come to those in the spiritual world before He is born a boy in the world. When they are asked whether they only who are in the world will be led into Canaan, they reply that they will then return into the world, and they will dwell with them in the land of Canaan. When they are asked whether they will then be again born, they say they will not, but that they will descend to them, believing that thus they will be men like them. When they are asked whether Canaan will be capacious enough for all who have been born from that nation from the time of Abraham, they say that the land of Canaan will then be enlarged. When they are asked how the Messiah, the Son of Jehovah, can dwell with such evil persons, they say that they are not evil. When it is said that Moses in his song said that they were the worst, and do they read it and sing it as was commanded by Moses, they reply that Moses was angry when he wrote that, because they departed from him, and therefore they do not read it, but run through it quickly. When it is said to them that their origin is from a Canaanitess, and from whoredom with a daughter-in-law, they then are angry and depart, saying that it is enough that they are from Abraham and Jacob. They say that Moses and David will also return and go with the Messiah, one at His right and the other at His left. They narrate many fabulous things concerning the Messiah, how He will introduce them into the land of Canaan, and how rich Christians will follow them freely, if they give them their money. Nevertheless many of them who know that Christ who is the Messiah rules all things in the heavens, say that they wish to receive this, but cannot; they hear it from Moses, who sometimes appears above with a rod, and teaches this, and when they hear, they go away in various directions. They said to me, "Why did He suffer the cross?" I replied, "Because He was the greatest prophet, and therefore He carried the iniquities of the people, like the prophet who lay on his right side and on the left, and ate bread made of barley and filth, of whom it is said that he bore their iniquities; likewise other prophets, one who took a harlot to wife, who put on ashes, who went barefoot, who thus bore their iniquities; in like manner it is said of the Messiah" (Isa. 53). When they heard this they said that they would go off among themselves and consult together. They who have not become foul from filthy avarice, and who have not become devils from hatred, fraud and revenge, are tolerated below the heavens where their habitations are, because they regard the Word as holy, and they who suffer themselves to be instructed concerning the Lord, are transferred to societies where they are instructed, and are sent back to those who have not yet received. Their business is dealing in diamonds and precious stones as in the world. They procure them for themselves from heaven. They learn that they have that business, because they regard the Word as holy, because the sense of the letter corresponds to those stones and signifies them. Therefore the more holy they regard the Word, the better do they succeed there in that business.

DEGREES. There is a natural kingdom, a spiritual kingdom, and a celestial kingdom.

In the natural kingdom are men whilst they live in the world. In the spiritual kingdom are spiritual angels; in the celestial kingdom are celestial angels; for there are these three universals, the natural, the spiritual, and the celestial.

In each kingdom there are two degrees, in the natural two, in the spiritual two, and in the celestial two; thus in the three kingdoms there are six degrees. All these degrees are discrete, or discontinuous, and are called degrees of altitude. Discrete degrees are to each other as thought to speech, or as the affection to gesture, or as the affection of the mind to the countenance; and in the material world as the ether to the air, or as a nerve to the fibers of which it is composed. All compositions in the whole natural world and in the spiritual world are of this character, and they consist either of two or three degrees of this kind in their order. These degrees are called prior and posterior, higher and lower, interior and exterior; and, in general, they are as cause and effect, or as a substance and a substantiate, or as the aggregate from substances, or as a principle and the principiates, or the thing formed from principles.

There are also continuous or cohering degrees; each discrete degree has its continuous degree. The continuous degree of each discrete degree is as light verging to shade, and at length to the obscurity of night; and also as the rational thought which is in light to sensual and, as it were, at length to corporeal thought, which is in a dense shade according as it descends to the body. In such a degree continually decreasing is the human mind. In a similar degree, but lower; are man's sight, hearing, smell, taste, and touch; in like manner his speech and his singing; for man has a tone like the tone of a lyre, and like the sound of a drum. It is also similar with harmonies and beauties; for they proceed by continuous degrees from the highest harmony and beauty, to the least. These degrees are of the cause in itself and of the effect in itself; they are distinguished from the former degrees, because these are of the cause and the effect in themselves. Continuous degrees are called degrees of what is purer or grosser. An idea of these degrees can be had chiefly from light and shade, and also from the aerial atmosphere in its lower and higher regions; for in the lower region it is grosser, denser, and more compressed, and in the higher region it is purer, rarer, and more extended.

Unless one procures a knowledge of these two kinds of degrees, he cannot have an idea of the interiors and exteriors of man, thus neither of the soul and the body, nor indeed of causes and effects. Nor can he have an idea of the distinction between the heavens, nor of the wisdom of the angels in the heavens; nor can he have any idea of correspondences, of representatives, of influx, of order, thus he cannot have an idea of those things which are of order, both in the natural world and in the spiritual world, thus scarcely any just idea of anything.

Few hitherto have had any other idea of degrees than of continuous degrees, which is, as was said, from what is pure to what is gross, or from greatest to least. From which it follows that only one kind of degrees has been known, and that the natural degree and the spiritual degree are distinguished only as what is pure and gross; in like manner the difference between the heavens, and also in the wisdom of the angels. Whereas the difference is according to discrete degrees, the nature of which we shall presently show from experience.

There are, therefore, as stated above, six discrete degrees, two in the natural kingdom, two in the spiritual kingdom, and two in the celestial kingdom; but these degrees are those in which men and angels are, as to their thoughts, their affections, and their wisdom therefrom. Degrees are as follows: Below these six degrees of life, there follow similar degrees, and also material, even to the ultimate, and above those six degrees ascend degrees of the infinite even to the Divine itself. For the Divine itself cannot flow into any angel or man from itself but by discrete degrees; for if it flowed in immediately, or by what is continuous, both angel and man, from the ardor of the Divine love, and from the light of the Divine wisdom, would be entirely consumed. This would be as though the sun, of the world, from its fire, were to flow immediately into the objects of the earth, and not mediately through the atmospheres according to distinct discrete degrees.

There are three natural atmospheres arising from the sun of the world, and there are three spiritual atmospheres arising from the sun of heaven, which is the Lord. The three natural atmospheres arising from the sun of the world are the purer ether, which is universal, from which is all gravitation; the middle ether, which forms the vortex around the planets, in which are the moons and the satellites, from which is magnetism; and the ultimate ether which is the air. By these three atmospheres all the corporeal and material things of the earth are held together, which are so composed as to be applicable to those three degrees. The three spiritual atmospheres arising from the sun of heaven, are those in which are the angels of the three heavens. In the two higher atmospheres are the angels of the Lord's celestial kingdom; in the third and the first natural, which is pure ether, are the angels of the Lord's spiritual kingdom, and in the atmospheres following those two which are the middle and the ultimate ether, which is the air, are men while they are in the natural world.

But it should be known, that the atmospheres arising from the sun of heaven, which is the Lord, properly speaking, are not three, but six, there are three above the sun of the world, and there are three below it. The three below the sun of the world constantly accompany the three natural atmospheres, and enable a man in the natural world to think and to feel. For the atmospheres arising from the sun of the world have not life in themselves, because they originate from a sun which is pure fire; but the atmospheres arising from the sun of heaven, which is the Lord, have life in themselves, because they originate in the sun, which is pure love and pure wisdom. The atmospheres which originate from the sun of the world, which is pure fire, cause those things on the earth, and in the human body, to subsist and be held in connection together, and they are not changed except according to the laws of natural order. Hence is the difference between things in the natural world and in the spiritual world, concerning which difference more will be said in what follows.

That in the spiritual world which is above the natural world, there are also atmospheres, is evident from the light and heat there, which before the eyes and senses of the angels appear similar to the light and heat before the eyes and senses of men; and angels are spiritual, but men are natural, and there cannot possibly be any light and heat with their differences without atmospheres. That there are also spiritual atmospheres is evident from many appearances in the spiritual world, as from the appearance of colors there, of meteors, of clouds both thin and thick, of winds, of gravities, pressures, and consequent consistencies, which although they appear entirely similar to such things as are in the natural world, nevertheless, they are spiritual and not natural; although before the angels, because they are spiritual, they appear similar. That there are spiritual atmospheres, is evident especially from the respiration of angels and spirits. For angels and spirits breathe in like manner as men in the world; but angels breathe from their atmospheres, and men from theirs. The angels in the celestial kingdom breathe from their atmosphere which is more pure, but the angels of the spiritual kingdom breathe from their atmosphere which is less pure.

But the things which we have hitherto said concerning degrees and atmospheres are, for the most part, theoretical; but all theoretical things should be drawn and concluded from the facts of experience, and also be confirmed by them. For unless the facts of experience, as it were, lead the hand of man in coming to conclusions, he may be deceived in theoretical things, and from some imaginary hypothesis, be carried away into false principles entirely opposed to what is true, which he can then confirm by fallacies and appearances of every kind; for false principles may be confirmed by appearances and fallacies to such a degree, that a man may believe that they are truths themselves. I wish, therefore, now to produce some facts of experience, by which not only what has been said may be confirmed, but also by which everyone who is in the light of the mind or who has natural ability, may draw conclusions as to many other things.

In the natural kingdom in which men are whilst they live in the world, and in the spiritual kingdom where the spiritual angels are, and in the celestial kingdom in which are the celestial angels, similar things appear, so much so that there is scarcely any other difference than that the like things in the spiritual kingdom are more perfect than in the natural kingdom, and in the celestial kingdom still more perfect than in the spiritual kingdom. A spirit or an angel appears like a man in the world, even so that he knows no otherwise than that he is a man of the world. He has a similar face and a similar body, and in the face similar eyes, nostrils, ears, lips, mouth, and similar hair; and in the body also a similar breast, abdomen, loins, hands and feet, and also similar organs of generation; in a word, he is a man in external form altogether like a man of the world. He has similar lungs, because he breathes; and he has a similar heart, because it pulsates. The other interior viscera of the body are also similar, because there are societies in heaven which equally correspond to these viscera. There is likewise a ruddiness in the face, hands, arms, and body, as if from blood in the arteries and veins. There are also similar fibers, nerves, and muscles, because in like manner a spirit moves his limbs like a man in the world. Moreover, he has similar sight, hearing, smell, taste and touch. He also has similar speech and singing; he has also a similar power of imagination, thought, intellect, and will, also affection and cupidity. In a word, an angel or a spirit is so similar to a man of the world, that he himself knows no otherwise than that he is a man of the world. Conjugial love is also similar with all its effect; moreover there is not propagation, but in place of it unition of minds, and thence an increase of intelligence and wisdom. Thence it is that in the Word in its spiritual sense by marriage is meant the conjunction of truth and good, and by daughters goods, and by sons truths, and so on.

Their garments also are similar to the garments of men; they have tunics, mantles, breeches, stockings, shoes, caps, tiaras and undergarments like those in the world, with some difference as to colors, especially of the tunics. The reason is, because colors signify the appearances of truth from good, and garments signify truths, and hence the clothing of the understanding.

They have also similar houses, in which are apartments and chambers with courts as in the world, and within there are tables, benches, utensils, and various decorations. In heaven there are palaces so magnificent that palaces in the world cannot be compared to them. These palaces are of a magnitude so great, and of such symmetrical and architectural beauty, both without and within, and are decorated in such forms with gold and precious stones, that no picture painter on earth could possibly express them. There are also marble houses and houses of a blue color. The use of every apartment is known from its decorations.

They have also similar food and drink as in the world, and various kinds of food and drink are named.

In the spiritual world are likewise earths, mountains, hills, plains, grassy fields, paradises or gardens, groves and woods. There are ways everywhere tending to various societies, some are guarded. These ways then first appear to a spirit when he goes into his own society. There are also in that world fountains, lakes, and seas.

There appear likewise animals of the earth and all kinds of flying things, greater and smaller. There also appear compound animals, such as are described in the Word, there are also various insects or worms.

In a word, in the spiritual world there are not only similar things as in the natural world, but innumerable others; and everything exists with infinite variety and harmony, from which there breathes forth delight. In a word, in heaven there is a heaven in all and in each thing, in general and in every particular. Thus every external sense has its own heaven, and everything of the internal sense has also its own heaven, and an angel is a heaven in its least form, and each one, as he has heaven in himself, has also heaven outside of himself.

But it must be known that all things, and each now mentioned, are not material but spiritual, or are from a spiritual origin; and yet spirits know no otherwise than that they are material; the reason is, that when what is spiritual touches or tastes what is spiritual, it is altogether like when what is material touches or tastes what is material. Concerning this appearance I have often had a discussion with spirits, who believe that the things which they see and touch are material. I have shown them by various methods, and by various reasons even to the life, that nothing in the spiritual world is material, but that everything there is spiritual. I demonstrated it to them by the houses, which in a moment are formed, and in a moment are destroyed and dissipated; also by their garments, which in a moment are put on, and in a moment are changed; new garments are also given in a moment. In like manner I have demonstrated it from their dinners and repasts, showing that the tables upon which is the food, exist in a moment, and are afterwards dissipated in a moment; and that the spirits themselves can enter into the houses through the walls, and oftentimes not entering in through the doors. There was a certain individual known to me, with whom I conversed when his body which he had in the world was being buried, and I told him that he was now being buried, when he replied that he did not know what of him was being buried, because he had all things with him, a similar body as before, and other things similar, for he, like others, did not know otherwise than that he was still material, whereas he was spiritual. He was soon instructed that his material body, which he carried about with him in the world, and which then clothed his spiritual body, was being buried.

WONDERFUL THINGS [CONCERNING THE LANGUAGE OF SPIRITS]. Spirits and angels do not know otherwise than that they speak the same language they did in the world, write as they did in the world, and think as they did in the world, when yet they speak the spiritual language, in which there is no expression similar to any in the world; and they write by letters and characters; but it differs so much from writings in the world, that there is nothing whatever that is similar, except the letters and some points. Yea, they think altogether otherwise than in the world, so differently, that no thought is similar; but still they do not know otherwise than that all things are similar. That it is so I have often experienced by this, that spirits and angels when they are with me, are in my natural state; and it was said to them that in their spiritual state they should speak words and sentences, and retain the words with me in the natural state; and then there was not a single word alike, nor did they understand one of their words. They like-wise wrote a sentence in the spiritual state, and when it had been written it was shown in the natural state; there was nothing similar but the letters and points. Likewise when they thought in the spiritual state, they could not bring forth any idea of thought in the natural state. As for example, they say Rocky and to wish life [vitam velle]. Scopulosum in the spiritual language signifies that he casts out of doors, and vitam velle, that it is afar off. When they retain these expressions in the natural state, they do not understand them, nor any expression in the natural state when they come into the spiritual state. When they write scopulosum, they write —-, and when they write vitam velle, they write —-, and they suppose that they have written it fully. They write the sense of the words by alphabetic letters, each one of which signifies a thing —-. They write also by many signs, so that the greater the angelic wisdom is, the more things of wisdom they understand in the writing; the Word is thus written.

From these things it may be concluded that there is no ratio given by continuity between the natural and the spiritual; and that spirits and angels who are with men do not know that they are with them, nor an angel or a spirit that he is with a man. These wonderful things were disclosed to me before those in the spiritual world who were with me today, because they could be with me in my natural state and not before.

It is altogether similar between the thought, speech and writing of the angels of the Lord's celestial kingdom and of the angels of the spiritual kingdom, as there is between those who are in the spiritual kingdom in relation to those who are in the natural kingdom. This also has been confirmed by experience. 334-1

THE ENGLISH. The garments of the English are not like their garments in the world, neither those of the virgins nor of the women. They are adapted altogether to their general affection. When viewed in the spiritual state they appear graceful and beautiful, because they are altogether in agreement with their genius. But when the same are seen in their natural state, they do not appear so beautiful. The reason is that garments signify truths, and therefore all are clothed according to the reception of truth.

In London there are ten moderators of similar authority.

The understanding teaches the will and does not lead it, or faith teaches, but does not produce good works. For man can discern and see what is good and evil, but still act contrary there to, and then he either shuns it, or holds it in hatred, the will in the understanding is then opposite, yea in time dissipates it. Truth seen is what one acknowledges, but this is not the truth of life. But what once becomes of the will is either evil or good, this is stirred up by the sight and by the understanding, or the thought, and then the will is stirred up, and thence it exists in the thought. It is thus effected in all things reborn. It then appears as if the will was aroused by the thought; but it is not so. It is as if the sight should teach the feet to walk cautiously, and the hands to do the work. It appears as if that leads, but it does not lead, but shows and teaches. It is altogether like the heart and the lungs. The lungs do not respire unless the heart also acts, nor can there be given a reciprocal conjunction from the lungs but from the heart. See more below.

It is to be observed, that there may be anything either spiritual, moral or civil whose effect man has produced and thence has loved; the man hears it from another, or he reads it in a book. Thence it becomes his thought. In the thought there is raised up a perception of it, because this was the first of that thing. His affection is in the perception, thus the affection of truth. This affection which is called the affection of truth is from the affection of good, which is of the will, thus from the will in the affection of truth there is effected the conjunction of good and truth, in which conjunction the will and the understanding or good and truth act as one. Thus one is concealed in the other, within, and all are aroused from the ultimate, even through the hearing and sight, that is, the rousing up, namely because the will is concealed inmostly in the hearing, and thence in the thought, and it goes forth not otherwise than the spiritual sense and the celestial sense from the natural sense into the hearing, and thence sight is simultaneous. But it does not produce; production is effected by the will or the affection of good into the affection of truth, thence into the perception and from this into the thought; but not vice versa. From these things it is evident whence are appearances.

Thought is also given from hearing, and within the thought is perception, and within the perception is the affection of truth, and not at the same time the affection of the good of that truth. The affection of its good can be given with the love of self, of reputation, honor, and gain, but this is not marriage, but adultery. The reason is that this good which is merely natural, can be opposite to the good of truth itself, which is spiritual in various ways and respects. Examples may teach this.

When man is in his natural good, which in itself is evil, he then either does not know that [spiritual good], or denies it. He does so when he is in his proprium.

There is given the affection of knowing and understanding truth on account of glory, gain, and remuneration. The love of knowing and understanding is the love of natural light; the love of knowing and understanding truths is the love of spiritual light, which love is especially given with those who are in the love of good, but it is also given with those who are in the love of glory. From experience it has been given me to know that the love of light on account of glory as also of use is given with those who are in the love of evil; but with them the love of evil is then hidden or is lulled to sleep. It touches only the surface, as beauty from various colors, and the more it is hidden or lulled to sleep, the more it can feel delight. The love of knowing and understanding truths is from the external, which can be given provided the internal is hidden or is lulled to sleep; but it is a spurious love; it is like some filthy object covered over with a beautiful color, yea, with gold, underneath which surface there is evil. Therefore when good is in evil, one cannot know and understand those things, yea, he holds them in hatred, for he then confirms himself against truths. Thus the internal dissipates the external. Yea, there is given a holy external and a profane internal, the internal is lulled to sleep, but not the external; the external is not asleep.

IN THE TREATISE ON THE TEN COMMANDMENTS. It must treat of faith and of the understanding of truth.

What faith is. That there is conjunction with good works, and there is so much of faith as there is of life. That life is the soul of faith. That faith separate is not faith, it is inanimate. It is the dragon; it is the he-goat; it is Philistia; it is Cain; it is Reuben. What is faith? It is truth. At this day how sterile [is faith separate], and religion is nothing.

In heaven they altogether reject the dogma that the understanding is to be held under obedience to faith. All things of theology can be comprehended by the understanding. Not only by the spiritual understanding by the angels, but by the rational understanding by men. Otherwise from theological authority they could say whatever they wished.

FOODS. There were some in the lowest heaven, to whom the atmosphere above appeared like water. I spoke with them and they said that they have choice foods, and they take them from the table and keep them until evening, and eat therefrom at will; but it is not allowed them to hide them until morning. This is what is meant in the Lord's prayer, "Give us daily bread." Concerning the manna it is said that it bred worms when it was kept. Then they were to burn up what was left of the paschal lamb; neither should they let anything from the sacrifices remain over; also that the bread of faces should be replaced anew every day. Thence it is evident why everyone is provided with spiritual daily bread by the Lord, and that it is not given as their own, and thus there should be no care concerning tomorrow, what they should eat and drink. Thus and not otherwise are good spirits in their works, and in their life and faith. Nothing is given to the evil, but only to him who is in work. Thus also all are held in bonds, thus every use is remunerated. [Marginal Note:] Some are nourished at the tables of others, but those who are evil and hateful sit at the table and do not see the food.

MARRIAGE AND ADULTERY. Adultery is hell itself, thus it is the Devil himself and Satan. It has been shown by many things as also by experience, that all in hell are adulterers, that they rage like furies when they perceive conjugial love; which is a sign that they are from hell; that they desire to violate chaste marriages, and many other things; then that they are in the marriage of evil and falsity. Marriage is heaven itself because all there are in conjugial love, everyone in his own degree. That love is the fundamental love of all the loves of heaven, because an angel by it becomes love in form, because they who are in marriage are in good and truth; and therefore heaven cooperates in marriages and nuptials and hell in adulteries and whoredoms. Thence it follows that as far as a man detests adulteries as a diabolic sin, and looks to the Lord, so far he is in a like degree in heaven.

Marriage and adultery must be treated of especially, because he who is in marriage is in the conjunction of good and truth but he who is in adultery is in evil and falsity. And because adultery is all sin against the Decalogue, for he who is in that is in all the evil of the Decalogue and vice versa; and because these are involved and as it were contained in marriage and adultery in summaries, therefore they must be treated of especially. At this day in the Christian world adulteries are more prevalent than in any other religion, because they separate good from truth or charity from faith; and when these are separated, then from influx it cannot be otherwise. Therefore they confirm adulteries and not marriages; and therefore it is not known what conjugial love is, it must be shown how the faith of the present day separates and thus falsifies the Word, then how it perverts man's rational, thence adulteries are delightful, but not so marriages.

Adulteries are the worst of all abominations, because the seed of man is his life which is conjoined with the life of the wife, so that they are not two but one flesh; but when the lives of many men are immitted into one woman, there becomes such foulness that on account of the abomination it cannot be described, it becomes such before the angels. 348-1

TO DO GOODS AND NOT TO FIGHT AGAINST EVILS IS TO DO GOODS FROM SELF AND NOT FROM THE LORD. It is believed by many that they will be saved because they have done goods, as that they have given to the poor, benefitted their neighbor, acted sincerely and justly in their duty and work, and yet have never fought against the evils opposed to their goods; believing that thus evils are removed. It appears to them, moreover, as if goods removed evils; saying in heart, "If I do good then I shall avoid evil." Nevertheless the case is as follows: that such a one does good from obedience to the precepts of the Lord, yet not from the Lord but from himself, thus not from any spiritual law except only apparently, but from a moral and civil law actually. In this case his evils nevertheless remain; for although he does not do them, yet he is not averse to them. Consequently when the love of evil with its delight returns, he does not resist the evil, but either excuses it and does it, or omits doing it on account of himself and the world; moreover, he does not then know that it is evil. The case is otherwise when he fights against evil from the spiritual law; for, insofar as he does this, he censures evil, and he then loves good and its truth; and in proportion as he does good from the Lord and not from himself, in the same proportion the Lord, by the good and truth in the man, removes his evils.

I have heard spirits saying, that they know no otherwise than that to do good is to shun evil. But they receive for reply, that in this case they no otherwise shun evil than that they do not do it; but that nevertheless they do not hold evil in hatred, and reject it as sin, unless as far as they have fought against it. By fighting against it evil is removed, and then good succeeds, that is, by combat the devil is removed and the Lord enters. To do good, and not to fight against evil, is to do good only in externals and not in internals; but to fight against evil and thus to do good, is to do good in internals. Man is not made spiritual except by combat. Some of those who have been sincere, just, chaste, and have not fought against what is insincere, unjust, and unchaste, are after death let into combats, and then it clearly appears how much they have done good from themselves, or on account of themselves, or from the Lord; and by combats they are reformed.

Footnotes

334-1 Following n. in Tafel's Latin text is a paragraph "On the Spiritual Sense;" this and numbers following 339, 347, and 355 properly belong to The Word of the Lord from Experience, where they will be found in this volume. Nos. xxi., xxii., xxiii., xxiv. and xxvi. We make our numbering of paragraphs consecutive.

336-1 Following n. 328 in Tafel's Latin text is a paragraph "On the Spiritual Sense;" this and numbers following 339, 347, and 355 properly belong to The Word of the Lord from Experience, where they will be found in this volume. Nos. xxi., xxii., xxiii., xxiv. and xxvi. We make our numbering of paragraphs consecutive.

348-1 Following n. 326 in Tafel's Latin text is a paragraph "On the Spiritual Sense;" this and numbers following 339, 347, and 355 properly belong to The Word of the Lord from Experience, where they will be found in this volume. Nos. xxi., xxii., xxiii., xxiv. and xxvi. We make our numbering of paragraphs consecutive.

Before this they do not come into the affection of truth; nor their hearts into the perception and knowledge of it; nor are they taught what evil is and what good is. Their former state is thus one of ignorance.

Man does good from obedience, and he does good also from affection. He does good from obedience before he has fought against evil. This is the first state of man, and it may be a state of reformation; and he who is in this state and does not do evils is regenerated in the other life by combats against them or by temptations. To do good from affection takes place only when man has fought against evils; this is the state of man's regeneration and this state is the inverse of the former.

To do good from obedience is not from freedom, because not from affection; in it there is the thought of reward, and consequently afterwards of merit. In proportion as man shuns evils as sins, in the same proportion he does good not from himself but from the Lord. In proportion as man shuns evil, in the same proportion his works become works of charity.

No one can do good from himself; it is the Lord with man who does the good, and no one comes to the Lord but he who removes evils from himself by combats against them. Hence it is that in proportion as anyone thus removes evils, in the same proportion he does good from the Lord; and this good appears in like manner as if it were done by the man, but nevertheless the man always thinks of the Lord, and the angels have a perception that is from the Lord.

THE DELIGHT FROM THE GLORY OF BEING WISE, AND THE DELIGHT OF COMMANDING. The delight from the glory of being wise, and the delight of commanding I have sometimes seen that when they were in the delight of the love of ruling, they acted like foolish persons, believing then that they were wiser than others. But when they were turned about they were led back into their understanding. They then saw that they had been foolish. But because they more greatly loved that former delight which was foolish, and turned themselves continually to that foolishness, they then seemed to be in that wisdom, thus by turns, and still their understanding could not lead them back, but the will led. Concerning this many may be named from experience, as Charles XII., Benz, and others. This is a manifest sign that the will acts into the understanding, and not the understanding into the will. Nor is it so that they are converted by the Lord in the understanding by an influx of light into the voluntary, and that they are converted by hell to the delight of the will.

THE TEN COMMANDMENTS. The Ten Commandments As far as man fights against evils as sins, and shuns evils as sins, so far the works which he does are goods, and so far they are charity.

As far as a man shuns evils as sins so far his spiritual mind is opened. -So far his life becomes spiritual moral. -So far he is in heaven, thus in the Lord, and the Lord is in him. -So far he comes into the light of heaven, thus into the affection of truth on account of the truth. -So far he is being regenerated, and is regenerated. -So far the order is inverted and he acts from the will of good, and as if from the understanding. -So far he is purified by truths. -So far hereditary evil is removed. -So far he increases in intelligence and wisdom. -Many similar things from the heavenly doctrine where it treats of what is meant by truths. -This is done successively, and afterward to eternity. -So far he has faith.

THE MORAVIANS. They said that they were the remains of the Apostolic Church, and therefore they call each other brothers. Therefore some from their society who were below the earth, were sent to those who had been converted in the time of Paul and the Apostles and were of the church.

First they came to the church which was with the Collossian nations, and they spoke with them at first as if they were of such a church, but they were questioned concerning the Lord; they said that they pray to the Father for the sake of the Son, and that they do not go to the Son. They answered that they go to the Lord, because He said that He is the way, the truth and the life; and that no one cometh to the Father except through Him: then that one must have faith in Him, and that they cannot go to the Father immediately, thus it is that they ascend above what is permitted. They were questioned about charity. They said that they have charity among themselves, and therefore they call each other brethren; but they said that this is friendship and not charity, and they asked whether they do not know that charity is to do good, and that this is primary, and that they should call good brother, and truth companion. But when they said that to do good effects nothing for salvation, thus charity effects nothing, but faith alone, and that faith is that the Lord was sent by the Father that He might take away the damnation of the law by the passion of the cross, it was seen that they are no longer under any law, then being indignant they drove them away, calling them fanatics and not Apostolical.

They who were of the Thessalonian church said the same of them. But these only inspected them from above and they recognized similar things with them, and being indignant they turned themselves away, as from those who are to be altogether guarded against.

Afterwards they came to a certain Apostolic church, which was in Galilee not far from Tyre. There they did the same, asserting that they were in a like doctrine with them. But they were questioned concerning the Word, they said that they had the Epistles of Paul, in which is their doctrine itself, and that he spoke from the Holy Spirit. They were asked what they believe concerning the Gospels, they answered that the Lord there spoke from Himself. They were asked whether He spoke from the Father, thus from the Divine or from the Holy Spirit. They said that He spoke from Himself. They asked how; [they replied] simply as a man, and that He did not speak from the Father nor from the Divine, because He wished them to have faith in Him, and wished to be equal to the Father. They asked whether He was conceived from the Father; they said that they would think of this as they wished, they did not dare to say that [they thought] as the Jews did, nor did they dare to say that they hold in low estimation what He spoke. They were questioned about the Old Testament, whether it is holy, they said that the Jews regard it as holy because [it was given] through them; but that they do not regard it as holy, and that it is evil to believe that it is holy by itself. They were asked whether they know that there are many things therein concerning the Coming of the Lord; they said that it is about the Coming of the Messiah, and that by the Messiah is meant God the Father and not the Lord, denying that the Father was in the Lord, according to His Word. When passages were quoted therefrom concerning the Lord, they turned themselves away and said that they understand it differently from them. In a word they reject the Word of the Old Testament as not holy, and as having nothing there concerning the Lord. Some things which they answered, because they hurt the ears, I pass by. Afterward they heard concerning their faith, and they said that it does not at all agree with their faith and that it is nothing, and being indignant that they had said they were of their church, they commanded them to depart, and otherwise they would drive them away, because they see that they are not Christians at all, calling them antichrists.

Zinzendorf heard all those things which they spoke with this and the former Apostolic church, and he grieved, saying, "I know not whence such things have come to pass since I was in the world;" and seeing that there was nothing for them but hell, he grieved. They said they would not turn to them, because they would thus disturb them, and misfortunes would happen to them.

They said they take something from the Gospels, the prophecies and the histories of the Old Testament in their preaching; chiefly things which confirm their dogmas; something also on account of the rest of Christians, lest they should give offense, and that they may allure to their side.

It was asked whence they could become such in the world, when yet they pray to the Father, and are religious. Answer was made them, because they deny the Divine of the Lord. And they were instructed that there is a general efflux from hell against the Divine of the Lord, against charity towards the neighbor, and against the holiness of the Word, and that they may know from this whence they have the confirmations against those three things.

Some hundreds of them came out and went to a society where charity reigns, and they were in the persuasion that they were living and those who were in charity were dead. From that persuasion the angels of the society of charity appeared before their eyes as blackish, and they themselves in some degree exteriorly as angels. Their persuasion has this in it, that as they draw near they appear to themselves from their persuasion as if they were living, and the rest before their eyes as if half dead. When they perceive this, they pray to the Lord that the newcomers be removed from them, therefore those over them are commanded to go away; but as they depart and are at a distance, they appear monstrous, so that they are scarcely men, and that monstrous appearance increases even until their entrance under the earth, which was a cavern; and when they come thither the monstrosity remains and appears before their eyes and the eyes of their brethren; and afterwards for a long time they are punished many times, nor do they approach anymore to other societies and by persuasion induce others to such things, and thus allure them to their insane dogma, and believe that they are living; and those who are in charity are unwilling to be continually with them. The punishment continues until they affirm that they will no longer do thus; for their greatest desire is to allure and lead over to their side by various cunning ways and arts; they are deceivers.

FAITH. 366-1 The Lord from eternity, who is Jehovah, came into the world that He might effect the Last Judgment and at the same time glorify His Human, and without this no mortal could have been saved; and they are saved who believe in Him and do good from Him. This is the faith of the New Jerusalem.

As far as faith is separated from the goods of charity it differs from that faith. Let him explore it who is able. Faith separate supposes: That God the

Father and God the Son are two, both from eternity. It supposes that God the Son came into the world from the will of God the Father that He might make satisfaction for the human race, otherwise from the Divine justice, which they also call vindictive, it would have perished in eternal death. It supposes that satisfaction was made by the Lord's fulfilling the law and by the passion of the cross. It supposes that the mercy of God the Father was on account of those things of the Son. It supposes imputation, the ascription of His merit to them who are in that faith, and who from it pray to the Father to have mercy for the Son's sake. It supposes the justification of those who thus pray from trust and confidence. It supposes the operation of the Holy Spirit with them. It supposes the remission of all sins with them and thus salvation. It supposes that then they will have an endeavor to do good, which deeply hidden operates, but not manifestly, and moves the will of man. Others, whom they believe to be less learned, suppose a manifest operation. But most of those who confirm themselves in that faith, suppose that no one can do good from himself which is good, unless it is meritorious, thence that no good work saves, but faith alone; they say nothing about evil and about good of life, nor do they think of it. Some suppose that the influx of faith is instantaneous, and also that it is given in the last hour of death, and that their salvation is by faith alone howsoever they have lived. [Marginal Note:] They suppose there is something of temptation, and that liberation is by that faith.

In a summary, that God the Father sent the Son to make satisfaction for the human race, and that they who believe in Him are saved from His merit.

They divide into parties concerning instantaneous salvation by faith and vindictive justice.

Their books are full of these things, but they write confirmations of these subjects only.

Faith places the understanding under obedience to this faith, and he does not understand what the truth of faith is.

THE MORAVIANS. I spoke with them of their brotherhood, whether it is of love or charity, they said no, but only of friendship, because they are of one opinion; they do not admit the expression love and charity in religion. Argument Concerning the Judgment By the judgments which have preceded, preparation has been made for the universal judgment. Concerning the new heavens which they made for themselves. Concerning the going forth of some before the Last Judgment, who were in faith separate. And that they were first visited and separated. Who they were that made for themselves heavens]. It was seen that they acted there as in Sodom. There were seen rocks carried away like a cloud. Those who were in faith alone betook themselves upon rocks. How they dwelt there. Earthquakes preceded. The wicked spirits in the plain were cast out. And the good reserved by the Lord were taken up in their place, and this is to open the sepulchers The destructions which preceded the Last Judgment. How the Divine sphere enters into them and thence opens up their interiors. The quality of those upon whom the Last Judgment was effected. The arrangement of the Reformed before the judgment, also where and how they were arranged. How they were first led forth. The casting down of those in faith alone. And then exploration. Likewise others. Likewise others. Likewise others. How they were then seen]. Their dispersion. The angels wondered at such faith. They have no conscience. The purifying of the middle lasts a long time. Some were seen at a table, clothed as with wedding garments, but within they were robbers. They were cast down. They appeared as if sincere, yet they are wolves within. Their lot. The exploration of the Reformed as to their quality, and their distinction into classes. Their ideas of the Lord. Of those who were in piety and external worship. Their lot. Hypocrites, their lot. Priests who read the Word only that they may preach it. Their lot. They are separated according to the internals of life which are affections. Dragons, how they are explored. Who those are who are in confirmation and in pride. What they are. What is draconic. Anyone can know what charity is, that it is not to steal, etc.. The good who were left were allotted their habitations. Those who have understood and known many things, and with whom there was no will of good. Their lot. Those who have not acknowledged the Lord, and have no good of charity; their rebellion and conjunction with the papists and Mohammedans. Something said of the combat of the dragon with Michael. The Lord seen in a cloud. A representation of a tail. Those who are in faith alone and in the love of commanding look downward. How they are distinguished according to their idea of God. Five classes. They persecuted me by inspirations and at the same time respirations and pulse; experience thence. The thought of those who are in faith alone described. Their quality was such although they had not thought wickedly. Such were let out of the hells, they believing that they would then act well, but in vain, they were in anguish. The arrangement into societies. The purification of societies. The arrangement takes place according to the affections of the life. Not according to the affections of the understanding. The nature of their ways afterwards. The most perfect arrangement is that of the Reformed. The reason is that they have the Word and they go to the Lord. How they are taken up into heaven. The Word of the Lord, they who have faith as a seed of mustard. The goats and their combats. In like manner ,the dragon. Why it treats of them in Revelation. Draconic spirits. The power of truth in the spiritual world. Those who have little of life, how life is inspired into them. The religion of those who are in faith alone, it is only knowledge. They who combat against evils receive the law as if inscribed on themselves. Conducted into a mansion of heaven. What is the opinion in the third heaven concerning those in faith alone; it is only knowledge. According as they lived in the world so is their heaven. The quality of those who are in faith alone, and its quality as it interiorly appears. How the Epistle of James appears to them. They are received who believe in charity, provided they have lived the life of charity. One was turned about but he turned back afterwards. The arrangement of those who are in the faith of charity. In their factitious heavens there was a wintry light. The hells where they continually wrangle about their faith. Their quality. By experience those who believed that they had faith, it was given them to know that they had no faith. Their interiors were closed. They had a religion of the memory. They were sensual. Faith alone of the church is not given, from experience. Those who are in no affection of truth, and yet reason much about truths, experience. Those who are in faith alone have no conscience. Those who believe in charity and do not live the life of charity, are not much unlike [those in faith alone]. How faith separate leads to evil of life. I spoke with Melancthon about faith alone, how false it is. Those who are in faith alone cannot be saved, what their quality is. Because all the societies of heaven are arranged according to the differences of love. An Englishman who wished to conjoin charity with faith, but it was not recognized. I read before the English their prayer before the Eucharist, and my discourse with them. English presbyters who made an idol of their faith. Discourse with the English concerning faith alone. The nature of their arguments for faith alone. Those were explored who confessed faith in the last hour of death; their quality. After the judgment many of those from faith alone were collected and rejected. Afterwards many wished to receive charity, but in vain, the reason. The endeavor after justification. Free will with them. It is not allowed them to preach; the hearers go out. The deserts where those are who are in faith alone. They were explored whether they know anything true and it was found that they do not. Conversation with angels concerning the progression of truth to good. How the English write their discourses. That faith saves no one, a few things. It is like a dark chamber]. Their miserable state who have regarded evils as allowable, and their internal. All the states of love return after death, thus the states of faith if it enters the love. At this day they crucify the Lord. The ideas at this day concerning God, heaven, love, faith. The first state of man after death. Love produces the knowledge of every good in the thought. They who are in the love of self cannot be admitted into heaven. They who are in the love of self can equally speak of the Divine, but yet after death they are against the Divine. They are enemies of the Lord]. Two opposite dominions of love. Their interiors and quality. Examples from those in the equestrian order. Love corresponds to flame, faith to light. The quality of those who worship the Lord from spiritual love. Affection makes the man, from changes induced and correspondences. The delight of the love of commanding exceeds every other delight. The delight of the love of commanding, into what it is turned after death. Everyone after death comes into his own love. Fr. Gyll, his mode of praying. The quality after death of him who is in the delight of commanding. Dreadful example [of hatred] against the Lord with those who think nothing from religion in their life.

Footnotes
366-1 Following n. 326 in Tafel's Latin text is a paragraph "On the Spiritual Sense;" this and numbers following 339, 347, and 355 properly belong to The Word of the Lord from Experience, where they will be found in this volume. Nos. xxi., xxii., xxiii., xxiv. and xxvi. We make our numbering of paragraphs consecutive.

www.ingramcontent.com/pod-product-compliance
Lightning Source LLC
LaVergne TN
LVHW011330080426
835513LV00006B/267